Passchendaele
The Hollow Victory

A walk in the Salient.

Passchendaele
The Hollow Victory

Martin Marix Evans

Campaign Chronicle
Series Editor:
Christopher Summerville

Pen & Sword
MILITARY

First published in Great Britain in 2005 by
Pen & Sword Military
An imprint of
Pen & Sword Books Ltd
47 Church Street
Barnsley
South Yorkshire
S70 2AS

Copyright © Martin Marix Evans 2005

ISBN 1 84415 368 1

The right of Martin Marix Evans to be identified as Author of this work has been asserted by him in accordance with the Copyright, Designs and Patents Act 1988.

A CIP catalogue record for this book is available from the British Library

Printed and bound in England
By CPI UK

Pen & Sword Books Ltd incorporates the Imprints of Pen & Sword Aviation, Pen & Sword Maritime, Pen & Sword Military, Wharncliffe Local history, Pen & Sword Select, Pen & Sword Military Classics and Leo Cooper.

For a complete list of Pen & Sword titles please contact
PEN & SWORD BOOKS LIMITED
47 Church Street, Barnsley, South Yorkshire, S70 2AS, England
E-mail: enquiries@pen-and-sword.co.uk
Website: www.pen-and-sword.co.uk

Contents

List of Illustrations and Maps

Maps

Acknowledgements

I am grateful to David Fletcher of the Tank Museum, Bovington, for first drawing my attention to the history of the tanks in the Third Battle of Ypres and guiding my reading on the subject. He is not responsible for my errors. Peter Doyle revealed the importance of the underlying geology to me and Henrich Dirksen sent me valuable German accounts of the events in the salient, which Michael French rendered vividly in English. Ian Parker has kindly granted permission for the use of his father's words. David Stanley and his volunteers made me welcome to and gave me the run of the archives of the Oxfordshire and Buckinghamshire Light Infantry in Horspath, Oxford, which enabled me to reproduce detailed mapping of their operations. The sources of the illustrations are given in the captions and I am obliged to the institutions concerned for permission to use them.

When I undertook this work I anticipated a task of selection and collation of eye-witness accounts which would produce a clear story. Instead it became a search for coherence and a sifting of conflicting views, an attempt to balance the detailed with the broad picture from which each reader can generate a personal opinion, for firm conclusions do not emerge, except for the fact that most of the firm opinions expressed in the past are mistaken.

Specific enquiries on the source of a given quotation or statement, with page references, may be addressed to the author care of the publishers, which may help readers in place of footnotes.

Martin Marix Evans, Blakesley, October 2005

Background

On 14 October 1914 Lieutenant General Sir Henry Rawlinson's IV Corps came into being when the 7th Division and the 3rd Cavalry Division entered Ypres and positioned themselves astride the Menin Road to face the oncoming German Fourth Army. On Rawlinson's right was Major General Hubert Gough's 2nd Cavalry Division of Lieutenant General Edmund Allenby's Cavalry Corps and on his left Lieutenant General Sir Douglas Haig arrayed his I Corps. To Haig's north General Marie Henri de Mitry's Cavalry Corps was in position alongside the Belgians. The German assault began on 21 October and continued until 15 November. Rawlinson was recalled to England before the end of October to organize the new 8th Division, and so the final phase of the battle was under Haig's control alone. It was a close-run thing, but the Germans were stopped and the Ypres Salient was established, from the canal north of Boesinghe at Steenstraat, east past Langemarck to a point just west of Poellcapelle, then southwards to pass east of Zonnebeke, north of Polygon Wood, east of Sanctuary Wood and then south-westwards towards Croonart. The First Battle of Ypres was Haig's victory, and a notable one.

On 22 April 1915, while the Salient was held by Lieutenant General Sir Herbert Plumer's V Corps, the Germans released 160 tons of chlorine gas, against which the French troops in the northern part of the Salient had no defence. The burden of resistance devolved on the Canadian Division and in spite of the reinforcements sent by General Sir Horace Smith-Dorrien, Second Army during the following weeks, the size of the salient was much reduced. By 25 May the front line left the canal at Boesinghe, wobbled south-east to Hooge and passed through Sanctuary Wood and south of Hill 60 before rejoining its former course. By then Plumer had replaced Smith-Dorrien, who was made a scapegoat for the retreat, and it was Plumer who stabilized the new positions. The fighting on this front then became spasmodic until the hostilities of 1917 began and the three men who were to exercise the principal influences on the renewed fighting returned to the scene of former triumphs.

Background

The Terrain

The challenge of fighting in the Ypres Salient was complicated by the geology of the area. The town of Ypres, a port in mediaeval times, stands on a canalized river that drains into the North Sea at Nieuport. The town is encircled to the south and east by a ridge which rises to a mere 52m (170ft), but which nonetheless affords a superb view of Ypres and the coastal plain beyond: a view appreciated by the British who held, for a while, Hills 60 and 62 (197ft and 203ft high respectively) to the south-east of the town. If military necessity had been the sole arbiter of decision, it could have been argued as prudent to abandon the place to the Germans, but this was one of the only towns on Belgian soil left in Allied hands and thus its defence was mandatory. The area had been mapped geologically at the turn of the century, and the maps of the Commission Géologique de Belgique were used by the military engineers.

The floor of the area is of Ypres or Ypresian Clay, which is impervious, generally speaking, meaning that water easily sits on its surface and does not easily drain away, making it suitable for engineers to dig deep dugouts. The ridges are formed of sands or sandy clays, in layers — known to the pre-war scientists as Paniselian deposits — over the Ypresian Clay. These soils were capable of becoming waterlogged, rainwater passing through them until they met the clays beneath. Where the Paniselian clays met the Ypresian clays, the water emerged as springs.

Ypres is thus sitting on a clay plain through which water will not pass or soak away, the soils for cultivation becoming waterlogged except where run off can be provided by suitable watercourses. Where these are destroyed, this surface covering of soils quickly becomes mud. The higher land is made of layers of clay and sand or just sandy soil, which holds water and again, if it cannot drain, makes mud. The top of the Passchendaele Ridge is a layer of sand similar to that at Wytschaete, and so known as Wytschaete Sand, which is freely draining and relatively dry, so once right up on the ridge the chances of good going are much improved.

The interest in the soils was stimulated by two possible requirements. First, the military engineers were interested in digging trenches, shelters or tunnels and it was reckoned that only the Ypresian Clay was suitable, although an overlying clay might be found that gave them a chance of success. However, when the Paniselian clays were wet even a shallow trench collapsed. The dugouts could be one of three types, a shallow burrow in the side of a trench (a 'funk-hole'), a cut-and-cover ditch roofed with corrugated iron or a deep dugout with soil cover of some 5.4 yards (5m). The first gave some cover from small-arms fire and shrapnel, the second would protect against shell fragments

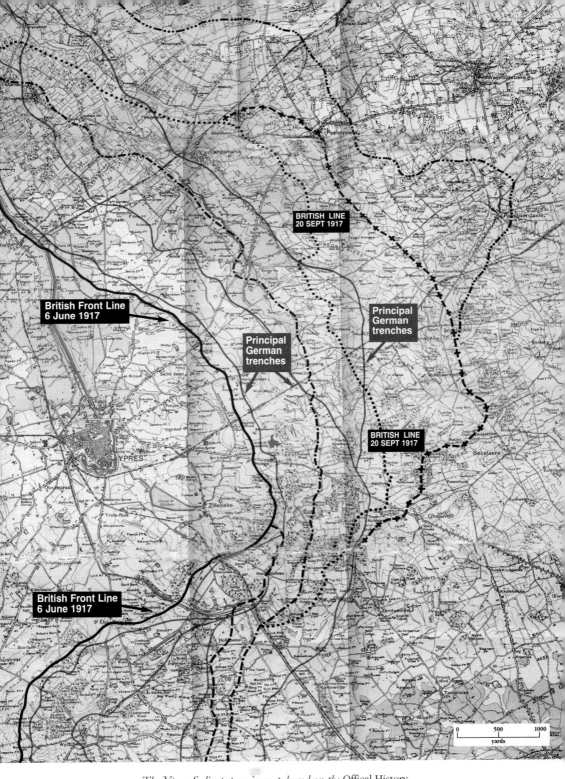

BRITISH LINE
20 SEPT 1917

British Front Line
6 June 1917

Principal
German
trenches

Principal
German
trenches

BRITISH LINE
20 SEPT 1917

British Front Line
6 June 1917

0   500   1000
yards

The Ypres Salient: terrain map based on the Offical History

and the third gave shelter from direct shelling.

The second interest was in the acquisition of resources such as water or building aggregates. The latter were lacking here and roads had to be made of wood. In the Ypres Salient water came either from purified surface supplies or from bore-holes reaching through the Ypresian Clay to the sand formations some 38.2 yards (35m) below, but this was a difficult proposition, as these sands were fine and tended to clog the pumps. If shelling broke through the clay to the sand beneath, a new spring could be created and water would come up, adding to the problems generated by rainfall.

German trenches at La Boisselle on the Somme front, 1915.

The ridge surrounding Ypres is a watershed, with numerous little streams flowing north-west and south-east from its slender mass, and so the terrain over which the British decided to advance in the summer of 1917 consisted of various shallow valleys reaching up towards the ridge, across which much of the first advance was made at right angles, and along which (or parallel to) later attacks were carried out. The progressive destruction of the drainage system and the resultant waterlogging of the terrain was not a matter studied, it would appear, prior to the campaign. If it rained the shell-pocked clay held its water in the hollows while the undrained sandy clays became a morass.

The landscape today is a fair indicator of what it was like before the battle of 1917. The urban areas are larger and a major four-lane highway has been carved across the scene, but the agricultural nature of the land has reasserted itself. The Ypresian clay, overlain with loam, is ploughed and cultivated once more, and the sandy soils of the ridges, less suited to planting crops, bear woods again. The arable land is drained without the aid of a complicated network of drains: those are found on the lower land along the Yser towards the sea. A simple system of field-side ditches and streams, properly maintained, does the job here as it does on clay-based farms throughout Europe. It is vulnerable, as the events of 1917 demonstrate, but those events were still far-off when plans for the campaign were made: so the outcome — apparently so obvious in retrospect — required a considerable leap of insight and imagination. The lakes of mud and the chaos of shattered woodland were not easy to visualize, especially for people who had fought here successfully as recently as 1914.

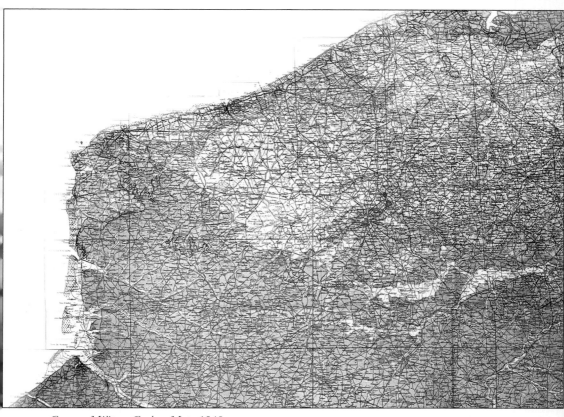

German Military Geology Map, 1940.

The Weather

The First Battle of Ypres was fought in dry, bright conditions and mud played no significant part in it. The British Expeditionary Force Meteorological Officer, Colonel W Gold, set up his first weather station in St Omer in 1915. The observations for rainfall there show figures of 53.8mm (2.12in) for July, 38.1mm (1.5in) for August and 129.8mm (5.11in) for September. In 1916 there was a weather observation facility in the Second Army's area, that is, the Flanders sector, for which there are figures that can be compared with those for 1917 at Vlamertinghe, immediately to the west of Ypres. The figures are:

	1916	1917
July	25.9mm (1.02in)	79.8mm (3.14in)
August	73.9mm (2.91in)	127.0mm (5.0in)
September	55.9mm (2.20in)	40.1mm (1.58in)
October	69.1mm (2.72in)	106.9mm (4.21in)
Three-month total	224.8mm (8.85in)	353.8mm (13.93in)

Background

Just how reliable these figures are is open to question. The total of the daily records for August at Vlamertinghe comes to 111.1mm while the figure in Lloyd George's memoirs is given as 105.9mm (4.17in) and yet another figure of 123.4mm is cited by a recent academic study. The former Prime Minister's figures appear to be unreliable, and the suggestion that a monsoon fell every year, regular as clockwork – as it did in 1917 – was dismissed decisively by Colonel Gold. What is clear is that 1917 was a significantly wet year – just as 2004 was. The figures for central England for 2004 were 2.7in (69mm) for July, 5in (128mm) for August, 1.9in (50mm) for September and 6.2in (158mm) for October: a total of 15.9in (405mm) for the period.

The weather in Flanders differs little from that in southern England: the two areas are very close. Those familiar with attempts to forecast the English weather will, therefore, share the view that early in 1917, the British commanders could do little more than assume it was bound to rain sometime, but that, with luck, there would not be so much rain as to interfere with operations in the field. The variations were simply those natural to the climatic region.

The Experience of War in 1916 and 1917

The fighting of 1914 and 1915 exhausted the strength and manpower of the British Regular Army and the requirements of the Allies were then met with Dominion troops, like the Canadians and the Australian and New Zealand Army Corps (ANZAC), men from many parts of the British Empire, such as India, and volunteers who responded to Lord Kitchener's famous appeal: 'Your Country Needs You!' The most notable common characteristic of these forces was their lack of military training and experience. Indeed, the Australian force, by law, excluded serving men of the country's regular army and thus consisted of territorial (i.e. part-time) soldiers, recruits, and regulars so eager to serve, they resigned and re-enlisted, usually with considerable loss of rank. This contrasts markedly with the German Army, which was largely composed of regular soldiers or soldiers who, having completed their compulsory service, were then reservists.

British Army commanders were all too aware of their men's inexperience and they feared for them, hesitating to demand anything too complicated or tactically sophisticated. Both commanders and the commanded had to learn what was possible.

The learning requirement applied to the technical aspects of the war as well. The machine-gun was a relatively new piece of equipment that had only had

6

Background

one period of war service in which to demonstrate its strengths and weaknesses: the South African War of 1899-1902, known to the British as the Boer War. That war was also the testing ground for the first of the modern quick-firing guns, field artillery able to absorb the recoil on firing without movement of the gun-carriage over the ground. In that war also the principal French heavy gun, the 155mm Creusot, had its first operational outing. Entirely new in warfare was the aircraft. Observation balloons had been used before and would play a significant part in this conflict, but observation from a flying machine was another matter, and by 1917 one of the most exciting of modern inventions, the wireless telegraph or radio, would enhance the usefulness of aeroplanes as reconnaissance devices. The evolution of new machines, and of their employment, was a constantly changing influence on the conduct of the war. In this context of uncertainty the battles of 1916 and early 1917 were fought.

The events of 1914 had created the Western Front, a line of trench fortifications running from the North Sea across Belgium and France to the Swiss border. Almost all of Belgium and much of industrial France lay behind German lines, so the ejection and defeat of the enemy was the only course open to the Allies. A number of costly battles took place in 1915, but more important was the gathering industrial power of Britain's war effort. General Erich von Falkenhayn, commanding the German Army, formed the opinion that a decisive blow had to be struck in 1916, before it was too late. The objective he selected was calculated to provoke the French to imprudent reaction: Falkenhayn chose Verdun.

On 21 February the German Fifth Army, a million men strong, unleashed the bombardment of more than 1,000 guns, concentrating on the Verdun sector, its late nineteenth century forts and its 200,000 defenders. The French response was exactly what the Germans had hoped for: a commitment to regain this valueless ground, no matter what. General Henri-Philippe Pétain was given command, and put in hand an artillery-based defence supported by determined logistical supply efforts. The General did what he could to shield his men from the ghastly conditions of the fight, limiting time in the line and relieving units frequently, but nonetheless the suffering was fearful. The Germans redoubled their efforts, culminating in a massive attack in April, which the French halted. In May the decision was taken by the French to move into the attack and General Robert Nivelle replaced Pétain. After some gains were made the Germans struck again, using phosgene gas for the first time. Again they were held, and renewed French aggression chipped away at the German positions until, in December, the original line was, in effect, restored.

Background

By then the French had suffered 362,000 casualties, the Germans 336,800, and the line was much where it started before this infantry and artillery battle began.

The effect of the Verdun campaign on the British was twofold. A major offensive in the Somme region was already planned for 1916, but it was to be a combined Franco-British affair. Now the French were in desperate need of such a battle in order to detract from the German strength to the east. The British were thus under pressure not only to hasten their assault but also to conduct it with minimal support from their ally.

The German line on the Somme was, for the most part, based on the chalk ridges and hills overlooking valleys. The excavation-friendly terrain had been thoroughly dug and tunnelled to provide the defenders with substantial dugouts and well-founded trenches, the whole strengthened and augmented with numerous machine-gun emplacements in recent months, as a result of British preparations being observed. This line was, the British believed, vulnerable to artillery bombardment, which would cut the barbed wire and destroy the dugouts before the infantry assault went in. The main burden of the fight would be carried by Rawlinson's Fourth Army, with Allenby's Third Army mounting diversionary attacks to the north and the French Sixth Army attacking along the Somme valley to the south. An eight-day bombardment was to precede the assault and mines placed beneath German strong points would be blown just before the infantry attack.

On 1 July 1916, at 7.30am, the battle began. In the south, at Montauban and Mametz, the German front line fell, but further north, at La Boisselle, Thiepval and Beaumont Hamel, success was either minimal or overturned by the end of the day. The British losses to shell- and machine-gunfire were horrific: 57,470 casualties, of which 19,240 were fatal. The preliminary bombardment had, in most cases, failed to cut the wire, the dugouts had survived, and the defenders had emerged to mow down the attackers as they advanced in long, slow-moving lines. As the battle continued in the following weeks and months, the British approach changed. The concept of the creeping barrage – a moving shield of shellfire behind which the infantry could go forward – was introduced. Infantry tactics were revised and the structure of the infantry unit changed. The battle continued to gobble up men: Australians, British, Canadian and New Zealanders. Rain began to fall in mid-August, adding mud to their miseries.

An entirely new weapon, the tank, made its first appearance on 15 September. Most of the machines broke down, but a few – enough – broke into German lines and helped achieve an advance of 2,000 yards (1,820m). In a final flurry of aggression, Gough's Reserve Army took lines disputed on the first day along the River Ancre and the campaign squelched to a close in late

Mark I Tank: moving up before the attack on 15 September, Battle of the Somme (Tank Museum)

November. Although it had not lasted as long, the Battle of the Somme had inflicted more casualties than the fight at Verdun. The British total came to 419,654 men, of whom 35,939 were Australian, 26,574 Canadian and 9,956 New Zealanders. The cost to the Germans, which because of methods of computation is not exactly comparable, was 419,989 men. The French had suffered 195,000 casualties.

The German response to the Somme was to withdraw to what the British called the Hindenburg Line: a band of fortifications to their rear that they had been building since late summer, and to which they retreated in February 1917, burning and destroying everything as they went. They shortened their line, reduced their manpower needs, and took up occupation of formidable defensive positions.

General Nivelle, the victor of Verdun, was full of ideas for great gains in 1917 of which, unfortunately, he spoke freely. A great pincer movement was planned, with the British pushing eastwards from the region of Arras and the French striking northwards from the River Aisne to entrap a mass of Germans in the middle. The British went first, on 9 April, with the Canadians seizing Vimy Ridge and Allenby's Third Army advancing astride the River Scarpe. The Canadian attack was assisted by tunnels constructed to move men forward under cover, close to the enemy lines, and by the vast improvement in artillery shell fuzes, which gave them an effective wire-cutting weapon. Along the Scarpe tanks were useful while ground conditions remained favourable, but as the battle continued through April and into May, gains became fewer and losses greater. The troubles experienced by the French in the other half of the

9

Background

campaign encouraged persistence where a suspension of aggression would have been more prudent. By the end of the battle British casualties numbered 158,660 and the German losses were 180,000.

The French assaulted the heights above the River Aisne, crowned by the Chemin des Dames, on 16 April. Only four days later their effort ceased, for although they had clambered out of the valley, the casualties inflicted upon their gallant men came to 187,000 against German losses of 163,000. It was, finally, too much for the French soldier to bear. At first individual units – then whole formations – refused orders. If attacked, they defended themselves, but they were not going to undertake more assaults. German attacks on the French front continued for more than two months and included a massive assault on a wide front along the Chemin des Dames on 4 July. All these were resisted and overcome, as were the attacks on the French positions in the Verdun sector though July and August, so it remained unknown to the Germans the French Army had, in effect, mutinied. Petain replaced Nivelle and set about repairing the damage. Remarkably few men were executed for their military crimes, as major reforms slowly brought the men round, but meantime the prosecution of the war on the Western Front fell to the British. This was the background to the events in Flanders in the second half of the year.

The Learning Curve

The experience of war had a significant impact on the way both sides fought. The Battle of the Somme had given rise to a series of studies, which resulted in instruction manuals for the British forces similar to the documents circulated in the French and German armies. In December 1916 *Instructions for the Training of Divisions for Offensive Action* (SS135) came out and in February 1917 *Instructions for the Training of Platoons for Offensive Action* (SS143) was published. The former made use of the critical analysis of the artillery performance and set out the concept of the creeping barrage as opposed to the lifting barrage used the previous July. That had fallen on the German front line trenches and then moved on in a single bound to the support line, in accordance with the theory that 'artillery conquers, infantry occupies.' In practice, the two arms fought separate battles with the shellfire proceeding according to its own programme, and leaving the infantry at the mercy of German defenders unscathed by a faulty bombardment. Moreover, British counter-battery work – the shelling of the enemy's artillery – was poor, partly because German locations were hard to identify. The greatest of all deficiencies was, however, a simple lack of material of war: there were too few guns and too

Background

few shells. Twelve months later much had been done to remedy these faults, but even as the Battle of the Somme unfolded, new tactics were tried and proved. On 25 September Morval was attacked with a creeping barrage, which XV Corps followed so closely, it was in amongst the enemy before he could break cover and bring his machine-guns to bear.

Infantry tactics were studied in detail. The infantry battalion of 1916 had about four Lewis guns and a couple of trench mortars. The manual of February 1917 set out a new platoon structure consisting of a command group and four specialized sections. One section comprised nine riflemen, of whom one was a scout and another a sniper. A second section was made up of bomb (grenade) throwers, and a third section was equipped with four rifle-grenades served by nine men. The fourth section was armed with a Lewis gun and thirty pans or magazines of ammunition. In simple terms, when faced with a strong point, this formation could lay down heavy fire with the machine-gun and covering fire from rifles to enable the bombers to get close enough to blow the enemy out of his defences. This flexibility and mobility was enhanced by lightening the loads the men carried to a basic fighting requirement. Towards the end of the fight for Passchendaele in 1917 German aircraft shot at a line of greatcoats, much to the amusement of the troops, who had hung them up on some barbed wire before going into action untrammelled by their sodden weight.

The use of the heavy Vickers machine-gun changed during the course of the Somme battle and was used to lay down a barrage in the attack on High Wood in August. The following month saw the introduction of the tank to the battlefield, where it was used to suppress enemy machine-gun nests and trench-based light arms fire, enabling the infantry to advance. These early machines were unreliable and most of them suffered mechanical failures, but those that kept going proved themselves useful not only in practical terms, but also in raising the morale of the troops.

Messines

On 1 May Sir Douglas Haig wrote to the War Cabinet to set out the situation and his plans. He remarked:

'Preliminary measures to enable me to clear the Belgian coast have been in hand for some time and are fairly well advanced; as soon as Russia and Italy have come in my main efforts must be concentrated on completing these measures so that the operations may be commenced at as early a date as possible. . . .

'The guiding principles on which my general scheme of action is based are those which have proved successful in war from time immemorial, viz, that the first step must always be to wear down the enemy's power of resistance until he is so weakened that he will be unable to withstand a decisive blow; then to deliver the decisive blow; and, finally, to reap the fruits of victory.'

The idea of penetrating the Belgian front had been discussed as long ago as 13 January 1916, shortly after Haig became Commander-in-Chief. General Plumer had argued that, given the impossibility of squeezing between the North Sea and the floods south-east of Nieuport, it would be necessary first to take the Messines Ridge, then the Gheluvelt Plateau and finally the Passchendaele Ridge. He then revealed that, in order to take the Messines Ridge, tunnelling had started in 1915 to place mines under the German defences. In November 1916 the subject of this campaign was revived and Plumer was asked to prepare plans. These included the capture of the Pilkem Ridge, north of Ypres, as a further preliminary to the action at large. The scheme he submitted was not well-received at Haig's headquarters and his Chief of Staff, General Sir Launcelot Kiggell, wrote to Plumer on 6 January demanding a revision and a less cautious approach. He said:

'it is essential that the plan should be based on rapid action and entail the breaking through of the enemy defences on a wide front without any delay.

2. The plan, as submitted by you, indicates a sustained and deliberate offensive such as has been carried out recently on the Somme front. In these circumstances the enemy will have time to bring up fresh reinforcements and construct new lines of defence.

3. The object of these operations is to inflict a decisive defeat on the enemy and to free the Belgian coast.'

He went on to lay down an attack by two armies, the Southern Army to take the Messines Ridge and the Northern Army to undertake the decisive attack. The Northern Army was that of Rawlinson, and the two army commanders, although they revised the plans, stuck to a slow-but-sure approach: between Messines and the Pilkem attack a pause of about a week would be needed to move the artillery. On 30 April Haig, unwilling to accept this, told Gough he would command the northern assault. On 1 May Haig, in the light of the failure of Nivelle's offensive plans, noted the content of a letter sent to the War Cabinet when he wrote up his diary:

'The enemy has already been weakened appreciably, but time is required to wear down his great numbers of troops. The situation is not yet ripe for

Background

the decisive blow. We must therefore continue to wear down the enemy until his power of resistance has been further reduced. . . .

'I recommend that the pause which is forced upon us in vigorous offensive operations is utilised to complete measures for clearing the coast this summer. Success seems reasonably possible.'

The precise nature of the new arrangements was made clear by Haig at a conference at Doullens on 7 May where the Messines attack was seen as a separate operation. Major General C H Harington, Plumer's Chief of Staff, recalled:

'I remember a conference on 7 May, 1917, when he [Haig] told us that the Second Army was to capture the Messines Ridge, for which we had been making preparations for some time beforehand, and he asked General Plumer for the earliest date he could do it. Plumer replied: "Today month, sir." We returned to Cassel in great heart, and we did indeed spend a busy month.'

Plumer earned a reputation for meticulous preparation and for the excellence of his staff and their work. Harington observed:

'There was not a detail of those preparations which the Army Commander himself did not supervise. Every gun position, every light railway for ammunition, every railhead, hospital and back arrangements he visited. He consulted corps, divisional, and brigade commanders as to the best hour to attack, the pace of the barrage, and the various objectives and other details, and then decided himself and told me to issue the orders. . . . before the attack, every subordinate commander was able to feel he had at any rate been consulted and that no doubt the final decision was the best.'

The month's activity was the culmination of work that had started eighteen months before. Gough and his staff, about whom commentators were less enthusiastic, would have from 13 May to late July to make their preparations for a vastly more ambitious undertaking.

By the first week in June the Second Army was poised for the assault. In the north was XX Corps, in the centre IX Corps and in the south II ANZAC Corps. The artillery had begun its bombardment on 26 May, and the plan for the attack itself was closely modelled on that used for the successful battle at Vimy Ridge. Rehearsals on 3 and 5 June provoked German retaliation – not as great as expected – but enough to reveal more than 200 enemy battery positions against which counter-battery fire would be directed. The British guns numbered 2,266, or one to every 7 yards (6.4m) of front. The Royal Flying

Background

Corps aircraft, 300 machines — outnumbering the Germans by almost two-to-one — carried out extensive reconnaissance and reported with photographs and eyewitness observations. Radio, although somewhat primitive, supplemented the dropped message used since the start of the war. Early in the morning of 7 June the twenty-one mines were blown. Two failed to go up, but the others produced what very possibly would remain the world's largest single explosion until the atomic bomb was dropped in 1945. Harington wrote a brief memoir of the event:

> 'I always remember the eve of the battle of Messines — bed at 9.30pm — breakfast at 2.30am. I can see now the glare in the sky as the mines went up. The Army Commander was not with us; he was on his knees in his room, praying for those gallant men who were scaling the Ridge. The troops had been successful all along the line. The Messines — Wytschaete Ridge, under which our troops had lived since the winter of 1914, was ours at last. . . . The explosion must have been terrific. The crater at Spanbrokemolen, which had been preserved, was an amazing sight. In a German concrete dugout, close by, I saw four German officers sitting up round a table — all dead — killed by shock. In an officer's pocket was found the copy of a message he had actually sent at 2.50am saying: "Situation comparatively quiet." He was literally living on a volcano, poor fellow. The pleasing feature was that all objectives were taken, and that our losses were only about one-tenth of what we had expected and feared.'

The impact of the mines was such that almost all units succeeded in gaining their first objective within the thirty-five minutes planned. The Blue Line, the next objective, was scheduled to be taken one hour and five minutes later and it was more difficult to keep to the timetable as resistance increased. The New Zealanders, in particular, had a tough target in assaulting the ruins of Messines itself, where strong points had been constructed amongst the wreckage of the houses and a steep hillside had to be scaled. The advance paused for two hours before, at 7am, the drive onwards across the top of the ridge took place. Tanks were able to assist the next phase over this comparatively sound terrain. By 8.40am the first troops began to work their way down the eastern side of the ridge and by 9am the whole ridge was secured.

The next phase of the advance demanded the bringing up of artillery pieces to new positions, and meanwhile the ridge grew congested with victorious troops. German artillery and machine-gun fire did severe damage as the men dug furiously to take cover. At 3.10pm the forward movement began again, although some formations, the Australians in the main, never received the orders to pause and had already been taking out blockhouses one after

14

Background

another, and now that their men were on the move the British staff had difficulty in maintaining proper artillery support for them. Indeed, there were many casualties as a result of so-called friendly fire. By 11 June the last of the Germans had withdrawn to more defensible positions and the Battle of Messines was over.

The cost had been small on the first day, some 11,000 casualties, but mounted as the battle continued until 25,000 were killed or wounded. German losses were similar. General Erich Ludendorff's summary of the battle attributed British success to the mines alone:

'At the beginning of June increased activity on the part of the enemy was noticeable in the neighbourhood of our salient at Wytschaete, south of Ypres. The straightening of this salient really ushered in the great Flanders battle in June. As long as it remained in German hands every British attack at Ypres and to the north of that town was outflanked from the south. The tactical position of the German troops in the Wytschaete salient was by no means favourable. There were some thoughts of evacuating it and withdrawing to the chord position. The Army, however, was of the opinion it could be held. Repulsed attacks are always to the advantage of the defending side, owing to the immensely heavy losses they entail for the enemy. . . . We should have succeeded in retaining the position but for the exceptionally powerful mines used by the British . . .

'The moral effect of the explosions was simply staggering; at several points our troops fell back before the onslaught of the enemy infantry. Powerful artillery fire raining down on the Wytschaete salient hindered effective intervention by our reserves and the recovery of the position. The line following the chord of the arc was then taken up with our consent. I refused to countenance any suggestion of further withdrawals. The 7th of June cost us dear, and owing to the success of the enemy attack the drain on our reserves was very heavy.'

As the attack was not immediately followed up, Ludendorff assumed it was intended only to improve the position before the larger assault.

Sir Douglas Haig concluded his coverage of the battle in his despatch of December 1917 with the words: 'By this operation [the last attack of 14 June] the Second Army front was pushed forward as far as was then desirable. Henceforward our efforts in this area were directed to putting the line in a state of defence and establishing forward posts.'

His despatch omits the events he recorded in his diary after he had, on 8 June, asked Plumer to proceed with the attack on either side of the

Background

Bellewaarde Lake at once. Plumer wanted three days to move his artillery and went to see the Commander-in-Chief. Haig wrote:

> 'General Plumer came to see me about noon after conferring with his corps commanders. The enemy having brought up reserves, the observation at Stirling Castle (south of Menin Road) cannot be captured without methodical preparation and systematic attack.
>
> 'I therefore decided that Gough should take over the troops on the northern sector of the Second Army front.'

Haig's earlier view of the men who had held the salient for so long had been recorded in his diary entry of 22 May: 'I felt the leaders have been on the defensive about Ypres so long that the real offensive spirit has to be developed.'

There was now a long pause before the next phase of the campaign . . .

The Campaign Chronicle

———◦•◦———

H aving received his orders from Field Marshal Sir Douglas Haig on 13 May, General Sir Hubert Gough moved his headquarters to La Lovie Château, some 2 miles (3.2km) north of Poperinghe. He described it as:

'A large, pretentious, ugly square building, with a lake in front of it, which must have made it an easy mark for hostile aeroplanes or long-range guns. A Belgian Count and his family were still in residence. He was a soft-looking, unfit little gentleman, and his wife was a gentle and kind lady. There were sinister stories of their secret influence with the Germans, which was supposed to account for the chateau having been spared from all bombardments when every building in its vicinity had been pretty well knocked about; I do not believe there was a word of truth in these stories, though it remained a mystery to me why and how the chateau escaped destruction.'

It seems to have been a curious choice for army headquarters.

1 June 1917: Gough Prepares a Massive Blow Against the German Fourth Army

The campaign in Belgium, as set out by Sir Douglas Haig at Doullens on 7 May, had been planned to take place in two phases. First, the Second Army, commanded by General Sir Herbert Plumer, had to take the Wychate-Messines Ridge. This would secure the southern flank of the next phase, the 'Northern Operation', with which Gough was tasked in the Ypres Salient, while General Sir Henry Rawlinson was to be responsible for an attack along the Belgian

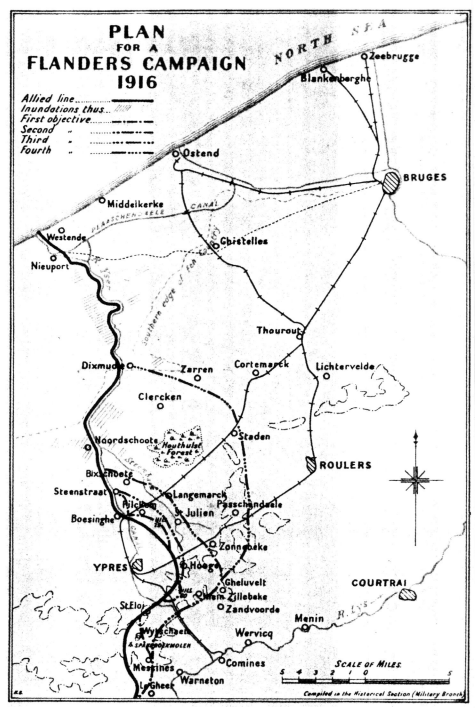

PLAN
FOR A
FLANDERS CAMPAIGN
1916

Allied line
Inundations thus
First objective
Second "
Third "
Fourth "

NORTH SEA

Zeebrugge
Blankenberghe
Ostend
Middelkerke
Westende
Nieuport
Ghistelles
BRUGES
CANAL
PLASSCHEN-DELE

Dixmude   Zarren   Cortemarck   Lichtervelde
Clercken   Thourout
Noordschoote Houthulst
              Forest   Staden
Bixschoote   ROULERS
Steenstraat   Langemarck   Passchendaele
Pilchem
Boesinghe   St Julien
                            Zonnebeke
YPRES   Hooge
              Gheluvelt   COURTRAI
St Eloi   Zillebeke
              Zandvoorde
Wytschaete   Wervicq   Menin   R. Lys
SPANBROEKMOLEN
Messines   Comines
Le Gheer   Warneton

SCALE OF MILES
5 4 3 2 1 0   5

Compiled in the Historical Section (Military Branch)

Map of the Projected Flanders Campaign: after the campaign map in published in the Official History.

18

coast. The eventual objective was 'securing the Belgian coast and connecting with the Dutch frontier'. Gough recorded the directions given to him as follows:

'The operations were 'for the capture of the Passchendaele-Staden Ridge and the railway Roulers-Thourout.

The object of these operations will be to facilitate a landing between the Yser River and Ostend and, in combination with a force so landed, to gain possession of the Belgian coast.

'The front of your attack will extend from Observatory Ridge to (probably) Noordschoote.

'The right of your attack should move on the high ground through Gheluvelt, Becelaere, Broodseinde, and Moorslede. As your advance progresses this high ground will be taken over from you by the Second Army, which will then be charged with safeguarding your right flank and rear against attack from the south.

'Your left flank should be directed to the south of Houthulst Forest.

In combination with your advance it is intended to arrange for an offensive along the coast from Nieuport, if possible by British troops. It is also hoped that the Belgians may carry out an offensive from Dixmude.

'It is unlikely that either the Dixmude or the Nieuport offensive would commence before your advance has made considerable progress.'

The directions went on to request Gough to study the problems associated with this plan, consulting Plumer and visiting the area of operations. Assurances were given about the transport infrastructure and the resources, particularly artillery, that would be placed at his disposal. The broad plan was clear: the British and their allies were to retake western Belgium. Field Marshal Haig's attitude of mind was revealed in his despatch of 31 May 1917 dealing with operations since 18 November 1916, largely the German retreat to the Hindenburg Line. He wrote:

'The retreat to which the enemy was driven by our continued success reintroduced on the Western Front conditions of warfare which had been absent from that theatre since the opening months of the war. After more than two years of trench warfare considerable bodies of our troops have been engaged under conditions approximating to open fighting, and cavalry has been given an opportunity to perform its special duties. Our operations south of Arras during the latter half of March are, therefore, of peculiar interest, and the results achieved by all arms have been most satisfactory. Although the deliberate nature of the enemy's withdrawal enabled him to choose his own ground for resistance, and to employ every device to inflict losses on our troops, our casualties, which had been exceedingly moderate throughout the operations on the Ancre, during the period of retreat became exceptionally light [falling from 7,000 a week to 4,000 at the end of March: footnote]. The prospect of a more general resumption of open fighting can be regarded with great confidence.'

Given 'operations south of Arras' now, at the end of May, included the costly battle at Bullecourt, Haig's vision of light casualties and open warfare may be regarded as optimistic, but there is little doubt about his general view of the evolving situation and thus the prospects for the 'Northern Operation'. The tactical approach he favoured was outlined in his diary entry for 3 May, when he reported discussions with General Pétain about a continuation of the campaign initiated by General Nivelle:

'Next as to the "method"? I aim at capturing and consolidating as much ground as can be prepared by our artillery – then push on advanced guards. Meantime, bring forward guns in preparation for another advance. The advance will probably soon be held up, but as the wearing-out process of the enemy continues, a moment will come when our advanced guards and cavalry will be able to progress.'

On 7 June the attack on the Messines Ridge succeeded, and in its aftermath a crucial decision was taken. It had been the intention to exploit the new situation by seizing the Gheluvelt Ridge along which the Ypres to Menin road runs. However, Plumer asked for three days' pause to redeploy his artillery and Gough, after six day's study, was in favour of including this feature in his area of operations as the mention of Observatory Ridge (east of Zillebeke) implied, but refraining from action until his whole attack was undertaken. From Second Army, II and VIII Corps had been transferred by Haig to Fifth Army on 8 June, expressly to have the attack carried out, but then, at a conference at Lillers on 14 June, Gough's proposal to delay was approved on the grounds that success would place the troops in a vulnerable salient. The need to occupy this ridge was clearly a prerequisite to the success of the overall plan. Indeed, Haig had contemplated an attack by massed tanks to take it, but Captain G le Q Martel had reported the area unsuited to such an effort because of the defiles between the wrecked woods and the unsuitability of the terrain of the woods themselves. Gough continued to worry about this flank and, arguing the front was too restricted, was granted an extension from Observatory Ridge down to Klein Zillebeke, a distance of some 1,500 yards (1,372m) on 4 July.

In consultation with his Corps commanders, Gough modified the original plan and decided to pivot on his left flank, where the French First Army was added to his command, advancing along the Passchendaele Ridge and passing east of the Houthulst Forest to head northwards. They planned to attack on 25 July, being unable to match the French forecast of 21 July, but keen to move as quickly as possible to limit the Germans' opportunity to prepare for the assault. That the Germans were aware was certain. Twelve days after the cessation of the Bullecourt battle on 17 May, Field Marshal Crown Prince Rupprecht, commanding the northern group of German armies, transferred three divisions and six batteries of heavy guns to his Fourth Army on the Ypres front, and a further two divisions and fifty-one gun batteries moved north. As Haig himself remarked in his despatch of 25 December 1917:

> 'On no previous occasion, not excepting the attack on the Messines-Wytschaete Ridge, had the whole of the ground from which we had to attack been so completely exposed to the enemy's observation. Even after the enemy had been driven from the Messines-Wytschaete Ridge, he still possessed excellent direct observation over the salient from the east and south-east, as well as from the Pilkem Ridge to the north. Nothing existed at Ypres to correspond with the vast caves and cellars which proved of such value in the days prior to the Arras battle, and the provision of shelter for the troops presented a very serious problem.'

The British intelligence reports, now archived in the Australian War Memorial in Canberra, were detailed and supported by aerial reconnaissance. The strengthening of German defence lines and the increasing concentration of artillery beyond Gheluvelt were precisely reported.

Gough's plans for the battle were subjected to detailed scrutiny. In a memorandum of 26 June the head of Haig's Operations section, Major General J H Davidson, advised a more modest ambition for the operation than Gough's 4,500-yard (4.1-km) first-day dash. He observed:

> 'we should not attempt to push infantry to the maximum distance to which we can hope to get them by means of our artillery fire, our tanks, and the temporary demoralization of the enemy. Experience shows that such action may, and often does, obtain spectacular results for the actual day of the operations, but these results are obtained at the expense of such disorganization of the forces employed as to render the resumption of the battle under advantageous circumstances at an early date highly improbable.
>
> 'An advance which is essentially deliberate and sustained . . . will in the long run be much more likely to obtain a decision.'

He went on to suggest advances of between 1,500-3,000 yards (1.3-2.7km) should be planned, and that a series of operations of about a mile (1.6km) at a time should be undertaken. Artillery should be moved up as part of a continuous process, rather than in a number of big jumps, so they could provide cover uninterruptedly. The barrages prior to attack could, given the depth of the objective, be kept short and concentrated. He pointed out that tanks were best deployed over ground that had not been destroyed by shellfire and therefore they should be used sparingly at the outset and then held back for use in the final stages of the battle when risks would be justified: 'Rapid and effective blows struck at him one after the other at short periods are likely to destroy his troops at a far greater pace than spasmodic efforts.'

Gough replied to this two days later. He declared himself in agreement with the broad principles of Davidson's argument, but proceeded to reject its specific recommendations. Gough's plan was, as was usual, set out in terms of the 'lines' to be attained by the attackers: the first stage, the 'blue line', was at 1,000 yards (0.9km), the second 'black line' objective was another 1,000 yards on and the third 'green line' an additional 1,500 yards (1.3km) in the centre, but only 1,000 yards on the left. There was even provision, if circumstances permitted, for a further advance to a 'red line' from Langemarck to Broodseinde. In his response to Davidson's memorandum Gough referred to these lines, saying that if only the black was taken on the first day, and then the green and the red were each subjected to separate assaults at intervals of some days, the artillery would have to be moved on a greater number of occasions, whereas if the red could be taken, three days would suffice to have all the artillery forward for further attacks. He insisted successive attacks were, in fact, the underlying motor proposed for the capture of the Passchendaele-Staden Ridge and that, while they would not always be at three-day intervals, 'deliberate and organized attacks on a large-scale every ten days as long as our strength lasts, or until the enemy is exhausted' were anticipated. He finished by supporting a scheme for laying light railways to aid the speed of their forthcoming progress. The matter was later discussed at a conference with Haig, his Chief of Staff, Kiggell, and Plumer. Gough's account states:

> 'We discussed the question of the objective for the first day's attack — in fact, whether we should try to go through, or confine ourselves to a more regular and systematic series of attacks, each with a limited objective. Plumer was of the opinion that after so much preparation we should be allowed to go "all-out", but I was firmly of the opinion that the methodical advance and the limited objective was the sound policy. Haig eventually supported Plumer, and it was decided in consequence we were to aim at

the green line. I think that the more cautious policy would have paid us better . . .'

There appears to be some conflict between what Gough wrote at the time and this later recollection which even detailed analysis and energetic research has failed to resolve. Nor is there mention here of the Gheluvelt Plateau, to which, in Haig's opinion, Gough was giving too little attention in spite of it provided an excellent observation point for the enemy. Haig wrote of mentioning the Gheluvelt Plateau in his dairy entry of 28 June and on 7 July he recorded:

'I held a conference with General Gough regarding the date of attack. The guns of the XIV Corps on his left were he said suffering considerably from enemy's fire, twenty-seven guns out of thirty-six had been damaged. He asked for postponement for five days. I pointed out that the date of attack could not be definitely fixed now. We had first to gain supremacy in the air, and then dominate the enemy's artillery. Much depended on the weather. We were now engaged in the artillery battle and must expect losses . . .'

10 July: German Assault at Lombartzyde Thrown Back at the Heavy Cost of Two British battalions

On 20 June the British 1st and 32nd Divisions had relieved French units at Nieuport, taking over the front between St Georges and the sea. To their right the line stretched away along the railway line towards Dixmude, and their right flank rested on the area flooded by the Belgians in 1914. The position held was north-east of the River Yser, in front of Lombartzyde, and secured the sluices that controlled the floods. The front was divided by waterways: from the Yser itself on the right, then the Passchendaele Canal and finally, at right angles to the Yser between Nieuport and the sea, the Geleide Creek, which ran just to

Flooded land north of Dixmunde (Taylor Library).

the left of Lombartzyde. The effect was to cut up the terrain into potentially isolated areas should the bridges between them be destroyed.

Sergeant George Ashurst of the 16th Lancashire Fusiliers, 1st Division, wrote of the forward positions to the right of Geleide Creek, which they occupied shortly after their arrival at Nieuport:

'we moved into the front line crossing a bridge over the canal on which it was suicide to stay one moment longer than was necessary. My company also had to cross a swamp on duckboards and then proceed up a communication trench that Fritz [i.e. the Germans] could fire straight into. There were good trenches in the line, however, and also good small concrete pillboxes. This front was fairly hot and one had to be most careful when moving about. Night patrols and listening posts went out every night, and working parties were busy wiring and digging.'

Next to the sea 2nd Battalion, King's Royal Rifle Corps held the line some 600 yards (549m) forward of the Yser, and 1st Northamptonshire Regiment were on their right. At the end of the first week of July the weather became rough and the Royal Navy flotilla was obliged to pull away from the coast to avoid shipwreck, thus depriving the British of naval artillery cover. On 8 July the Germans unleashed a bombardment of gas, including mustard gas for the first time, plus high explosive shells. Ashurst's battalion was now billeted in a tunnel in the town of Nieuport and he reports:

'The great advance was due to be made in a few days or so when suddenly, without the least warning, Fritz opened a terrific bombardment on the town, also raining shells on the front line, the reserves, and the new gun emplacements. We really thought Fritz was forestalling us with an attack, and the order came along for every man to be ready for the line at once. Quickly and excitedly we strapped on our equipment, fixed our gas masks in position for immediate use, and waited for the order to move. Very soon the order came. . . . "Come on, lads!" Off I went. At the end of the tunnel we dashed into the open street. Shells seemed to be falling everywhere; bricks and slates and glass were flying all over the place and the air was thick with dust and powder smoke.

'Aeroplanes roared high up in the sky dropping great bombs that seemed to rend whole rows of buildings asunder. . . . Madly we ran for the canal bridge, but awestricken we hesitated as salvo after salvo came screaming about it. However, it had to be crossed, and preparing ourselves for the mad dash we ran like frightened rabbits, not feeling our heavy loads as we pictured in our minds those terrible shells racing for us.'

Campaign Chronicle

Once over they sheltered under the canal bank and waited for the rest of their little band to come over. Most made it:

> 'Our next move was over that terrible swamp on the duckboards, right in the open. I glanced over the bank to see how the land lay in that direction. Shells were falling fast, churning up the muddy swamp; the duckboard track was broken up in places, and shrapnel balls were pit-patting into it like hailstones.'

Ashurst decided to take a longer route by way of a communication trench. It was slower but much less exposed. It saved most of their lives:

> 'The front line was having a nasty time of it. Trenches had been blown up in places and one had to dash across the open, risking the sniper's bullet. Fritz kept up the bombardment and we crouched in the low pillboxes. Some shells hit the top of them but the 2 feet [60cm] of reinforced concrete held and we just received a nasty, dull thud in our heads, or when a shell burst near the entrance we felt the mighty draught through our shelter.'

Bridges over the Yser and the Geleide Creek were smashed and the barbed wire in front of the defenders was cut. At 7.45pm on 10 July the 1st German Marine Division attacked, their crescent-shaped line hitting the King's Royal Rifles first and most heavily. Sergeant Benjamin Cope of the Northamptonshires swam the Yser to warn the troops on their right, the

German graves: laid out in the Belgian sand dunes, summer 1916.

Lancashire Fusiliers, of the nature of the assault, enabling them to take position to enfilade the attackers. Meanwhile the KRRC and Northamptonshires fought on, suffering great loss. Captain Aylett, C Company, 1st Northamptonshires, had taken the precaution of ordering the Lewis gunners to button their tunics around their weapons to keep out the sand, so these machine-guns were able to function. The 16th Lancashire Fusiliers were not attacked directly and were able to maintain fire on the Germans. From the Nieuport side, west of the creek, a soldier swam over with a rope and this allowed a number of the British to make their escape, but the majority were killed, wounded or taken prisoner: more than 1,000 of them in all. Of the two battalions on the extreme left only four officers and sixty-four men got back over the Yser. In just over an hour a section of front about 1,400 yards (1,280m) wide, between the creek and the sea, had been taken by the Germans.

Further inland, east of Geleide Creek, German progress had been less impressive. What ground they gained was soon lost again and the crucial locks controlling water levels inland remained in Allied hands. Another attack on 13 July failed and the front fell quiet. Haig stated the loss of ground would have no effect on the proposed coastal campaign, and Rawlinson revised his plans to start his advance from the Lombartzyde front – still in British hands – regaining the ground to his left as he proceeded. On 18 July Haig agreed and a date of 8 August was set, for planning purposes, as the launch of the operation. In the event the ill-fortune that attended the attack at Ypres put a stop to further operations on this front.

17 July: British Bombardment on the Ypres front Begins – Fifth Army Gathers for the Attack

During July the supplies, arms and manpower for the attack by the Fifth Army accumulated in the salient, building to nine British divisions with six French divisions of the French First Army on their left. The artillery totalled 3,091 guns and the bombardment, which continued unbroken fire until the attack took place on 31 July, began on Tuesday, 17 July.

The environs of La Lovie Château became the base for 1st Tank Brigade because their intended camp at Oosthoek Wood had been shelled persistently by the Germans, allegedly because of information supplied by a captured British soldier, said to be a certain Sergeant Phillips. The personnel were therefore moved to La Lovie but the tanks had to stay put. Second Lieutenant D G Browne, G Battalion, 1st Tank Brigade had arrived early in the month:

'We reached our destination at Oostheok Wood, beyond [i.e. east of]

Campaign Chronicle

Poperinghe, about 3 o'clock of [sic] a blazing July afternoon, at the exact moment when a German aeroplane was attacking one of our observation balloons, which hung immediately overhead. There was a hideous racket of futile rifle and machine-gun fire: along the whole line of balloons stretching northward observers were descending in parachutes; and two dissolving spirals of black smoke above the trees showed where a couple of the fragile gasbags had already been destroyed.'

The wood lay north of the Poperinghe to Vlamertinghe road and was some 4 miles (6.44km) from the front line at Boesinghe:

'It was bisected by a timbered military road (a splendid piece of work, capable of taking three lorries abreast) which ran from the direction of Lovie Château across . . . to Vlamertinghe. Beside this road a double line of rails had been laid from Peselhoek railhead to a new and very conspicuous detraining ramp built at the entrance of the wood for the use of our brigade. Half a mile [0.8km] further north a second ramp served the 3rd Brigade.'

The arrival of the tanks themselves was an operation spread over three successive nights, for all movement by day was under German eyes. The machines arrived by train and were, on occasion with difficulty, detrained and guided by means of a hand-held light to the wood where they were parked. The drivers' vision was limited at the best of times, and any orders were drowned by the boom of the engines. Signalling them to locate between the trees – in the dark – was a destructive business. Although camouflage nets were spread over them and the foliage of the woodland was dense, the German shelling did some damage and caused the death of five men of 3rd Brigade in the coming days.

The officers of the tank battalions undertook detailed reconnaissance in preparing for action. Of the condition of the ground, Browne later wrote:

'The whole countryside was waterlogged: reclaimed from the sea, for even Ypres once had been a port, its usefulness and habitability depended in normal times upon an intricate system of drainage, for whose upkeep the farmers were responsible, and for the neglect of which they were heavily fined. This drainage had now been destroyed, or had fallen into desuetude [i.e. disuse] and decay, over the whole area about the front lines. During our reconnaissances in July the deplorable results were not at first very apparent. The weather was fine, and the surface soil dry and crumbling: we walked, so far as it was safe, over what seemed to be solid earth covered with the usual coarse grass and weeds; and then, from observation points in well-constructed trenches, peered out through our binoculars upon a barren and dun-coloured landscape, void of any sign of human life, its dreary skyline broken only by a few jagged stumps of trees. From this desolation clouds of dust shot up where our shells were falling. It was much the same as any other battlefield, to all appearance. But even then the duckboards under foot in the trenches were squelching upon water; and a few hours' rain dissolved the fallacious crust into a bottomless and evil-smelling paste of liquid mud. And rain was the least offender. It was our own bombardment which finished the work of ruin, pulverised the ground beyond repair, destroyed what drainage there was left, and brought the water welling up within the shell holes as fast as they were formed. Long before any prolonged downpour had fallen, indeed after the hottest spells of weather, the little white discs on the aeroplane photographs were multiplying daily from end to end of the field of operations.'

Lieutenant Ernest Parker had volunteered in response to Lord Kitcher's appeal in 1914 and served first as a private soldier and then as a non-commissioned

Northampton Farm: aerial photograph, 7 July 1917. See square 15 on the map on page 51 for the position of the farm (Tank Museum).

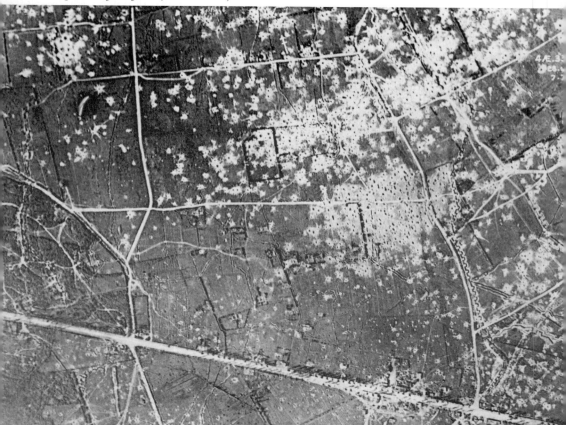

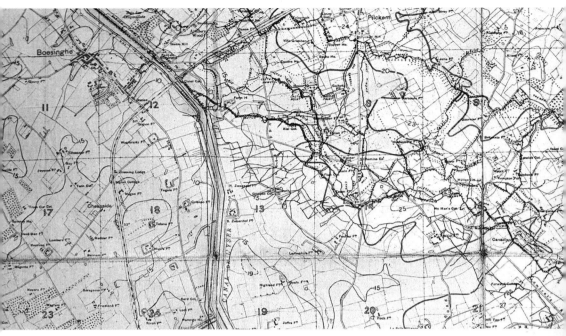

Caesar's Nose: top right, square 13, mapped April 1917.

officer in the 10th Durham Light Infantry. Now commissioned, he was returning to the front with Z Company, 2nd Royal Fusiliers. They entered the line opposite a small salient marked on Parker's map as 'Caesar's Nose'. A few days later Parker was asked to lead a raid on that feature and the pillbox at its tip. The first attempt had to be abandoned when their own comrades laid down a heavy Stokes mortar barrage on the enemy wire, obliging them to stumble back in the darkness to the safety of their own trenches. Another attempt was made the following night and this time British 18-pounders shelled the German line. Again they were forced to retreat and in his report Parker pointed out the impossibility of raiding an enemy trench when his own side was shelling it. In response Brigadier General R G Jelf, commanding 86th Brigade, visited Parker's post in person and undertook to ensure an interval of quiet to allow the young man to carry out his task.

Once again Parker, with two of his men, crept forward through the night. They lay down close to the flat-topped pillbox and watched for half an hour before Parker eased through the barbed wire. Suddenly a Very-light shot skywards under his very nose and he froze still. In front of him the head and shoulders of a German soldier in characteristic helmet could be seen, the man's eyes fixed on his flare. As it fell to earth the German sank out of sight.

Parker withdrew. Lying alongside his men once more he saw a succession of flares fired as the enemy soldier worked his way along the trench. He was alone!

A German Divisional Strength

At the outbreak of the war German divisions were made up of two brigades, each of two regiments, containing three battalions: thus equal to a British division of twelve battalions. The artillery strength of seventy-two guns was four less than the British. German strength of 17,600 all ranks compared with a British strength of 18,073 men. By March 1915 the Germans had already begun to decrease the number of battalions in each division by having only three regiments, that is nine battalions, and thirty-six guns giving a strength of some 12,500 men. By July 1917 this was the general rule.

Next day, as a result of Parker's report, Brigadier Jelf appeared once more, this time to ask him to carry out a more thorough raid and offering a box barrage for the party's protection. Parker said the barrage was not needed, so it was agreed the guns should be kept in readiness, in case they met resistance. The lieutenant wrote:

'Special raiding stores arrived at midday and from these were distributed revolvers, bowie knives, knobkerries, and sandbags for souvenirs. Besides these we all received suits of plain service dress without badges, and in a small package were corks, unfortunately divorced from their bottles, with which our faces and hands were to be blackened.'

On 19 July Parker took his raiding party forward into the front line, now held by the Middlesex Regiment. He left Corporal Green with the Lewis gun to cover them if a hasty withdrawal should be needed, and they picked their way through the barbed wire and dropped into the empty German trench:

'leaving the left clearing section to form a block while I explored in the other direction with six men trooping behind me.

'Gingerly I groped my way along the dark trench, working round its traverses nervously keeping a light pressure on my revolver trigger. In time my eyes saw further into the darkness and soon I came to the dugout, in front of which the flarelightman had fired his Very light on the previous night. Pushing aside the entrance curtain, I knelt down and crept into the intense blackness of the interior . . . with relief finding it unoccupied, I crawled into the second chamber, where I found nothing beyond a few scraps of paper . . .

'The roles of our two sections were then reversed . . . In this new direction the German trench bent away from our front line leftwards . . . Sooner or later we must run into the tenants of the German front line, and with this in mind I pressed on, relaxing a little now that the darkness and the nature of the trench line were becoming familiar.'

On they went, from time to time climbing over earthfalls caused by British shelling. The area on either side of the trench was pitted with shell holes, so Parker guessed that regular repairs were made to the trench itself. Time was running short and Parker hurried on, opening a gap between his men and him, when suddenly he saw the silhouette of a German soldier trotting forward to the trench. He opened fire and the man surrendered. He was sent back to the British lines but, alerted by the shots, a group of Germans came running to help their comrade:

'I emptied my revolver, wounding and killing one or two, while the rest dived into the trench ahead of me. On this I drew a bomb [grenade] from my pocket and lobbed it over, following it with a second. Now I was weaponless until I could reload my revolver. As I knelt down and reloaded the rest of my party came up and delivered a fusillade of Mills bombs. I sent them forward to examine the casualties and began to turn out the pockets of the nearest dead German.'

The German plan was clearly revealed: a front line lightly manned but studded with pillboxes to create a flexible defence.

The vast supplies on which the assault depended were moved up by night by the Army Service Corps. Driver L G Burton recalled:

'I was with a motor lorry [truck] ammunition column and our job was to get the stuff up. We took everything – shells, rifle ammunition, Mills hand grenades, mortar-bombs, duckboards, narrow-gauge railway-line sections, wood, and loads of large gas or liquid-fire cylinders. Day and night we worked from dumps to depots and depots to dumps near the front fighting line. We used to go through Ypres at night with no lights on our lorries, of course, as the road was under enemy observation from the various hills around. But there would be plenty of Very lights from the fronts going up and down continuously all around us, the flashes from our own guns and Howitzers in the ruins, and enemy shells bursting among the wrecked houses and roads. It was just fumes and dust and smells all the time, and sometimes there was gas too, sometimes incendiary shells. . . .

'It was so important to get the ammunition and supplies up that we were taking chances and running the lorries right up to Hellfire Corner, on the other side of Ypres on the Menin Road.'

The operation was not without penalties. German shelling hit one convoy, hurling trucks off the road a scattering dead and wounded men everywhere. Burton stubbornly stayed there, under fire and against orders, while surviving casualties were loaded to be carried to a dressing station.

All this while the British artillery maintained the bombardment. At Bayenghem, between Calais and St Omer, the London Rifle Brigade (1st/5th Battalion, the London Regiment) was in camp. Aubrey Smith, a ranker in the transport section, had just rejoined his battalion from England. He wrote:

'nobody had the least doubt but what the great offensive [at Ypres] was imminent and we were to take part in it at an early date. There were all the familiar signs of preparing for the fray. Limbers had been painted and repaired, respirators examined, equipment polished, iron rations replenished, new identity discs reindented for; the divisional band came to play in the village street to make glad the heart of man. The only question was, when would we take part and how long should we be kept up there?

'To the east there was a perpetual rumble which had been going on for some days. . . . It was the preparatory drumfire for the great attack. All day long as we rode to the watering place or attended to our work the dull rumble kept our thoughts continually on what was happening in the Ypres Salient.'

Lieutenant Browne was contemplating the move of G Battalion up to the start line for the attack. A great deal of information had already been assembled as some of the officers had already been here for a matter of weeks. His 9,144-metre (10,000-yard) approach from Oosthoek Wood to Frascati Farm beyond the canal was to be carried out in two stages. The first was to a field surrounded by trees and hedges north-west of Brielen:

'which we called Halfway House. Here the tanks of 19 and 21 Companies were to spend X-day, or the day but one before the battle. During X − Y night they were to move forward again along Rum Road, past Murat Farm, across Marengo Causeway, and so to Frascati, lying-up throughout Y-day under the trees there. The remaining stage of the approach-march to the front line at Forward Cottage was a mile [1.6km] in length.'

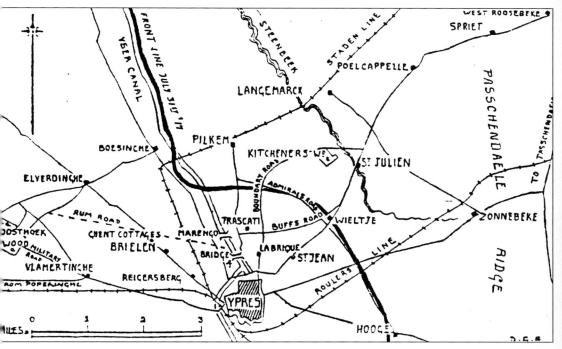

Lieutenant Browne's Sketch Map.

They spent days reconnoitring the ground. By way of Reigersberg, north-west of Ypres:

'we used to push forward on foot to another unhealthy spot, Bridge 4 over the canal. This was a timber structure for infantry and field guns, built over the wreck of a sunken steamboat. It was constantly shelled . . . Owing to the causeways which blocked the canal lower down, the water here was stagnant and chocked with weeds; but in fine weather, if the German guns were quiet, men usually were bathing in it . . . Beyond Bridge 4 we entered the annihilated region of the real salient.'

When another officer fell ill, Browne took his place and with it the command of *Gina*, G46, a Mark IV 'female' tank of G Battalion. The Mark IV was the first substantial improvement over the original model used on the Somme in September 1916. The fuel was carried in an armoured container outside the main body of the machine instead of inside and it had thicker and harder armour overall, which could resist the impact of German armour-piercing bullets. The 'female' tanks were armed with six Lewis guns and carried 276 drums each filled with forty-seven rounds of .303 ammunition. The refinement of having fewer than two cursing, sweating men to change gear had yet to come. Perhaps the most striking innovation was the unditching beam, a great baulk of timber carried across the top of the machine which could be attached with chains to the tracks to provide a solid hold for getting out of muddy holes, which kept a significant number of tanks mobile in poor conditions. G46 had just been delivered to the front and given the vigilance of German aircraft and the vigour of German shelling, it was impossible to test-run the tank. The driver, Johnstone, retuned the engine until it went perfectly, but the transmission was to prove troublesome.

The Mark IV Tank

A succinct specification is given by Heinz Guderian in *Achtung – Panzer!*:

'The standard tank in the autumn of 1917 was the Mark IV. It resembled the Mark I of autumn 1916 in external appearance, but its armour was proof against the SmK [German armour-piercing] round, and it carried an unditching beam which could be attached to the tracks to enable the machine to haul itself out of trenches. The tank weighed twenty-eight tons, and the 105hp Daimler engine gave it an average speed of 3 kilometres an hour [2mph], and a maximum of six [4mph]. The crew consisted of an officer and seven men, and it was armed with two 58mm [6-pounder] guns and four machine-guns in the "male" and six machine-guns in the "female". It had a range of 24 kilometres [15 miles].'

Browne's section, No. 10 of 21 Company, G Battalion, was in the first wave. The section's orders were:

'After crossing the German front line, No. 10 Section will split up. The left-hand pair, G45 and G46, pass to the north of Kultur Farm and take the northern end of Kitchener's Wood, giving special attention to Boche Castle and strong point; then proceed round the wood and mop up in conjunction with the infantry until the barrage at line S lifts at zero plus 4.1, when they will advance with the infantry, giving special attention to Regina Cross. The right-hand pair, G47 and G48, passing to the south of Kultur Farm, will take the southern end of Kitchener's Wood, and on the

'Male' Tank on exercise: illustrating use of the unditching beam (Tank Museum).

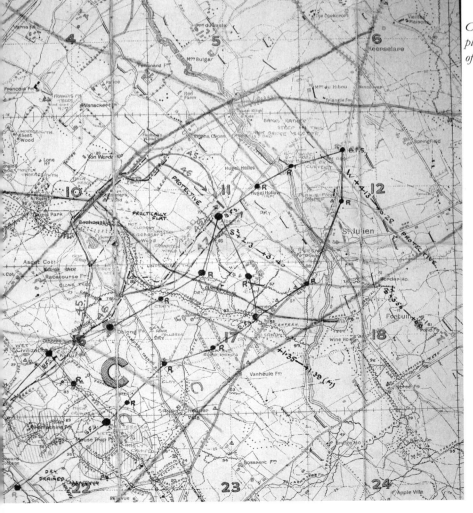

Captain Kessel's plan for the attack of 31 July.

35

lifting of the barrage on line S at zero plus 4.1, will devote their attention to the strong point at Alberta, and push forward at the discretion of the commander towards Hugel Hollow.

'As soon as the infantry are consolidated on the Steenbeek Line, tanks will rally at C11d 20.90 (north of Alberta).'

Browne comments:

'I despair of making anyone unfamiliar with the salient understand what lay behind these clear and apparently simple instructions. . . . every tank had to cross the enemy's front line by a single narrow gap between two flooded areas which marked the sites of Hampshire and Canadian Farms – themselves utterly demolished. . . . And once across, things would become even worse. For sixteen days before the attack the whole Pilkem Ridge was blasted by heavy-calibre shells. . . . As a result, everywhere behind the German line the water was welling up and spreading until the whole surface was a mere crust that would dissolve at a touch. The final barrage at zero, which as usual was to fall at dawn, would finish the work.'

25 July: Six-Day Delay Ordered – Battle to Commence on 31 July

The fact the Battle of Pilkem Ridge did not start until 31 July, when heavy rain began to fall, has been cited in retrospect as the reason Gough's ambitious plans were not to be fulfilled. He said in his memoirs:

'The French troops arrived late on our front; they could not get their guns or ammunition supplies into position in time to attack on the 25th July, and to suit them the attack was postponed until the 31st.
'This delay of six days turned out to be fatal to our hopes. They were moderately fine days, but on the 31st the weather broke . . .'

Sir Douglas Haig's despatch gives a different story. He reported the British airmen were spotting effectively for their artillery and

'So effective was our counter-battery work, that the enemy commenced to withdraw his guns to places of greater security. On this account, and also for other reasons, the date of our attack, which was fixed for 25th July, was postponed for three days. This postponement enabled a portion of our own guns to be moved farther forward, and gave our airmen the opportunity to locate accurately the enemy's new battery positions. Subsequently a succession of days of bad visibility, combined with the difficulties experienced by our Allies in getting their guns into position in their new area, decided me to sanction a further postponement until 31st July.'

The three-day delay was initiated by Gough although he appears to have forgotten about that when writing his book. Neither of them draws a distinction between the left of the line, the Pilkem Ridge, and the right, the Gheluvelt Plateau. The open country on the left was easily observed and here the British artillery was effective. On the right the shambles of smashed woodland and the hidden ground beyond the ridge rendered observation much more difficult and the overcast skies and strong westerly winds limited what the aircraft could achieve. The wind also made sound ranging inaccurate, so batteries that could not be seen went unscathed.

27 July: The Guards Cross the Yser Canal

The German front line came down off the ridge and ran along the eastern bank of the Yser Canal opposite Boesinghe. Aware of the British preparations, they withdrew from it to avoid the inevitable bombardment and, finding the trenches vacant on 27 July, the Guards seized the opportunity to take them over. Counter-attacks did not shift them and seventeen bridges were built across the water that night. A serious obstacle to Gough's left had ceased to be.

The Guards crossing the Yser Canal (Taylor Library).

Campaign Chronicle

On 28 July, at 9pm, the tanks moved forward towards Halfway House. Browne led with 10 Company, 19 Company following. Within the hour fifteen tanks were on the move: one remaining behind while a fault with its differential was sorted out. They drove through the clear, misty, starlit night. It was moonless and tank commanders walked in front of their machines to guide them: something pale, like a folded map, tucked into the webbing straps on their backs to make them visible. Once out of the wood and on the road, Browne noticed the leading tank, M'Elroy's, of 19 Company was missing:

> 'Entirely unknown to me, a singular accident had happened. A few hundred yards farther back in the wood we had crossed a broad gauge military railroad. As M'Elroy's machine was actually astride the metals a light engine came down them at a fair speed, struck the tank broadside on, pushed it into a hedge, and was itself derailed. The tank was uninjured, except for a bent plate on the sponson, but several of the crew were cut about, and all were badly shaken. . . . It was not for another hour that 19 Company overtook me again.'

By 2am they were parked up at Halfway House, camouflage nets slung over the machines. Only the 'eternal uproar' of their artillery broke the peace. They retired to their camp and came up once more the next day, at dusk. It had rained and the sky was clouded over. In fits and starts they moved towards the canal, G46 having trouble with her clutch, and then the first accident happened. The way to Marengo Causeway, their crossing place, was by a narrow lane off Rum Road, which had a thick hedge on one side and a deep ditch on the other. A tank slid on the greasy surface and ended in the ditch. It was 1am and they had to be in shelter at Frascati before dawn or they would be sitting ducks for German artillery. The unditching beam solved the problem and they crossed the canal without further difficulty. The route beyond had been taped out by reconnaissance officers, to whom Browne was deeply grateful:

> 'The broken ground, which had looked nasty enough by day, became appalling in the pitchy darkness; and I recall this final stage of the journey as a long, black nightmare of fatigue and apprehension. There was no track, and in many places even the tape had vanished, displaced or buried by the leading tanks. Over the communication trenches still in use, narrow wooden bridges had been built, and these required skilful navigation. As I walked along in front of G46, knowing that all my driver could see of me was the faint white patch on my back, I was continually falling into shell holes, tripping over debris, or getting hung up on wire; and with the tank lumbering blindly along a few feet behind me, these accidents put me in

infinite terror of being run over.'

One tank commander fell victim to an accident that might have killed him. He got caught in wire and although his tank just missed him, the wire was caught in the track and hauled the man around with it. Luckily the driver stopped before he was badly hurt. Then German shelling began, the 'soft detonations' characteristic of gas shells. They put on their respirators and attempted to press on peering through goggles. At long last, as dawn was about to break, they came to Frascati. It had taken almost seven hours to travel 5,000 yards (4,570m).

Under grey skies, overcast but rainless, the Fifth Army readied itself for battle. In the north, alongside the French, was XIV Corps, under Lieutenant General the Earl of Cavan, with the Guards Division on the left and the 38th Division on the right. It had no tanks allotted. Facing the Langemarck/St Julien sector was XVIII Corps, under Lieutenant General Sir Ivor Maxse, with the 51st Division on the left and 39th on the right. It had 1st Tank Brigade, D and G Battalions. The sector between St Julien and Freezenberg with the Ypres to Roulers railway on the right was that of XIX Corps, under Lieutenant General H E Watts, 55th and 15th Divisions, with 3rd Tank Brigade, C and F Battalions. On the other side of the railway, facing the Broodseinde Ridge, was II Corps, commanded by Lieutenant General Sir Claud Jacob. Alongside the railway was the 8th Division, astride the Menin Road but to advance north-east of it while the 30th Division was on their right with 18th Division in support, ready to pass through when the first objective, including Glencorse Wood, had been taken. A defensive flank to the south was to be formed by the 24th Division with its right near Klein Zillebeke. Second Tank Brigade, A and B Battalions, were with II Corps. Further south Second Army, X, IX and II ANZAC Corps, were ready to undertake limited operations on the flank.

Facing them was General Sixt von Arnim's Fourth Army, which was organized in four groups. It had its right flank, the North Group, the Marine Corps, on the coast. Fourteenth Corps, consisting of four divisions and one and a half counter-attack divisions, formed the Dixmude Group and alongside it was the Ypres Group, III Bavarian Corps, of three divisions and two counter-attack divisions. On the German left was the Wytschaete Group, IV Corps, with five divisions and three counter-attack divisions. On the eve of battle British intelligence reported that in opposition to the nine British divisions ready to attack, there were five German divisions in the line, four more in close reserve and four in reserve, while the artillery numbered 1,150 guns.

The impact of the war on German troops had been as serious as that experienced by the Allies. In May 1917 26-year-old Hans Fink, who had been a law student in Marburg, wrote:

> 'On account of our continual losses the company commander has the difficult, unceasing task of fitting reinforcements into the company. There are no old, experienced men left — nothing but deputy-reservists and recruits. The officer himself has to create an efficient body of NCOs. And what soldier nowadays has any self-reliance? All impetus must come from an officer, whose influence is more important than it ever was. . . . It is quite a novel sensation to find that with one glance one can make chaps advance under the fiercest fire.'

31 July: Battle of Pilkem Ridge — Massive British Assault Achieves an Advance of 3,000 Yards (2.7km)

Weather: Overcast; temperature 69°F (20°C); rainfall 21.7mm (1.067in)

The move to the attack began at 10.45pm on 30 July for the 1st Tank Brigade. As they moved towards Forward Cottage, where they would cross the front line, Browne could not help being impressed with the scene:

> 'The night was very quiet, for there was a lull in the gunfire. The sky was clouded and dark; but unceasingly, around the curve of the salient — to our right and left and even our rear — the Very lights rose slowly and hung for a space and faded, their diffused radiance reflected in the crater pools and imprinting continually along the horizon ephemeral silhouettes of naked and eerie trees. . . . In fact the Ypres Salient, depressing in its utter ruin in the daytime and infinitely dreary and forbidding toward dusk, assumed an inhuman beauty when night had fallen and this semicircle of wavering incandescence began its deliberate and irregular rise and fall.'

The British bombardment had alerted the Germans to the imminence of the assault and preparations were made. Gerhard Gürtler, a twenty-year-old student of theology from Breslau, was an artilleryman:

> 'We spent the whole of the 30th of July moving up to the wagon-lines, and that night, at 2.30am, we went straight on to the gun-line — in pouring rain and under continuous shellfire; along stony roads, over fallen trees, shell holes, dead horses; through the heavy clay of the sodden fields; over torn-up hills; through valleys furrowed with trenches and craters. Sometimes it was as light as day, sometimes pitch-dark. Thus we arrived in the line.
>
> 'Our battery is the farthest forward, close behind the infantry, so that we can see the English position on the left. Our position is a perfectly level

spot in the orchard of a peasant's ruined farm. In the square of trees, on each side of the road which runs through the middle, stand two houses. One is a mere blackened heap of bricks; the other has three shattered red walls still standing. The whole place is in the middle of arable fields reduced to a sea of mud, churned up to a depth of 15 feet [4.7m] or more by the daily barrage of the English 6- to 8- and 11-inch shells, one crater touching another. To this the never-ceasing rain adds a finishing touch! Nothing can be seen far and wide but water and mud. From the position the hill rises gradually to the front line.'

Browne sat in his tank, part of a column running down the slope from Hill Top Farm towards Forward Cottage, waiting for zero hour. The whisky was passed round. The drumming of the engine shut out all noise, so it was the sight of it that showed them the bombardment of the German line had started:

'At 3.49am, when I looked at my clock for the last time, the night was dark and misty and very still. Heavier clouds had rolled up, and there was no sign of the dawn. Only the pistol lights still soared and died away about us. Precisely at 3.50 two or three thousand shells of every calibre burst virtually together in two great semicircles on or over the enemy's first and second lines – 10 miles [16km] or so of sudden flame and horror. . . . the very earth seemed to erupt. It spouted fire and fragments like a volcano. . . . And from out of this instantaneous inferno arose strings of green and crimson rockets – the SOS calls of the enemy. It was the apotheosis of the artillery barrage, although no one suspected it then: the greatest blast of gunfire ever concentrated at once on any battlefield, and . . . the last of its kind. The next offensive battle, at Cambrai, was to inaugurate a new order of things.'

Gerhard Gürtler had been working hard all night, consolidating the gun position, hauling tree trunks into place to hold the gun-trails and attempting to construct some sort of shelter:

'We can't have a proper dugout because the ground is so soft and wet, only a sort of rather superior wooden hut, covered with tarred felt, sand and leafy branches, so that when it rains, which it generally does, we simply have to lie in the water. . . .

'At last we thought we were going to have a rest – and then the great Flanders battle started! Nothing is as trying as a continuous, terrific barrage such as we experienced in this battle, especially the intense English fire during my second night at the Front – dragging shells and dragging shells, and then the actual artillery duel in the rain and filth.

Campaign Chronicle

'Darkness alternates with light as bright as day. The earth trembles and shakes like a jelly. Flares illumine the darkness with their white, yellow, green and red lights and cause the tall stumps of the poplars to throw weird shadows. And we crouch between mountains of ammunition (some of us up to our knees in water) and fire and fire, while all around us shells upon shells plunge into the mire, shatter our emplacement, root up trees, flatten the house behind us to the level of the ground, and scatter wet dirt all over us so that we look as if we have come out of a mudbath. We sweat like stokers on a ship; the barrel is red-hot; the cases are still burning hot when we take them out of the breech; and still the one and only order is, 'Fire! Fire! Fire!' — until one is quite dazed.'

On the left, alongside the French, the Guards Division advanced without serious difficulty. The chief resistance appeared to be from blockhouses along the Ypres to Staden railway line and from Abri Wood. Lord Gort, who would serve here once more over twenty years later as Commander-in-Chief of the British Expeditionary Force, commanded the 4th Grenadier Guards in the second wave. They made their advance at 4.30am and dealt with Abri Wood by using a smokescreen cover before making a flanking attack. Gort was wounded, but remained in command and having reached his objective, added 1st Grenadier Guards to his command and consolidated. By 2pm the new line was secure, some 2.5 miles (4km) from the start point. The Guards took more than 600 prisoners to crown a brilliant success.

Thirty-six tanks were allotted to XVIII Corps, twelve in the first wave, twelve in the second and the rest in reserve. The 51st (Highland) Division were on the left and the 39th Division on the right, where 10 Company, G Battalion, 1st Tank Brigade were so impressed by the initial barrage that Browne almost

When the barrage lifted: Pilkem Ridge, July 1917 (from Covenants with Death).

forgot to start moving forward. As it was to lift forward a the rate of 100 yards (91.4m) every four minutes, he was in danger of getting left behind. Their progress was slow, for although the barrage and the infantry were moving away up the ridge, the machines were stopping time after time. The reason soon became apparent, as Browne says:

> 'The [German] front line was not merely obliterated: it had been scorched and pulverised as if by an earthquake, stamped flat and heaved up again, caught as it fell and blown all ways; and when the four minutes' blast of destruction moved on, was left dissolved into its elements, heaped in fantastic mounds of mud, or excavated into crumbling pits already half full of water. There cannot have been a live man left in it. At our point of crossing there was nothing to be seen which remotely resembled a trench: before us yawned a deep muddy gulf, out of whose slimy sides obtruded fragments of splintered timber, broken slabs of concrete, and several human legs clothed in German half-boots. . . . Infantry were strolling about here in a very casual manner, smoking, eating, and ferreting for souvenirs. The battle seemed a long way off.'

Browne cast about to find a way over; it would be pathetic to become ditched so early in the day. Just then Captain Kessel, the company commander, showed up and helped them find a place where enough barbed wire and trench

Lord Gort's plan for the attack of 31 July (Private collection).

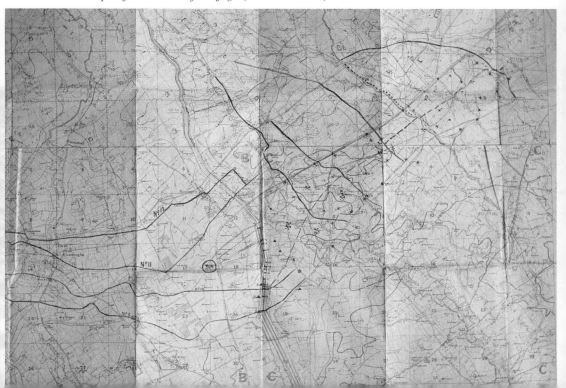

reinforcement survived to provide a semi-stable path. Once they were over, Kessel jumped aboard and remarked that it was great fun: a point which Browne observed had escaped him. The big problem was now seeing where they were going. There were no landmarks visible and Kitchener's Wood was obscured by smoke and dust thrown up by the barrage. What they saw was this: 'Indistinct groups of figures moved about in the gloom – signallers laying lines of wire, platoons in support digging themselves in, stretcher-bearers, runners, and walking wounded trailing back to the aid-posts. The damp air reeked of the pungent gases of high explosives …'

As they went on, leaving the shattered area of the old front line, the spaces between the shell holes grew larger and they made better speed, but they had no idea where they were or which way they were now facing. The land was a brown expanse of mud, without feature or slope. Then, suddenly, something they could recognize: Lone Tree! A round shrub that looked the same from all angles, which they knew was close to Kultur Farm. Much cheered they pressed on, pausing only to let Kessel out, hoping to catch up with the infantry near Boche Castle and assist with the attack on the second major line in front of Kitchener's Wood. The German artillery had now, at close on 5am, become a danger and Browne saw great fountains of earth thrown up and heard the

Browne's Tank (G64) bogged down: the picture was made in October 1917 but the damage to the track was caused by shellfire after the action of 31 July (Tank Museum).

sound of metal striking his tank. Something cut the lashings that held his unditching beam in place, and as they tipped forward into a shell hole it slid off in front of them. He got his entire crew out to manhandle the great timber back onto the tank, but the shellfire was too intense so they abandoned it. At about 5.15am they got to Boche Castle, the dark bulk of Kitchener's Wood to the right. The concrete tower built by the Germans had been uprooted and cast down by British shelling and G46 picked its way between huge holes and ploughed on in search of the infantry it was meant to support. Browne had been told to avoid at all cost the road heading north-east across the end of the wood, as it was reported to be mined. So he drove over it and turned right, parallel to the road and the light railway next to it. The ground was terrible, nothing but water-filled holes. They tried to regain the road, never mind mines:

'We arrived at length at a point abreast of the far edge of Kitchener's Wood: water lay everywhere about us; and immediately in front were two or three large shell holes, full to the brim. It being impossible to avoid them, G46, like a reluctant suicide, crawled straight into the first, which we could only hope was shallower than it appeared to be. The water rushed in through the tracks and sponson doors, covered the floorboards, and flooded the sump: the flywheel thrashed through it for a second or two, sending showers about the interior; and then the tank, not having been constructed for submarine warfare, gave up the struggle. The engine raced with an increased but futile noise, for the wet clutch had ceased to grip, and we did not move. It was nearly six o'clock, and the rain had begun to fall.'

Browne left his men in their tank and went back to G45, ditched near Boche Castle, to see if he could help and subsequently be helped. It proved to be impossible. A bunker at Von Werder House, north-west of Kitchener's Wood, was still in action and Browne half-crawled back to his own machine, only to see the bunker had been taken by kilted troops, possibly 4/5th Black Watch. His men were sitting knee-deep in oil and water. Browne had them draw lots to see who would stay behind with him while the rest made their way to the rear. Then they settled down, sending their two pigeons off with messages giving their location, to await events. They were disturbed by gunfire later in the day, showing the field artillery had managed to come forward and was now supporting troops on the Steenbeek. A platoon of infantry heading towards the front could tell Browne nothing of the development of the battle. At 4pm his crew turned up, having been ordered back from Hill Top Farm. They had to pass the night in the darkened tank and the next day welcomed them with slashing rainfall and steady shelling. The commanders of G45 and G46 decided, after a fruitless discussion with a salvage officer of amazing stupidity, to lock up their machines and withdraw.

From his gun emplacement Gerhard Gürtler witnessed the effect of the British attack:

> 'now came the sequel which follows every battle – and the Battle of Flanders not least: a long file of laden stretcher-bearers wanting to get to the chief dressing-station; large and small parties of slightly wounded with their field-service dressings – some crying and groaning so that the sound rings in one's ears all day and takes away one's appetite, others dumb and apathetic, trudging silently along the soft, muddy road in their low, heavy boots, which look like nothing but lumps of mud; others again quite cheery, knowing that they are in for a fairly long rest . . .'

As Browne suspected, XVIII Corps had reached the Steenbeek and 4/5th Black Watch crossed the stream. Their brigade had moved off the start line at 8am on 31 July and passed through the leading units to attack the third objective, the ridge beyond the stream. First Hertfordshire Regiment took part in that advance on the right of the Black Watch and Corporal Clifford Lane spoke of the experience:

> 'We went over the top. It was quite nice, we didn't have anybody firing at us, not for the first quarter of an hour or so, anyway. . . .
>
> 'We were told that we'd got to get to a stream called Steenbeek. We got there and were told to lie down prone. We were all lying there when suddenly I felt an object fall at my side. . . . it was a tin of Woodbines. I looked again and there was a padre. I'd never seen a padre taking part in an attack, and whoever he was he was worthy of the highest praise . . .
>
> 'We hadn't had too many casualties at that time, and then we saw a pillbox not far away, about a couple of hundred yards. We were told to make for that. We got up and got about 50 yards [45.7m] towards it, then we were told to lie down again. Then we were told to get up. As we got up we came under very heavy machine-gun fire from quite a distance away and practically the whole of our platoon was wiped out.'

On the left the corps's third objective had been taken and the advance had gone yet further, as far as the Steenbeek, but north of St Julien the German counter-attacks had forced them back, out of the village.

Browne and his companions were now, on 1 August, setting out to the rear:

> 'We were making our way obliquely across the front of the wood

[Kitchener's Wood] toward the Wieltje-St Julien road, which was to have been put in use immediately after the advance. It was out of our direct route, but with the rain still falling in torrents and the elemental mud something beyond the power of language to describe, any sort of stable surface on which to walk was an attraction. Tired and burdened [with Lewis guns] as we were, we could not face a struggle of 2 or 3 miles [3-5km] through pure slime. And presently signs of human and friendly activity were at length visible. We passed a few 18-pounders buried in shell holes or hidden behind pollard stumps. A little later a line of moving figures and vehicles, marking the road, came into view through the rain. We found the road congested, in fact, by opposing streams of mule trains and ammunition limbers, bringing their loads up to this new battery area and then returning for more.'

Once back at Frascati, Browne learnt of the fortunes of the other tanks with XVIII Corps. To his left two sections of 21 Company had been with the 51st (Highland) Division all the way to the Steenbeek, the effect on the enemy being so great that they abandoned their positions without the tanks having to fire a shot. Of his own section one tank, 2nd Lieutenant John Allden's G47, had got past Kitchener's Wood on the right and assisted the infantry in taking the strong point called Alberta. The report of the 39th Division runs:

'Lewis guns, rifle bombers and Stokes guns opened a heavy fire on the enemy machine-gun emplacements. Two tanks [G47 and 48] also opened heavy fire at very close-range and one of them (G47) advanced through our barrage and rolled out a lane for the infantry in the uncut wire. Meanwhile rifle sections worked round the flanks of the position and, on the barrage lifting, assaulted from both sides and captured the garrison which had been driven into their dugouts.'

Allden's report recounts the fire that distracted them early in their advance. It turned out to be the camouflage netting on top of their machine and having jettisoned that they pressed on towards Kitchener's Wood where they put an enemy machine-gun out of action. Emerging from the wood Allden:

'turned north-east towards Alberta, and now I had the opportunity of using my guns again. There were many of the enemy running for their lives up communication trenches and I stopped some or hastened their flight. . . . I now came across some of the officers of the 17th Sherwoods. I got to know them before we left Oosthoek and we agreed to look out for each other. They were glad to see us and told us Alberta was straight ahead. . . . After this I got a little too far to the right and was soon in our barrage. I straightened up a bit and made for Alberta, in front of which I saw the 17th Sherwoods who were waiting for the barrage to lift and for the machine-guns at Alberta to be silenced. I travelled along three sides of Alberta and poured in good fire, and as our own barrage had not lifted yet we reversed and went round the three sides again. Three machine-guns were certainly engaged about here, two in the strong point itself, and one on the right. We all had a chance of shooting. About this time five of our six guns were out of action and I was able to fire through the front flap with my revolver and it must have had good effect for when the barrage lifted the infantry were able to go to the strong point without any resistance and we soon saw a party with machine-guns come out and return towards our lines as prisoners.'

Nineteen Company had advanced through St Julien, but only two tanks, G10 and G11, which was commanded by 2nd Lieutenant Lynch, had climbed the slope beyond. G11 appeared to have actually reached Springfield, a fortified farm on the Langemarck-Zonnebeke road, but the infantry had been unable to keep up in the face of German fire and the tank had to withdraw. Then, at about 11.15am, G11 came face-to-face with a German 5.9 howitzer and took a shell through the front, killing all within.

Nineteen Corps had 3rd Tank Brigade in support. Tanks played their part in helping the 8/10th Gordon Highlanders and 9th Black Watch take Frezenburg and 7/8th King's Own Scottish Borders overcome Frezenburg Redoubt. Forty-Five Brigade passed through to attack the third objective but at about 11.30am there was trouble on the right flank where the 11th Argyll and Sutherland Highlanders were in action. Two tanks of C Battalion, *Canada* and *Cuidich'n Rich*, engaged machine-gun posts in the railway embankment successfully before themselves coming under artillery fire. Both machines were put out of action. A strong point called Beck House was the origin of much of this fire and *Caithness* worked with 6th Cameron Highlanders to take it. The tank eventually bellied down in the bog of Zonnebeke Stream from which *Carstairs* hauled her free. The advance continued as far as the third objective, beyond the Zonneebeke-Langemarck road, and tanks of C Battalion reached the Kansas Cross and Winnepeg strong points on the German Third Line, although the main body of the second wave were unable to advance quickly enough to support the attack on this objective. By this time communications were severely compromised. Telephone wire was repeatedly cut by shelling and observation was limited by the worsening weather. Although the gathering counter-attack forces were seen, the news could not be conveyed to the rear in time to organize a protective barrage. Vigorous German counter-attacks ensued and by the end of the day they were back to the second objective, holding a line from Beck House to Pommern Castle and Spree Farm.

Tank Availability

Both tank experts and more general commentators have criticised British commanders for frittering tanks away in 'penny packets' instead of using them en masse to create a breach in enemy lines. This assumes the machines were available in sufficient numbers to allow their use as a fleet of vehicles.

On 15 September 1916, during the Battle of the Somme, only forty-nine tanks were available, of which thirty-two reached their starting points.

On 9 April 1917 there were only sixty machines, some of which were Mark II training tanks.

By 31 July 1917, there were 136 tanks ready to take part in the Third Battle of Ypres.

On 20 November 1917, for the Battle of Cambrai, 378 machines could be mustered, the first time anything more than a 'penny packet' could be put into the field.

To suggest that tanks should not have been used at all before November 1917 does not make sense, and the experience of The Cockroft and of Springfield also undermines the 'penny packet' argument.

Source: Terraine, *The Smoke and the Fire*, p.150 et seq.

Second Corps, on the right of Fifth Army's line, was supported by A and B Battalions of 2nd Tank Brigade. The front they attacked stretched from the Ypres-Roulers railway on the left, across the Menin road and south as far as Kleine Zillebeke. On the left matters began well for the 8th Division with the taking of Bellewarde Lake by the 2nd Northamptonshires. Most of the advancing troops, however, got caught up in the debris of Château Wood, losing contact with the barrage, and would have faltered had not Acting Captain T R Colyer-Ferguson led six men straight up the Bellewarde Ridge beyond, keeping perilously close to the British barrage. The German troops were abandoning their positions and Colyer-Ferguson acquired one of their machine-guns, which he put to use in halting the counter-attack they attempted. The advance was limited to their second objective by the enfilading fire coming from their right, where Glencorse Wood remained in German hands. By the end of the day ground gained at Westhoek had to be yielded and the 8th Division fell back to the western side of Westhoek Ridge.

In the centre the 30th Division had the toughest task and was strengthened with 53rd Brigade of the 18th Division. The day started badly when the 21st Brigade lost contact with their barrage while struggling through the wreckage of Sanctuary Wood in the face of German shelling. Once out of the wood they had to take Stirling Castle, which was thronged with machine-gun nests. It took until 6am to do it, by which time all contact with supporting artillery fire had been lost. This exposed 90th Brigade on their left to fire, first from Stirling Castle and later from Inverness Copse. The problem was compounded by the fact that, in the shambles of Sanctuary Wood, 2nd Royal Scots Fusiliers became disorientated and attacked Château Wood, believing it to be Glencorse Wood. They reported Glencorse as taken. German shelling was continuous and heavy. The tanks faced an impossible situation. As pointed out by Martel long before, the woods precluded movement by tanks and the Menin road was dominated by a massive fortification near Clapham Junction: there were only three viable approach routes available. Of the machines coming through the Hooge Gap, four were knocked out by German guns. Some of the tanks of A Battalion got through and, where the Menin road bears right, forged onwards in the direction of the low ridge concealing Glencorse Wood from their sight. Corporal A E Lee recalls:

> 'one of our tracks broke through the soft ground and we went down into a deep hole. . . . We were completely helpless. We didn't even have our unditching beam because that had been shot away on the road up. Looking through the slits of the tank we could see the enemy, just about 100 yards [91.4m] away, and they were getting out of their trenches, running out of dugouts and massing for a counter-attack. . . . it was obvious we would be overrun . . . I had no intention of staying in the tank like a snail in the shell until the enemy winkled us out. We had machine-guns which could be taken out and used independently and we had with us . . . Pat Brady . . . [who] had been an infantry machine-gunner . . .'

Lee asked Brady to join him in getting out and firing on the Germans. Brady agreed on condition he had a swig of rum and the two emerged on the side of the machine away from the enemy and zig-zagged their way into shell holes. Expecting fire from the stranded tank, the attackers were startled when the Lewis guns opened up. Those not killed surrendered with the timely arrival of supporting British infantry. A second tank now joined Lee, but was hit by a shell: its unditching beam being dislodged as a result. Lee and his men made

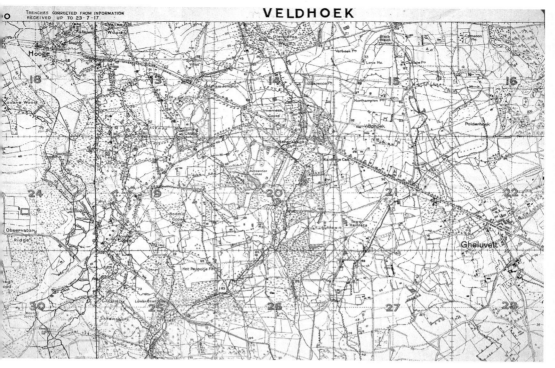

Veldhoek Map: showing the Menin road from Hooge to Gheluvelt, 23 July 1917 (Tank Museum).

use of the timber to extract their machine and were able to pull back.

Of the fifty-two fighting and supply tanks of 2nd Tank Brigade, nineteen were put out of action by German guns and twenty-two ditched, some due to mechanical failures. The 24th Division on the right was intended to create a defensive flank, but encountered heavy fire once out of Shrewsbury Forest. Groenenburg Farm was taken, but fire from Lower Star Post was so intense they did not even reach their first objective. The attack by II Corps had failed to make the necessary progress towards the Gheluvelt Plateau.

From the opposite side of the line things appeared no less miserable. Gerhard Gürtler wrote:

'And those men who are still in the front line hear nothing but the drumfire, the groaning of wounded comrades, the screaming of fallen horses, the wild beating of their own hearts, hour after hour, night after night. Even during the short respite granted them their exhausted brains are haunted in the weird stillness by recollections of unlimited suffering. They have no way of escape, nothing is left to them but ghastly memories and resigned anticipation.'

General Erich Ludendorff commented in his memoirs:

Campaign Chronicle

'On 31st July the English, assisted by a few French divisions on their left, had attacked on a front of about 31km [19.2 miles]. They had employed such quantities of artillery and ammunition as had been rare, even in the West. At many points along the whole front the enemy had penetrated with tanks. Cavalry divisions were in readiness to push through. With the assistance of the counter-attack divisions, the 4th Army, whose Chief of Staff was now Colonel von Losberg, succeeded in checking the hostile success and localizing its effect. But, besides a loss of from 2–4km [1.2–2.4 miles] of ground along the whole front, it caused us very considerable losses in prisoners and stores, and a heavy expenditure of reserves.'

Gough summarized the day in his memoirs with misgivings for the continuation of the battle:

'On the evening of the first day of the battle heavy rain began to fall, and in a few hours it was evident that further operations on any large scale could not take place until the ground had dried up, at least to some extent.

'As things turned out this was particularly galling, for the first day's attack had been decidedly successful; 5626 prisoners and a great many machine-guns and *minenwerfer* had been captured, and our troops had advanced against powerful entrenchments and a prepared enemy to the greater part of their objectives.'

He went on to say the delay in beginning the battle, which he attributed entirely to the French, had lost six crucial days. Further, he said the French played only a minor part.

As a summary of the first day, this has deficiencies. The signal success of his left, XIV Corps and the French First Army, receives insufficient acknowledgement and the effectiveness of the German counter-attacks in the centre goes unmentioned. While XVII and XIX Corps had pushed forward almost to their final objectives, they had not, lacking artillery support, been able to hold them, although their final positions were, by the standards of the time, a satisfactory result. On the right the advance was also impressive for that time, but well short of the desired positions: the German look-out positions on the Gheluvelt heights and their artillery to the rear remained secure.

But Haig was pleased:

'This was a fine day's work . . . As regards future operations, I told Gough to continue to carry out the original plan: to consolidate ground gained, and to improve his position as he may deem necessary for facilitating the next advance: the next advance will be made as soon as possible, but only after adequate bombardment and after dominating the hostile artillery.' On 5 August he wrote of news from his intelligence officer:

'Charteris reports that enemy is seen to be changing his divisions in the battle front very quickly. This may be due to large losses suffered in fruitless counter-attacks. State of German troops does not now appear to be so good that they can be trusted to hold a line for a prolonged period in the recent bad weather.'

Gough was correct in fearing the consequences of the rain. On that day 21.7mm (0.73in) of rain had fallen. The total rainfall for the whole of July the previous year in this area, Second Army's at that time, had been 25.9mm (1.02in). The tanks had already started to suffer from the conditions that resulted, and worse was to come. From 1–9 August a further 35.9mm (1.41in) of rain fell.

On Friday, 10 August, when 1.5mm (0.06in) of rain fell, the 18th Division tried to push forward astride the Menin road to take Glencorse Wood on the left and Inverness Copse on the right. Only on the left was any ground gained and held against the inevitable counter-attacks, but it still fell short of the wood. North of the 18th, the 25th Division managed to take Westhoek and the

Mules, the best transport: moving supports for fresh barbed wire, 31 July 1917 (Taylor Library).

quagmire of the Hanebeek valley beyond, preventing an effective German response.

At about the same time the commander of G Battalion, 1st Tank Corps, C D Baker-Carr, was giving a lecture to the Staff College Course at GHQ. At lunch afterwards he did nothing to conceal his view that, as a result of the conditions now prevailing in the Ypres Salient, the battle was 'dead as mutton'. Shortly afterwards he was summoned to see the Director of Operations, Major General John Davidson, who rebuked him for speaking as he had. Baker-Carr gives his recollection of the exchange, but if John Terraine's analysis of his observations on machine-guns are accepted, this report must be treated with caution. Baker-Carr says he replied:

'You asked me how things really were and I told you frankly.'
'But what you say is impossible.'
'It isn't. Nobody has any idea of the conditions up there.'
'But they can't be as bad as you make out.'
'Have you been there yourself?'
'No.'
'Has anybody in OA [Operations Branch] been there?'
'No.'
'Well then, if you don't believe me, it would be as well to send someone to find out. I'm sorry I've upset you, but you asked me what I thought and I told you.'

Baker-Carr returned to his headquarters, but whether any action was taken as a result of his remarks neither he nor anyone else can say.

The rainfall total from 11 to 15 August was 32.4mm (1.276in). Gerhard Gürtler had written his last letter home on 10 August. He said:

'The battlefield is really nothing but one vast cemetery. Besides shell holes, groups of shattered trees and smashed-up farms, one sees little white crosses scattered all over the ground – in front of us, behind us, to right and left. "Here lies a brave Englishman" or "Bombardier, 6,52". They lie thus, side by side, friend beside friend, foe beside foe. In the newspapers you read: "Peacefully they rest on the spot where they have bled and suffered . . . while the guns roar over their graves, taking vengeance for their heroic death . . ." And it doesn't occur to anybody that the enemy is also firing; that the shells plunge into the hero's grave; that his bones are mingled with the filth which they scatter to the four winds . . .'

Gürtler was killed on 14 August.

Aerial Photograph of Northampton Farm: 10 August 1917 comparet photograph on page 28 (Tank Museum).

16 August 1917: Battle of Langemarck – Fifth Army Secures the Steenbeek and Seizes the Village of Langemarck

Weather: overcast; temperature, 68°F (20°C); rainfall, nil

On 15 August Aubrey Smith of the London Rifle Brigade was driving a limber full of ammunition, pulled by two horses, Jumbo and The Grey. They left Zillebeke Lake to their left and plodded up to Hell Fire Corner, where enemy shellfire was falling. They went along the Menin road for a way before heading right towards Sanctuary Wood. In the distance they could see Glencorse and Polygon Woods, which were still in German hands:

'The track we were following was not only muddy, but dotted with shell holes, and only the fact that we kept moving prevented us from sinking dangerously and perhaps getting stuck. However, Pocock unfortunately had to halt us while he located the exact spot for dumping the bombs, and the limbers before me suddenly pulled up short, leaving my back wheel in a shell hole.'

Smith's horses could not heave the limber out: indeed they stood still, frozen with fear. Then Smith tried digging the limber out. It was futile. Then he unhooked the rear half of the two-limber rig and his beasts hauled the front half forward where, alone, Smith unloaded the forty-five boxes of grenades. The second half remained stubbornly stuck, so Smith unloaded that where it stood and finally turned for home. By then both horses were wounded, Jumbo slightly but The Grey, which Smith was riding, pouring blood from the shoulder. They cantered back and as they went down the hill towards Zillebeke, The Grey began to limp badly. Smith halted, attempted to bind up the wound and moved the saddle to Jumbo for the rest of the journey to the horse-lines:

> 'Throughout the afternoon the rumble continued up the line where several divisions were getting ready for tomorrow's attack, living every minute under conditions as bad as those of which, after all, I had only a taste that morning. To be up there with our batteries or in the trenches subjected to an unceasing bombardment like that was enough to shatter anyone's nerves in a few days. Yet thousands of men were enduring the endless racket as I had seen them that morning, huddled here and there behind mud banks or crouching in shallow dugouts and shell holes, fully expecting a wound of some sort before evening. What our casualties must be, in the course of an ordinary day's happenings in the salient, I couldn't imagine. On no part of the Western Front was the destruction of life more ruthless.'

In spite of the condition of the ground the attack intended for 14 August went ahead on 16 August. On the left XIV Corps made excellent progress. With French artillery cover to assist, 1st King's Own Scottish Borderers and 2nd South Wales Borderers attained their objectives and to their right the 2nd Hampshires and the Newfoundland Regiment advanced to take Japan House. To their right the 20th Division had a tougher fight. The 6th Oxfordshire and Buckinghamshire Light Infantry of 60th Brigade were given the task of taking the strong point of Au Bon Gite with the assistance of 59th Brigade in the course of their advance. The attack began at 4.45am. The battalion crossed the Steenbeek at a point held by the 11th Rifle Brigade. Second Lieutenant H W H Willes recorded their experience in his diary:

> 'At 4.45am it sounded as if someone had been careless about leaving the lid off hell. . . . The 11th RBs [Rifle Brigade] put up a smoke barrage and rushed forward to try conclusions with Au Bon Gite. Before describing our own movements, I will deal with the work of this company of the 11th RB, for no account of the Langemarck fight can be complete without justice

King's Own Yorkshire Light Infantry resting at Wieltje: waiting for the offensive, August 1917
(Taylor Library).

being done to the bitter struggle for Au Bon Gîte . . . [a] concrete block-house, excellently planned for defence, and held grimly by the Germans until surrounded and cut off. . . . Around it were five or six smaller posts, and from it to the stream a barbed-wire entanglement ran diagonally in such a way as to break up any attacking party . . .

'The capture of Au Bon Gîte seemed well-nigh impossible; the general advance went on regardless of it, and it was perhaps this fact that upset the calculations of the enemy and caused him to surrender an hour after the attack had been launched. Captain Slade and his company of the 11th RB, with the aid of a smoke barrage, succeeded in getting under the walls, and, after much discussion, the defenders agreed to surrender, when thirty-two Germans were made prisoners . . .'

The Ox and Bucks advanced past the strong point, and took serious casualties on the left until their comrades silenced the position. Willes said they 'kept well up to the barrage.' On the right losses were few up to the First Objective and they then moved on to the Green Line, the Second Objective and there consolidated. Willes went back to report to his commanding officer before returning to the line, where he found 12th King's Royal Rifle Corps, which had passed through to take the Third Objective, hard-pressed. C Company, 6th Ox and Bucks, was sent to reinforce them in anticipation of a counter-attack:

'The Boche counter-attack crumpled up beneath our artillery and rifle fire. The 12th RB threw two companies in on the right flank of the KSLI [12th King's Shropshire Light Infantry] and the 10th Welsh put a company into Au Bon Gite. By dark the situation had become less critical, and could be said to be in some measure safe. The enemy shelling kept up all the afternoon and night. So ended the fight for Langemarck.'

Willes later wrote of the work of the runners, the men who, at considerable danger to themselves, carried messages across the battlefield:

'I established an advanced runners' post . . . Three . . . men went with me to act as runners . . . They all behaved exceedingly well. Private Cox was especially useful to me, but had the bad luck to be wounded by a shell about the middle of the day. Private Claridge was hit through the neck, and staggered 200 yards [182.8m] through ground that would have taxed the strongest man. He gave in his message and then collapsed, dying before night. I consider this the finest action that has been brought to my notice with regard to these operations.

'I have recommended both the above lads for reward, but I am afraid that Claridge will go unrewarded. The VC is the only posthumous reward, and I can scarcely hope for that for him.'

Lieutenant Edwin Vaughan of the 1/8th Royal Warwickshire Regiment had heard three days earlier that they were to take part in the next attack, alongside the 14th Royal Irish Rifles, at St Julien:

'The imminence of the attack made me very frightened and I trembled so much that I could not take part in the discussion at first. But after poring over the map for a bit and passing on all the information to my platoon, I grew calmer. Before noon we had learnt every detail of the ground from the map and, incidentally, had been issued with private's clothing.'

In the early hours of 16 August they went forward to cross the canal:

'We were at Bridge 2A of the Yser Canal, a few hundred yards north of Ypres. The air was poisoned by a terrible stench that turned me sick. In the dim light the water appeared to be a dark-green swamp wherein lay corpses of men and bodies of horses; shafts of wagons and gun wheels protruded from the putrefying mass . . . After a few minutes of silence he

Position between St Julien and Freezenberg on 21 August 1917 (Tank Museum).

[Sergeant Major Chalk] said "what is the time, Sir?" "Four forty-five" I said, and with my words the whole earth burst into flame with one tremendous roar as hundreds of guns hurled the first round of the barrage.'

They moved forward, at first marching in fours on Buff's Road. Reaching Van Heule Farm, just over halfway along the road from Wieltje to St Julien on the forward slope of the ridge, they saw the first of the great pillboxes. They moved to the right of the road and, close to the German barrage, took cover as best they could: 'we all dived into shell holes right on the fringe of the shell-torn zone. With my head just over the edge of my shell hole I lay blinking into the shrieking, crashing hail of death 30 yards [27.4m] in front.'

Orders came to locate and occupy Border House, which was south-east of St Julien. A patrol found the objective. Vaughan recorded in his diary:

'Dully I hoisted myself out of the mud and gave the signal to advance, which was answered by every man rising and stepping unhesitatingly into the barrage. The effect was so striking that I felt no more that awful dread of the shellfire, but followed them calmly into the crashing, spitting hell until we were surrounded by bursting shells and singing fragments, while above us a stream of bullets added their whining to the general pandemonium. The men were wonderful!'

They passed almost unharmed through the thickest part of the barrage, but then men began to fall. Vaughan had to be pulled from a mudhole, in which he was sinking unnoticed till he fired his revolver to attract attention. They were getting through a gap in the barbed wire when Corporal Breeze was blown into the air by a shell and fatally wounded. A ditch appeared before them and they tumbled in, finding the 14th Irish Rifles in occupation. It was the Steenbeek. They could go no further, for the Irish were stalled and the troops to their right were yet further from their objective. Indeed, from there on south, virtually no progress had been made. Vaughan was ordered to move his men to the left, behind the 1/5th Gloucestershire Regiment and push forward after dark to deal with enemy machine-guns. Night had fallen by the time they had reached the position in front of St Julien, so they probed forward, exciting bursts of fire from the Germans. Vaughan went forward to see for himself:

'I took a couple of men and went out towards a spot where I judged a gun to be. In five minutes we were stumbling into deep holes full of water, and the noise we made dragging our bodies through the mud caused flares to shoot up all along his line and the ground was swept by traversing guns. . . . it was obvious that to attempt a night attack would be madness, so I took my patrol back.'

No tanks went into action that day. Baker-Carr recalled:

'On the 16th of August, I made a desperate effort to send a dozen tanks to assist an attack near St Julien, but, in spite of the most determined and gallant efforts of the crews, not a single tank managed even to reach our own front line. The infantry attacked without them, but the assault was driven back with heavy loss through the inability to capture a line of concrete pillboxes.'

General Gough wrote of the action:

'The attack on the 16th was successful along most of the front, but the II Corps, which had to meet not only greater difficulties of ground, but a more concentrated artillery fire than that which the XIV and XVIII Corps on the left were encountering, was not able to gain all it had intended, strong counter-attacks driving back parts of its line and holding up others.'

He went on to say that, on the left, they had been entirely successful and the village of Langemarck was now in Allied hands, but the state of the ground had prevented the use of tanks. It could not be concealed the attacks on the Gheluvelt Plateau had failed. On 17 August, at a conference of Fifth Army corps commanders, Gough in part attributed the failure to the unwillingness of some officers to cling on to their gains.

Meanwhile, Haig went visiting. At the headquarters of XVII Corps he was told by Major Harold Franklyn the concrete-reinforced farms and dugouts had survived the British bombardment, and at XIX Corps he saw Lieutenant General Herbert Watts, who confirmed the Irish divisions had not done well. Haig then wrote:

'But I gather that the attacking troops had a long march up the evening before the battle through Ypres to the front line and then had to fight from zero 4.45am until nightfall. The men could have had no sleep and must have been dead tired. Here also a number of concrete buildings and dugouts were never really destroyed by artillery fire, and do not appear to have been taken. So the advances made here were small . . .

'The cause of the failure to advance on the right centre of the attack of the Fifth Army is due, I think, to commanders being in too great a hurry! Three more days should have been allowed in which, if fine, the artillery would have dominated the enemy's artillery, and destroyed the concrete defences! After Gough has got the facts more fully I have arranged to talk the matter over with him.'

Gough also wrote in his memoirs:

'The state of the ground was by this time frightful. The labour of bringing up supplies and ammunition, of moving or firing the guns, which had often sunk up to their axles, was a fearful strain on the officers and men, even during the daily task of maintaining the battle front. When it came to the advance of infantry . . . only the shortest advances could be contemplated. In consequence I informed the Commander-in-Chief that tactical success was not possible, or would be too costly, under such conditions, and advised that the attack be abandoned.'

He says this advice was given repeatedly during those days, but that Haig replied that it had to be continued. Gough attributed this to the fact the British and Commonwealth troops alone remained to prevent a German victory: the wider need had to prevail.

The refusal to recognize the limitations imposed by the effect of rainfall on the terrain was chief among the causes for the failed assault. The poor weather, even when no rain was falling, added to the problems, as aircraft were unable to observe the enemy gathering for counter-attacks, and thus artillery cover for freshly gained positions was compromised. But it was not the success of counter-attacks that had frustrated progress on the higher ground on the right: German artillery and infantry fire had prevented any advance taking place at all. There was no realistic chance of success on this front, and the opinion that continued pressure on the Germans could only be pursued here, in the Ypres Salient, was open to question, as the action at Cambrai in November would show.

19 August 1917: Dramatic Success of British Tanks

Weather: cloud cover; temperature, 69°F (20°C); rainfall, nil

Colonel Baker-Carr wrote glowingly of General Maxse's understanding of the problems the tanks faced. The tank commander pointed out his machines had not been allowed on the corduroy roads but had been obliged to attempt the crossing of the mud. Firm footing was vital to success. Further, the problem of 16 August had been the supportive complex of pillboxes of the ridge beyond St Julien, pillboxes behind which, ran the remains of a few crucial roads. The attack was planned for 19 August. No rain fell on 17 or 18 August.

Maxse supported the idea. Baker-Carr wrote:

> 'First of all, he and I went to call upon the divisional commanders concerned. Both of these had actually prepared plans for another infantry and artillery attack, but neither was very confident of the result. Their estimate of probable casualties varied from 600 to 1,000.
>
> 'General Maxse . . . ordered me to outline my scheme. It was received with contemptuous silence, but General Maxse . . . was not to be deterred. He told the divisional commanders that this was 'Baker-Carr's battle' and that any demands I made were to be met. He further pointed out that the number of infantry to be employed was considerably less than half their estimate of probable casualties.'

The force to be used was a composite company of a dozen tanks under the command of Major Broome of G Battalion. They had to move up during the night of 17/18 August and lie up in the ruins of St Julien next day, ready to go into action before dawn on 19 August. It was not as simple as it sounded.

D G Browne was given command of G47, the machine that had done so well in the Battle of Pilkem Ridge, as John Allden was away at rest-camp. It was a 'female', armed with six Lewis guns. Once cleaned up and re-supplied, she was ready to join the other ten tanks moving forward. The twelfth machine was on the far side of the canal and a doubtful starter. They began their journey forward at 7.30pm, 17 August. Browne said it was one of the most wearisome treks he had ever undertaken with tanks. The carefully laid timber road was damaged when the tanks turned and the route was clogged with other traffic:

> 'We had collided, of course, with the usual nightly ammunition trains, going up loaded to the forward battery positions and returning empty. Even a mule could not travel at night cross-country in the salient, and there were only three or four roads for all this vast traffic. Buffs Road . . . was well choked with opposing streams of mules and limbers, when into it turned our eleven tanks. The result, I hope, can be imagined; it was something beyond the power of polite language to describe. . . . Hour after hour went by, the night grew blacker and blacker, dawn, even, was drawing near, and still we were embedded in mules. . . . When I turned off the road . . . at Bellevue, it was two o'clock in the morning. It had taken me five and a half hours to cover those 2,500 yards [2.2km] — on a road.'

They were close to the front line of 31 July.

Late in the morning of 18 August Browne and his fellow tank commanders were sent back to 48th Divisional headquarters for a conference. Browne hung about, waiting to be called, and used the time to get to know the platoon commander of the 7th Warwicks, with whom he was to work next day. The infantry were to hang back behind the tanks and wait until the objective had been subdued, an outcome that would be signalled to them by the waving of a shovel from the manhole on top of the machine they were working with, before moving up to occupy it. In the end only Major Broome was called to take part in the discussions. The final plan was, however, decided. Coutts and Willard of 19 Company would attack the Cockroft, Baker and Kane of 20 Company Maison du Hibou, Morgan and Close of 20 Company would go for Triangle Farm and Vancouver, Claughton of 21 Company was allocated Hillock Farm, on the road up to Triangle Farm from St Julien, and Browne himself was to attack a row of gunpits opposite Hillock Farm. Chaddock's machine was to follow Browne as back-up. They were to cross the Steenbeek to the left of St Julien on fascines, to be laid after dark, leaving the road to do so and then going on into the village.

Detail from Kessel's map: the Cockroft and Springfield (Tank Museum).

Campaign Chronicle

At 1am on Sunday, 19 August, they moved cautiously forward, as slowly and silently as they could manage. It was a clear, starlit night. They crept over the crest of the low Pilkem Ridge and down into the shallow valley, fearful of detection by the enemy. By 2.30am Browne was close to Vanheule Farm; still a long way to go. Willard's machine developed a leaking exhaust and had to be driven with all doors open to avoid gassing the crew. Eventually they reached the Steenbeek, just as it was starting to get light:

> 'This stream . . . presented . . . so forbidding a spectacle that I got hurriedly out of the tank to lead the way across myself. At one time an insignificant trickle of water a couple of yards wide at the most, but enclosed between banks 6-8 feet [1.8-2.4m] high, the pounding of our own barrage, followed during the past three weeks by that of the Germans, had multiplied its difficulties tenfold. There was little water to be seen now, only a sort of boggy surface, several yards across, beneath which the fascines laid that night by the engineers had already disappeared completely under the weight of the leading tanks. Some of these tanks were now climbing a perfect precipice of mud on the opposite side, the black nose of one pointing almost vertically upward against the rapidly brightening sky in the east.'

Two machines were stuck, Willard's and Kane's. Browne was told the fascines were, indeed, in place and they got over without difficulty, crawled over the ruins of a house and found themselves in St Julien exactly on zero hour. In front was G44, Claughton's tank, and the two machines immediately went into action. There had been no preparatory bombardment to warn the Germans of an attack and now the British artillery were firing smoke shells only. One fell short and temporarily blinded Browne. The road had been shelled for more than a month, but the central *pavé*, the cobbled part, had survived intact except where a direct hit had punched a hole. It was, however, covered with slime and careful driving was needed to avoid skidding off it. Trees had come down across the road and crashing over them reduced control and the power to steer, and so increased the danger of skidding into the ditch, apart from the peril of breaking a track. Browne wrote of his driver:

> 'Waller drove G47 over a succession of trees without a semblance of trouble. Everything loose inside, of course, including the crew, fell helplessly about each time we crashed; but this was a part of the ordinary day's work. The [carrier] pigeons . . . bore this repeated experience, which must have seemed to them like a series of earthquakes, with as much equanimity as anybody, although their basket usually was dislodged and upset.'

65

Browne knew the gun-pits he was seeking stood near a flooded tributary of the Steenbeek, across which the road went, and soon he saw the water to the right of the road. At the same moment the Lewis gunners opened fire and through his revolver loophole Browne could see a row of great mounds: pits for heavy artillery, he guessed, from which machine-gun fire was beating a tattoo on his tank. His gunners told him they could see Germans retreating with a machine-gun and after about fifteen minutes enemy shellfire on the positions confirmed they had been vacated. Up in front, G44 was firing at close range into the windows of Hillock Farm and soon the shovel was waving the infantry forward. Browne had thought about going on to help the attack on the Cockroft, but his orders were to return as soon as his objective was taken, and Claughton's tank filled the way forward. So G47 swung round to head for St Julien, Chaddock in support was doing the same and G44 followed up behind. At 5.45am they were passing through St Julien, going back to base.

At the Steenbeek the ditched tanks were still stuck, almost blocking the crossing. Browne's machine slid down the bank into Willard's immobile machine and had too little grip to back off. What was more, the stream was also the exact line of the German barrage. It took half an hour of digging, gathering bits of wood and trees and experimental efforts to get a grip before they could heave themselves free. At headquarters they learned that all objectives had been taken, and at low cost. The details emerged later.

Coutts attacked the Cockroft with his 'female' tank, leaving the road to get within 50 yards [45.7m] and opening fire with his Lewis guns. The garrison, in spite of the strength of the fortification, abandoned their position after the briefest of fights. Coutts's supporting infantry, however, failed to come up at his signal, and the tank commander was obliged to leave his machine and go on foot to find them. Maison du Hibou fell to Baker's 'male' tank. From the road little was achieved, but Baker left the hard surface and managed to get to the rear of the blockhouse before bogging down. From there his 6-pounders hurled some thirty or forty rounds at the door, forcing the garrison out to be captured by men of the 1/8th Worcesters or shot down by Morgan's 'female' tank. Morgan had been attacking Triangle Farm, which held out valiantly until the infantry penetrated this rather less solidly constructed position. Morgan moved on to help Baker but slid off the road and was ditched – fortunately with a good field of fire over the line of German retreat from Maison du Hibou. He then unditched and returned to St Julien. Meanwhile, Close went for Vancouver and he, too, ditched, but it was threat enough to cause the abandonment of the strong point. The casualties were trivial. Reports vary slightly, but Browne's figures are fifteen infantrymen wounded and of the Tank Corps there were two killed and one officer and ten men wounded. He points out the wounded included the entire crew of Morgan's tank, which had faulty armour-plate that scattered tiny splinters inside the machine when hit by German fire.

It had been a remarkable demonstration of just how effective tanks could be, given suitable terrain conditions for their operations. This condition escaped the notice of many and tanks were to be squandered in the coming weeks by the failure to consider the terrain in detail. An example of the way in which appreciation of the action was selective is provided in Browne's memoirs. He relates how General Gough visited the old tank park in Oosthoek Wood to congratulate them:

'As the general approached, his staff quite obviously shepherded him past Coutts and diverted him on to me. With his first question I realised the reason for this manoeuvre. He asked me if the infantry had supported me properly. I was able to testify, quite honestly, that they had . . . Some rumour must have reached the staff about the trouble at the Cockcroft, and Coutts, who might have made damaging revelations, was given no opportunity to speak. It was a little thing, but instructive.'

Browne himself was delighted with the outcome of the action, but unimpressed with the persistent pursuit of what seemed to him an unattainable objective:

'Higher Command . . . must have realised that von Armin, or whoever was responsible for the interminable series of pillboxes and concreted farms, had devised a method of defence which in such a country, and in combination with the barriers that our own artillery was augmenting daily, deserved at least as much credit for our discomfiture as that convenient public scapegoat, the rain.'

22 August 1917: Remaining Strong points on the Zonnebeke-Langemarck Road Attacked With Little Success

Weather: partly cloudy; temperature: 78°F (25°C); rainfall, nil

A similar assault, with more infantry than before, was attempted three days later. General Gough recollected this as another general attack by the three corps on the right of his front:

'The objectives in this attack had been reduced to those within a short distance of our line, as it was impossible for the men to go forward over any long-distance; my object was to spare the troops to the utmost

The Leicesters at Zillebecke, resting in the sunshine, 22 August 1917 (Taylor Library).

possible degree, while at the same time complying with my orders from GHQ to the effect that the battle must be continued.'

The element of surprise was now lacking and Springfield and Winnipeg, which might have fallen three days earlier, were better prepared and the approaches heavily shelled. Springfield was taken but fell to a counter-attack. The attack was also on a wider front with II Corps involved on the right. Here the assault went in at 7am, two and a quarter hours after that of XVIII Corps when, in full daylight and aroused by the action to the north, the defenders were alert. The objective was Inverness Copse, alongside the Menin road and Fitzclarence Farm to its left. Two tanks supported the 6th Somerset Light Infantry when, having taken the Copse, a counter-attack drove them back halfway through it. The 6th Cornwall Light Infantry were held up by fire from Fitzclarence Farm and supporting tanks were forced to withdraw when the infantry fell back. A renewed effort the next day, when [0.05in] 1.4mm of rain fell, saw three of four tanks ditched and the attack called off.

Calculation of Casualties

The term 'casualties' covers those killed, wounded, missing or taken prisoner. The system of recording casualties differed from nation to nation and was subject to a number of possible sources of error.

The British counted their losses almost immediately, listing as 'missing' all those not accounted for under the other two categories. The number of missing should have been adjusted if a man turned up wounded or regained his unit having been lost, but this did not always happen. Minor wounds that left a man fit enough to fight were not counted by the British, but were by the Americans. It is also worth noting that, on the Western Front, nine per cent of deaths and fifty-seven per cent of wounds were from causes other than enemy action.

German casualty figures were compiled some time after the action concerned, so the figure of missing tended to be a smaller proportion of the total, as the fate of these soldiers became known. The way in which lightly wounded were counted is disputed. The British *Official History* added 30 per cent to German figures to take account of the alleged exclusion of men wounded but likely to recover and rejoin their units, a calculation called into question by many. Towards the end of the war figures were falsified to confuse the Allies, and the collapse of the German state in 1918 led to statistics being lost or further corrupted. Precise casualty figures do not exist.

The most remarkable incident took place in the centre where a tank of F Battalion, on which the section commander, Richardson, was travelling to attack Gallipoli Fort, ditched without infantry support. It came under fire from the enemy, but, assuming it had been captured, the British fired on it as well. All attempts to signal from the tank failed or were misunderstood. The tank maintained fire against the Germans through the next day and at night the enemy clambered all over it but could not break in. By 24 August the situation in the tank had become critical with one man killed and all except Richardson wounded. Food and water were running short. The next night a man managed to crawl back to the British lines and report the true situation, after which

Richardson and his crew were evacuated. They had held out for seventy-two hours.

Of thirty-four machines in action on 22 August, eighteen became mired as soon as they left the road and another six were destroyed by shellfire.

25 August 1917: Inverness Copse Lost

Weather: partial cloud cover; temperature 68°F (19°C); rainfall, 0.1mm

On 24 August Inverness Copse was retaken by the Germans, in part because of 'friendly fire' falling on the 10th Durham Light Infantry, which was holding a line halfway through the wood while their supporting artillery believed they had retreated to the western edge. This set-back on the Gheluvelt Ridge precipitated change, but how the decision came to be made is somewhat obscure. Gough's memoirs appear to be clear:

> 'It was now evident that if we were to clear the ridge and get possession of all the high ground, it was essential to extend considerably the front of the II Corps. It was too narrow to hope for a successful advance, taking into consideration the concentration of German guns against it.
>
> 'It was essential that the Second Army on the right should push forward and so draw off a considerable proportion of the enemy's artillery fire. I put these conclusions to GHQ, and in consequence General Kiggell, the Chief of Staff, came over to Cassel, and there a small conference was held with myself and Plumer and our senior staff officers to discuss the proposition.'

He goes on to say that Plumer did not like the idea and Kiggell lacked the 'personality' to carry a decision, so the matter had to wait for Sir Douglas Haig, who 'saw the cogency of the arguments' Gough put forward. Writing after the Second World War, Gough said:

> 'As early as the end of August this fact [the need to extend the front southwards] became so clear to me that I asked to see Haig to make him, if possible, accept this proposal. Kiggell, then his CSO, came to discuss my fresh proposal as Haig had been called to London. After a discussion in which Plumer took part, my proposal was agreed to, and as a result Plumer took over in the middle of September the right of the Fifth Army on the whole breadth of the ridge . . .'

Haig's accounts do not coincide with Gough's recollections, neither do they

German 5.9cm Gun wrecked by a direct hit, Langemarck, 23 August 1917 (Taylor Library).

contradict them entirely. In his despatch of 25 December 1917 the timing of his decision is unclear, but the implication is that he formed the view that Plumer should assume responsibility for the high ground crossed by the Menin road after the Battle of Langemarck (16-18 August) but before the Cockcroft attack of 19 August. According to his diary he arranged to see Plumer on 25 August and Gough later that day to inform them of the change of frontages, presumably as a consequence of Kiggell's meeting with them the previous day. This was followed up with an order dated 28 August, which set out the new arrangements, but also gave Gough powers to continue to pressure the Germans not only on his remaining front, but also against the woods flanking the Menin road: a provision that was withdrawn two days later.

The *Official History*, which was not finalized until after the Second World War, says the second meeting Haig held that day was attended by both Plumer and Gough, when it was decided that II Corps should be transferred to Second Army 'early in September'. Plumer asked for three weeks to prepare for his first attack and Gough was ordered to remain active and to take the Menin road woods (Inverness, Glencorse and Nonne Bosschen) as well as to continue pushing towards Poelcappelle. The precise facts are thus difficult to establish.

The rain, having been trivial on 24 and 25 August at a total of 0.003in (0.1mm), now began to fall seriously. Sunday 26 August produced 0.7in (19.6mm). Another attack was imminent.

Campaign Chronicle

27 August 1917: Springfield Falls to the Worcestershires

Weather: half cloud cover; temperature 57°F (14°C); rainfall, 0.6in (15.3mm)

Gough, in response to what he understood to be Haig's wish that Fifth Army should continue to 'press the enemy' while Second Army made its preparations, undertook limited actions, declining anything more substantial until it became possible to move his artillery up to the Steenbeek. That depended in part on the weather, and in part on securing the ridge east of the stream. The elusive objectives on the Menin road were also attacked.

In the early hours of 27 August Lieutenant Vaughan went to get his orders. His battalion was already in its forming-up position near some gunpits west of the Steenbeek:

> 'The rain had stopped for the time being, but the ground was utterly impassable being covered with water for 30 yards [27.4m] at a stretch in some parts, and everywhere shell holes full of water. He [Pepper, his commanding officer] showed me the final orders which detailed zero hour for 1.55pm — a midday attack! My instructions were that at zero minus 10 (i.e. 1.45pm) I was to move my troops forward to the line of the Steenbeek. . . . While we were talking a message arrived from Brigade: "There is a nice drying wind. The attack will take place. Render any final indents for materials forthwith.'

The attack on the Menin road went in at 4.45am with the support of four tanks and was intended to get into Inverness Copse and Glencorse Wood. It failed. The tanks all ditched somewhere near Clapham Junction, well short of their objective.

To the north the troops had to endure more than seven hours of waiting before they attacked. Tanks in St Julien had the Poelcappelle road open to them, but the road branching right, towards Winnipeg, was blocked by a derelict tank and thus the Zonnebeke–Langemarck road, on which Springfield stood, could only be reached by heading north and turning right at Vancouver. At the appointed hour the British barrage began and immediately the German artillery replied. Vaughan and his men moved forward:

> 'Shells were pouring on to the St Julien–Triangle Road as we advanced, and through the clouds of smoke and fountains of water I saw ahead the lines of figures struggling forward through the mud. It only took us five minutes to reach the Boilerhouse [a pillbox], but during that time I saw, with a sinking heart, that the lines had wavered, broken, and almost

72

disappeared. Over our heads there poured a ceaseless stream of bullets from sixteen machine-guns behind, and all around us spat the terrifying crackle of enemy fire.'

The 1st Company, 414 (Württemberg) Infantry Regiment held Springfield with 3rd Company to their rear and 2nd Company to their left, near the Winnipeg road junction. The attack was expected and the men, concealed from twelve British observation balloons, were in readiness in shell holes, as Otto von Moser describes:

'At 2.45pm [German time] enemy fire becomes a storm. Communication between the support command and the front line is compromised. The scene is obscured by smoke. The commanding officer hears and feels the wave of fire passing the Wilhelmstellung and getting nearer and nearer. The front line is under pressure; he has to help. Seventh and 8th Companies move forward in tight formation . . .'

Vaughan sent three platoons forward from the Boilerhouse and then peered out, trying to make sense of the scene: 'With a laboured groaning and clanking, four tanks churned past us to the Triangle. I was dazed, and straining my eyes through the murk of the battle I tried to distinguish our fellows, but only here and there was a figure moving.'

Major W H L Watson, D Battalion, 1st Tank Brigade, described the journey up the road:

'It was lonely on the Poelcappelle Road, with nothing for company but shells bursting near the tanks. After the heavy rain the tanks slipped about on the broken setts, and every shell hole in the road was a danger – one lurch, and the tank would slide off into the marsh.

'Very slowly the tanks picked their way. Three tanks reached the crossroads . . . turned to the right . . . and, passing through the infantry, enfiladed the shell holes occupied by the enemy.'

The Germans suffered from the shellfire and – as von Moser reports – from gas:

'The gas masks were at the ready but, before the gas is recognised and before the clay-covered fingers can act, the gas does its work. Out of the skies the aircraft strafe the shell holes. And now, towards the flat horizon three monsters appear, going north from St Julien, but then turning along the regiment's front. Following them wave after wave of infantry. Everyone with a rifle or machine-gun fires until the barrels steam. Two light and two heavy machine-guns are with each company and 200m

[218.7 yards] from their front they force the enemy to ground. Now the rifles must stay in action and the machine-guns must be kept cool – coffee, soda water, anything – but it's not enough! Under the duckboards where the wounded are lying there is water. Bring a hatchet! The floor is torn up and the water scooped out in dixies to pour into the machine-guns. The brave machine-gunners still pin the enemy down.'

The tank commander doubted the effect his machines had on the course of events. He remarked the fire they laid down was no more than local, as the road was embanked. The enemy pulled back, he said, and suffered some casualties in doing so, but then fought back from the shell holes. The German view – courtesy of Otto von Moser – is expressed with greater drama:

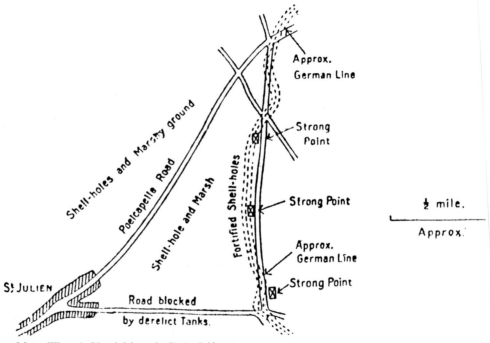

Major Watson's Sketch Map: the Springfield action.

'But what's happening on the right with 1st Company? Tanks! Turning our flank and pushing us to the left! First Company had seen the danger and deployed artillery and machine-guns, but the three tanks had hit the line between 413 and 414 Regiments where control was weakest. With machine-gun fire they spit death and destruction on the vulnerable line, smothering resistance, forcing surrender – the last at about 5pm. It was here Reserve Lieutenant Walter Layh received his fatal wound, and of

Campaign Chronicle

Lieutenant Eugen Linse of 1 Machine-gun Company nothing more was
heard.'

Back at their headquarters, Vaughan and his Commanding Officer had no idea
of what was happening:

'we waited on and on; the shells continued to crash around us, the sky
clouded and rain began to fall. Time after time he sent out runners to find
out what the position was, but none returned. Two tanks were stranded
on the road just beyond Hillock Farm, and in front, save for occasional
movement near the gunpits, there was no sign of life. The hours crept on;
our barrage had lifted from the German line and now was falling on the
Langemarck Ridge. At last . . . a runner arrived with a report from Taylor
that the attack was completely held up: "casualties very heavy".'

Vaughan was then ordered up to the gunpits and told to take orders from
Taylor once he got there, if he got there. Followed by his batman, Dunham,
and by eight signallers and runners, he hurried off through the mud:

'Immediately there came the crackle of bullets and mud was spattered
about me as I ran, crawled, and dived into shell holes, over bodies,
sometimes up to the armpits in water, sometimes crawling on my face
along a ridge of slimy mud around some crater. . . . Exhausted by my
efforts, I paused a moment in a shell hole; in a few seconds I felt myself
sinking, and struggle as I might I was sucked down until I was firmly
gripped round the waist and still being dragged in. The leg of a corpse
was sticking out of the side, and frantically I grabbed it; it wrenched off,
and casting it down I pulled in a couple of rifles and yelled to the troops
in the gunpit to throw me more. Laying them flat I wriggled over them
and dropped, half dead, into the wrecked gun position.'

There he found Taylor, pale but calm, with the news that the attack had not
even reached the German line. Vaughan was to take his company up the road
to the Triangle and then seize Springfield. He gathered what men he could. Of
his headquarters staff only he and Dunham survived. Sending Dunham back to
the Boilerhouse to fetch up the reserve platoon, he looked about and found
about fifteen men. Up the road they went, running into shrapnel as they got up
to the tanks:

'Up the road we staggered, shells bursting around us. A man stopped
dead in front of me, and exasperated I cursed him and butted him with
my knee. Very gently he said "I'm blind, Sir" and turned to show me his
eyes and nose torn away by a piece of shell. . . . At the Triangle the shelling

was lighter . . . several wounded men of the 8th Worcesters and 7th Warwicks jumped out of their shell holes and joined us.

'A tank had churned its way slowly round behind Springfield and opened fire; a moment later I looked and nothing remained of it but a crumpled heap of iron; it had been hit by a large shell. It was now almost dark and there was no firing from the enemy . . . As we all closed in, the Boche garrison ran out with their hands up . . . We sent the sixteen prisoners back across the open but they had only gone 100 yards [91.4m] when a German machine-gun mowed them down.'

Vaughan took over the pillbox as his headquarters. He crawled through the small doorway and found a scene of dirt and destruction within. Two Germans lay dead and a severely wounded officer, his left leg almost severed, lay in a machine-gun niche, victims of the tank's shellfire. Vaughan made the man as comfortable as he could and offered him his flask. The rum in it was refused, but water was gulped down. A German signal lamp was discovered and a man was sent out to flash '8th Warwick in Springfield' towards the rear. It was not acknowledged. An officer of the 8th Worcester was carried in on a stretcher and seemed cheerful in spite of a wound in his back. He asked for a cigarette and they put one between his lips. He died before they could light it. More Germans arrived to surrender. Vaughan stepped out to inspect his line:

'From the darkness on all sides came the groans and wails of wounded men; faint, long, sobbing moans of agony, and despairing shrieks. It was too horribly obvious that dozens of men with serious wounds must have crawled for safety into new shell holes, and now the water was rising about them and, powerless to move, they were slowly drowning. . . . And we could do nothing to help them; Dunham was crying quietly beside me, and all the men were affected by the piteous cries.'

Vaughan returned to the pillbox and resumed attempts to signal with the lamp. Finally, at about 11.30pm, came the sound of men ploughing through the mire; the 4th Berkshires had come to relieve them. As they made their way to the rear they pulled as many wounded as they could onto drier ground. Some cursed them for leaving them and were told, without conviction, that the stretcher-bearers were coming. From battalion headquarters Vaughan was sent to report to Brigadier Sladden at Cheddar Villa, who poured him whisky and quizzed him about enemy dispositions. The next morning he found that, of ninety men, his company now numbered only fifteen.

The Württemberger record describes the close of the battle thus:

'Until dark there was fighting along the Langemarck-Zonnebeke road.

From the Wilhelmstellung line 3rd and 4th Companies and 7th and 8th Companies attacked to bring the rest of 1st and 2nd Companies back in. Night, fog and rain, and sometimes a deathly quiet, cover the battlefield of 27 August.'

The *Official History* sums the day up as follows: 'the actions that took place on the 27th in accordance with the decision that activity should be continued were minor affairs; but they resulted in considerable further casualties and very little gain of ground.'

What gain there had been owed much to the few tanks involved which, while still able to keep to what had been roads, gave the infantry some cover and support. All machines were out of action by the end of the day.

From Tuesday, 28 August 1917 what almost passed for peace fell over the Ypres Salient. There were new attacks and a steady flow of casualties, but the fury of the previous four weeks faded away. Days, then weeks, passed. On 13 September General von Kuhl, Crown Prince Rupprecht's Chief of Staff, wrote: 'My inmost conviction that the battle in Flanders is at an end is more and more strengthened.'

It was an illusion. General Plumer had asked for three weeks to prepare for Second Army's renewal of the battle and his request was granted. There was much to do. On 1 September Haig summarized the achievements, so far as he saw them:

'Since the beginning of the Ypres battle forty-one German Divisions have been engaged on the Ypres front of which over thirty have been withdrawn to refit.

'Ten of the [German] Divisions brought in to reinforce this sector have been withdrawn from the French front . . .

'Documents recently captured show the heavy strain to which the enemy's troops are being subjected owing to losses, hardship, and the moral effect of our artillery and air superiority. These factors are having a steadily increasing effect on the German troops as they did during the Battle of the Somme, though in the present case they are more likely to have more important results owing to our greater superiority in material, and to the inferior value of the recruits which are now being drafted into German units.'

31 August: Second Army Publishes New Guidelines For Attacks

As early as 12 August General Plumer had been considering how best to respond to what were now recognized as new German defensive tactics. He set out his ideas in a memorandum to GHQ in response to its memo of 7 August. The product of this was *Second Army's Notes on Training and Preparation for Offensive Operations* of 31 August, and the next three weeks saw the training of his army in the application of the new approach. The nature of the problem was set out succinctly:

> 'The new system of defence adopted by the enemy, consisting of lines of shell holes in depth and a large proportion of his strength disposed in readiness for a counter-attack, is liable to produce a condition of affairs by which a) the farther we penetrate his line, the stronger and more organized we find him; b) the farther we penetrate his line, the weaker and more disorganized we become.'

Major General C H Harington, Plumer's Chief of Staff, went on to say that, lacking trenches for designation as objectives, the intention should be to secure ground suitable for repelling the inevitable counter-attack and the position selected should allow the British to consolidate and hold it. The ever-present threat of counter-attack meant the British attack had to be by forces arrayed in greater depth so that support was always readily available:

> 'The distance between objectives and consequently the areas to be cleared will decrease as the advance progresses on any one day. Further, the numbers of troops allotted to the final objective will be proportionately greater than those allotted to the first, so as to ensure that there are sufficient to hold on . . . and exploit success when the counter-attack is repulsed.'

The formations to be used were also to change. The leading wave of the attack was to be formed of extended lines to force the enemy to give his positions away and the following troops were to be in small parties or in file, ready to swing into action to take out enemy points of resistance. The approach was flexible and initiative was expected of junior officers leading small units. Detailed study of the ground and of aerial photographs was advised.

The nature of the fighting anticipated led to comments on the weapons to be used:

> 'Rifle and Lewis gun fire is becoming more and more important. The rifle grenade is most valuable for dealing with the enemy in shell holes. The hand grenade will only occasionally be required, and therefore the bombing squad should be trained primarily as riflemen.
>
> 'It has been proved that smoke grenades (No. 27) and an improvised 3-inch Stokes mortar smoke bomb (The Varley Bomb) are of great value for

blinding machine-gun emplacements and concrete dugouts during the advance . . .'

The former concept of stout lines of bayonet-wielding infantry pouring into the enemy trench, where hand grenades would rout the enemy out of his dugouts, had given way to a much more open vision, in which riflemen and light machine-gunners would eliminate strong points under the cover of smoke they themselves laid down at a distance.

A battalion now had thirty Lewis guns, eight Stokes mortars and some sixteen men with rifle grenades. The operations would be covered by the artillery, which was also to change tactics:

'The barrage must have much greater depth, and with the exception of the creeping barrage, the barrages must not move so regularly.

'There will be several barrages of different natures of guns or a combination of natures.

'The enemy must be driven to lie down at the bottom of shell holes and be drilled to always expect another barrage to pass over. This can be done by making barrages irregular and unexpected.

'His front system must be cut off and starved. All means of supply and reinforcement must be reduced . . .

'His batteries must be located and destroyed.'

In order to get at enemy batteries, which were located as far back as practical, the British guns had to be pushed forward. The other target for destruction by artillery was the pillbox. For success in both cases, good observation was necessary, and thus fair weather. As to the creeping barrage, the need to prevent it leaving the infantry behind was recognized and the state of the ground in determining the pace of the infantry advance was to be taken into account. On the other hand, the protective barrage might, it was suggested, be put further forward than normal. The achievement of these wise counsels was, perhaps optimistically, to be secured by putting a senior artillery officer at every divisional headquarters.

A passage dealing with the use of machine-guns followed. They were seen as laying down fire supplementary to the artillery barrage and were to be moved forward behind the advancing infantry: a bound of 800 yards (730m) could be made and the guns could be back in action in the space of thirty minutes, the memo stated. The document finished with a brief collection of points on communications, including the suggestion that relay posts used by message-carrying runners should be marked with large, coloured flags by day and coloured lamps by night. Given that German artillery observers oversaw the entire battlefield, this seems a remarkably dangerous idea.

There is no mention at all of tanks. Eleven short paragraphs by Harington set out the Operation Order No. 1 of 10 May for the capture of the Messines Ridge, one of which specified the use of two battalions of the 'Heavy Branch Machine-Gun Corps', the cover name used for tank formations before the formation of the Tank Corps. That was followed on 18 May by a document of greater length entirely given over to the use of the tanks. But now, with drying weather and recent experience of both the successes and the failures of tanks, Harington was silent. The other major weakness of the new tactical approach was in communications. References were made to ways of sending messages to the rear, but only contact between advancing units got additional attention. It was apparently accepted that contact between front and rear by telephone line would be tenuous if it worked at all, and that visual signals, by lamp or flag, would have to be relied on to call down protective artillery fire against counter-attacks. Failing that, the vulnerable runner was the only means left.

On 7 September Brigadier General H J Elles, commanding the Tank Corps, wrote to GHQ to say that the use of tanks before the end of the month could not be foreseen because of the state of the ground and he sought, and was granted, permission to withdraw five of his eight battalions for training, preparation for winter, and use in First and Third Army sectors. This was agreed, and on 11 September the three Tank brigades moved, leaving three battalions of I Brigade and one of II Brigade for the next phase of the battle.

Lieutenant Willes and the 6th Ox & Bucks had been relieved on 18 August and withdrew to Malakoff Farm and thence to Swindon Camp. The Battalion had a chance to rest and also to train. Willes was detailed to become a member of the Committee of Brigade Sports and 30 August-2 September passed in making preparations. On 3 September the NCOs did a compass march in the morning and the Six-a-Side Football took place in the afternoon. C Company won and was designated to represent the Battalion in the Brigade League. On 4 September the Battalion came third in the Cross-Country race. The Field Ambulance won and the Durhams came second:

'September 5th — Colonel Boyle turned up late last night, having left London about twelve hours before — good, quick work! He claims that we shall see great changes in the war in a month or two. I am very glad to hear it. I have known this war, man and boy, for the last three years, and I have seen precious little change in it yet — the same old mud and monotony.

'The Tug of War came off this morning. Our team got into the semi-finals, which will be pulled off later.

'Our football team succumbed to the 12th KRRC [King's Royal Rifle Corps], who were a lot better than our people.'

Campaign Chronicle

Training and sports occupied their days. On 7 September they gave a platoon-in-attack demonstration in the presence of the divisional commander. The sports took place the next day and the Battalion did very well, to Willes's gratification. At 8pm on 10 September they were moving back into the line, occupying dugouts on the bank of the canal near Bards Causeway. They were back at Malakoff Farm two nights later and then, on 18 September, they moved forward once again, in readiness for the attack of 20 September. Since 1 September they had had 33.7mm (1.33in) of rain, more than half of which fell on a single day, 6 September. On 19 September they had 5.1mm (0.2in) of rain, which gave Gough fresh worries, according to Haig:

> 'About midnight [on the night of 19/20 September] General Gough proposed that operations should be postponed on account of rain, but General Plumer between 1 and 2 am after consulting his corps and divisional commanders decided to adhere to plan.'

General Harington, in his memoirs, tells of such a conversation, although he does not state the date on which it took place and the time differs:

> 'General Gough was, I know, opposed to the attempts in such weather; he rang me up at about two-thirty one night, on the eve of an attack, and wanted me to ask General Plumer to stop it. The latter came down to my room and waited while I rang up and asked the opinion of each of our corps commanders.
>
> 'They all, with one exception, who did not express a definite opinion, agreed that it was impossible to get orders to them. General Plumer then took the telephone and I remember his words so well: "Is that you, Gough? The attack must go on. I am responsible, not you. Good night and good luck."'

An objection on the grounds of weather on 19 September seems to have been unreasonable and may have contributed to subsequent rejections of similar pleas when conditions were much worse.

The artillery support for Second Army's assault had been flooding into the area during this brief dry season. By this time they were, in Plumer's eyes, still some 140 guns short of requirement: he had asked for 1,339 weapons and only got 1,295, consisting of 575 heavy and medium guns and 720 field guns and howitzers. For the assault on Vimy Ridge the previous April there had been one gun for every 9 yards (8.23m) of front, and at Messines Ridge Plumer had had a gun for every 7 yards (6.4m). Now he had a gun for every 5.2 yards (4.75m) and for seven days' preliminary bombardment and the first day of the battle, 3.5 million rounds: four times the fire density Gough had employed on 31 July.

Campaign Chronicle

Clouds of dust marked the arrival of these materials.

There was also a massive programme of road-building, with 12,500 men of the Labour Corps and 1,000 men of the British West Indies Regiment added to the engineers and pioneers attached to the corps on this front. Elm or beech planks, 9 feet (2.75m) long and a foot (30.5cm) across were hauled up, as was broken stone, by cart. The stone was used to fill holes and the planks were laid on the mud and stone, four or five along the length of the road and then a final surface of crosswise planks secured with spikes. The ANZAC sector of the front received eighty trucks carrying 3 tons [3.04 tonnes] of planks a day to complete their roads by 19 September. The materials were taken to the front from the dumps by 120 wagon teams. Lest dust revealed their progress, the work had to be done by night.

The war in the air had tipped in favour of the British with the introduction of new aircraft, notably the DeHavilland DH5, and the improvement in pilot training. In July Manfred von Richtofen, recovering in hospital from wounds received when he was shot down on 6 July, wrote a report to bemoan the Germans' loss of technical superiority. The Sopwith Triplanes and Camels, the French SPAD XIII fighters and the Bristol F2Bs were, he said, all better than similar German aircraft. Nonetheless, bombing attacks were made by night by both sides while, during the day, the Royal Flying Corps was able to carry out photographic and reconnaissance missions, although with some interference, as Hugh Quigley of the 12th Royal Scots, 9th Division saw:

> 'In the morning, through a glorious clear sky of pale blue, we watched our own aeroplanes and the enemy's circling slowly and dropping outside our range of vision, heard the constant rattle of machine-guns and the crack of high shrapnel, white and black. All we could do was lie motionless on our back and pray the enemy had not seen us.'

This was written home from Vlamertinghe on 17 September, after Quigley had been in the salient for some days. He described the tortured terrain in which his unit was patrolling:

> 'The country resembles a sewage-heap more than anything else, pitted with shell holes of every conceivable size, and filled to the brim with green, slimy water, above which a blackened arm or leg might project. It becomes a matter of great skill picking a way across such a network of death traps, for drowning is almost certain in one of them. I remember a run I had at the beginning of this week – for dear life, if you like. Five of us had spent the night patrolling and were returning to Brigade HQ when the enemy sighted us and put a barrage along the duckboard track we

were following. Early dawn broke in the east, and a grey light filtered eerily through dim cloud-masses to a desolate world of brown, touching skeleton woods strangely, and blackening the edge of ridge where the German trenches lay. First one shell dropped 10 yards [9.1m] behind us, then one came screaming so close that we dropped in our tracks and waited for the end. I got right under the duckboard track, and the hail of shrapnel and mud on it was thunderous enough to frighten the most courageous. Then we stood up, all safe though muddy, and with a "Run like hell, boys," went off in a devil's race, with shells bursting at our heels, for half a mile [0.8km], dropping at last in complete exhaustion in a trench out of range.'

The shelling and shooting persisted throughout the 'quiet' period. Between 30 August and 30 September Second Army suffered casualties of 299 officers and 5,198 other ranks, while Fifth Army, which was more easily observed by the Germans, lost 521 officers and 10,135 other ranks killed, wounded or missing.

20 September 1917: Battle of the Menin Road

Weather: overcast; temperature, 66°F (18°C); rainfall, nil

The achievements of Thursday, 20 September were costly but raised hopes of a release from the awful, mud-ridden grind of the previous month. On Second Army's left was I ANZAC Corps under Lieutenant General Sir William Birdwood, attacking a front between the Ypres-Roulers railway and the Menin road itself. South of the road was X Corps, with the 23rd Division on the Australian right, then 41st Division and 39th Division moving forward from Shrewsbury Forest with the 19th Division of IX Corps forming a defensive flank to the south. To the north of the railway Fifth Army attacked.

Eddie Johnson was a signaller with S Department, 1st Australian Division. He left Dickebusch for the Menin road on 19 September:

'The day had been perfect when leaving, but towards evening a steady rain was falling, and the surface of the battlefield changed from dust to mud. Owing to weather conditions, etc., the previous cable line had badly deteriorated and had to be relaid from Halfway House to Hooge Crater. It was a very important line, and would be used by Brigadier Bennett at Hooge Crater for the hop-over, during the Ypres stunt the following day. It was situated close to the front line.

'At 3pm the artillery opened up with a terrific bombardment . . . Having

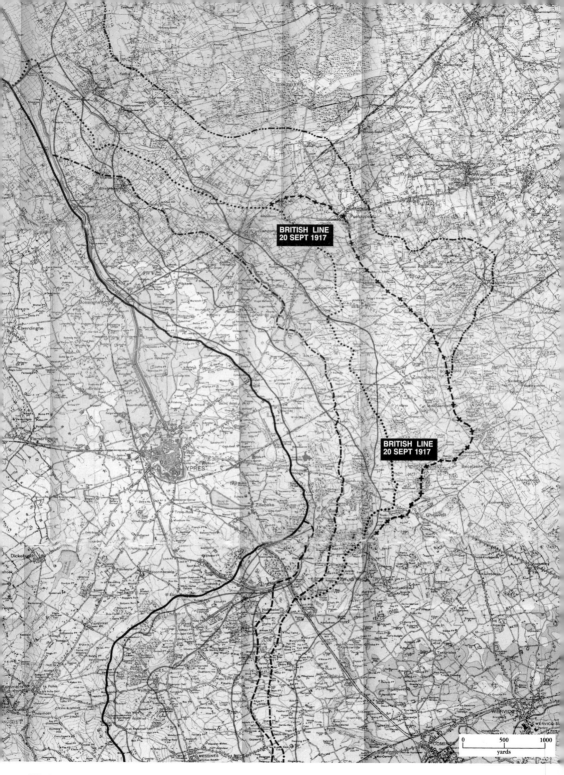

The Ypres Salient: terrain map based on the Offical History, *the dotted line shows front line of 20 September 1917.*

Campaign Chronicle

arrived safely near Halfway House we dismantled the four cable reels, and in a hurried departure the drivers and the cable wagon returned to Dickebusch. Then, ten signallers were detailed to lay four lines about 40 yards (36.5m) apart to make a ladder line to Hooge Crater. . . . We received a light bombardment from Fritz, but completed the line by approx. 11pm. Overnight we continued parading our line and mending any breaks.'

German Fourth Army headquarters had, some three days previously, formed the view that an attack was imminent; indeed, given the facility with which they could overlook the salient, they would have had to be startlingly insensitive to miss the evidence. At about 3am on 20 September an Australian officer of the 2nd Division strayed too far forward and was captured by a German patrol. The orders he had received for the attack by I ANZAC Corps were discovered in his pocket and the German divisional artillery opened fire at 4.30am. The alarm was sent to headquarters, but fortunately too late for a general defensive bombardment along the whole front to be put into action. I ANZAC Corps attacked at 5.40am. The frontage of the 1st Division ran from Nonne Bosschen on the left to Glencorse Wood on the right. The British counter-battery fire consisted of gas-shell and high explosive from 222 guns and howitzers and the barrage behind which the infantry advanced was of unprecedented depth – 1,000 yards (0.9km) – and density. Two belts of high explosive shell from the heavy guns crept in front of a belt of machine-gun fire from 240 weapons, and behind that were two belts of field artillery barrage. The timing of the attack was intended to coincide with the growing light of dawn, but mist obscured the battlefield and out of it, a German wrote, the Australians appeared 'like spectres'.

The 2nd Australian Division swept forward astride the Westhoek – Zonnebeke road, swiftly overrunning the German forward positions in the Hanebeek valley and swarming up the gentle slope beyond. The strong points of the *Wilhelmstellung*, Albert and Iron Cross, were blinded with smoke and their garrisons fled. On the left the defenders of ANZAC House, the chief German artillery observation post, were caught while trying to set up their machine-guns in the open and fifteen of them were overcome. Sniping from Garter Point did not persist for long: the 18th Battalion quickly took the position. To their right the 1st Division advanced towards what were called woods. By now these were almost entirely without trees, consisting of stumps and the odd sapling amongst the shell holes. Nonne Bosschen was crossed by keeping to the edges of the ponds in the shell craters and almost the only resistance came from concrete shelters along the northern edge of Glencorse

85

*Glencorse Wood: shell burst near
Australian troops, 20 September*
(Taylor Library).

Wood to their right, where the Germans set up a machine-gun on the roof of one of the shelters. It did not remain in action for long. Private R R Inwood of 10th Battalion took one strong point single-handed, killing several Germans and taking nine prisoner. Second Lieutenant F Birks of 6th Battalion and a corporal attacked a pillbox and the officer, when the NCO fell wounded, went on alone to get into the position and kill the defenders with a grenade. He then led a party in attacking another pillbox held by twenty-five Germans. Fifteen of them survived the assault. Both of these Australians were awarded the Victoria Cross. By 7.45am the ANZACS were on their objective on the outskirts of Polygon Wood where the *Wilhelmstellung* pillbox and shelter system was taken. The shelters (*Mebus*), unlike the pillboxes, were without loopholes and were simply for protection from shellfire. Eddie Johnson learnt from his officer that 'our objective had been gained by 7am.'

Along and to the south of the Menin road the 23rd Division made its attack at the same time as the Australians. Four tanks of A Battalion, II Tank Brigade were to be in support, but one failed to make it to the start line and the debris slowed the others to a pace outstripped by the infantry. One was lost to shellfire on the Menin road and the other two were of some service as supply vehicles. D G Browne was unimpressed:

'Tanks were to operate as on 31st July, following up the infantry to deal with the fortified farms along the second and third objectives. This was a

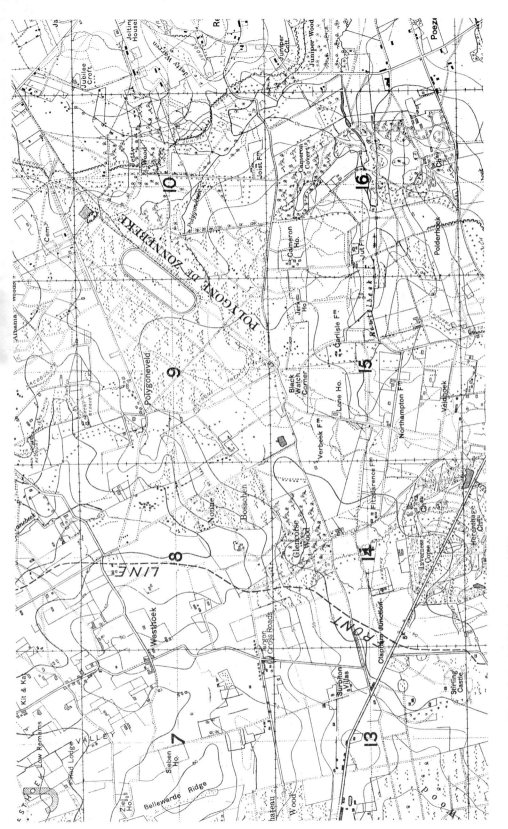

Polygon Wood: the battlefield, late September 1917.

reversion to the old bad manner, and in the event was an almost complete failure, although tanks endeavoured to keep to the roads. Four machines sent in by the 2nd Brigade went to swell the crowd of derelicts in the quagmire by the Menin road, known as the "tanks' cemetery". Of the nineteen tanks from E Battalion, thirteen were ditched and four hit; while only three out of fifteen from D ever got near the fight at all. The Germans had grasped very quickly some of the lessons of this road fighting, and trees had been felled across the roads in such a position as to offer the greatest obstruction to tanks.'

The 11th West Yorkshire Regiment, with the support of 69th Trench Mortar Battery, got into and through Inverness Copse, like the other woods now just a tangle of fallen trees and shell holes, but failed to mop up sufficiently and bypassed a significant number of Germans who did great harm to those following, the 9th Yorkshires. Some sixty Germans were eventually accounted for by the moppers-up. The attack rolled on to seize Kantinje Cabaret and, after some difficulty, pillboxes to the north. Northampton Farm fell to the 10th Duke of Wellington's. Dumbarton Wood was taken by the 11th Northumberland Fusiliers but beyond that, at the junction with 41st Division, the complex of fortifications at Bodmin Road, at the southern end of the spur from Tower Hamlets, caused real difficulties. The day began badly when the Division's 124th Brigade went into the attack at zero hour. After a while the usual trickle of wounded began to come back, but then, as Captain Harry Yoxall recorded in his diary:

> 'A terrible thing happened. An enormous crowd of the 124th Brigade suddenly appeared, retiring in disorder. We formed a battle stop with headquarters officers and men . . . & drove lots of them back. What things we did & what language we used during that hateful half hour I do not remember. We stopped as many as we could but many got round us.'

Exactly which machine-gun positions had caused this rout is unclear: the official diaries omit the incident entirely. The attacks in this sector were still going in during the late afternoon, but the day ended with the 23rd Middlesex consolidating their line short of the morning's objective. To the south the 39th and the 19th Divisions, not without serious loss, achieved their objectives.

North of the railway line Fifth Army also went into action at 5.40am. On the left, forward of Langemarck and to the right of the Ypres-Staden railway line, the 20th Division had to secure the flank and 6th Ox & Bucks were part of the action. They had the 12th Rifle Brigade on their right but lacked contact with the 59th Brigade on their left. Eagle Trench was the target for some 290 mortars hurling blazing oil, but the projectors were anything but precise in range and errors of up to 200 yards [182.8m] could occur. Lieutenant Colonel C R C Boyle reported:

'It was still dark, dawn just breaking. At 5.41am oil drums were discharged at Cemetery (U.14.c.0.0.). These lit up the sky and showed my men to the enemy. As soon as the leading lines came over the ridge, into view of Eagle Trench, they came under heavy machine-gun fire from five concrete houses in the trench. B Company, on the right, caught the worst of this, and soon lost all their officers and most of their NCOs. C Company, in the centre, gallantly led by Captain Brooks and 2nd Lieutenant Bevington, tried to get on, and were within 60 yards [50.8] of the trench, when they were finally held up, Captain Brooks being killed on the German wire. Second Lieutenant Bevington and three or four men succeeded in getting into the trench, but were wounded and could do no more.

'A Company got within 70 yards [64m], and were then held up; Captain Skuce was mortally wounded. D Company tried to get forward to reinforce and push on, but were unable to do this, and at 6.30am all companies were in shell holes west of Eagle Trench, digging in.'

Second Lieutenant Willes, the intelligence officer, was with D Company. He recorded the events thus:

'Just before daylight the attack began, the Trench Mortar Battery being well to the fore with petrol cans and other presents for a good Bosche. The whole attack got off all right, but the people on the left got hung up with a strong point, and the men did not seem to be able to keep up with the barrage, so from one cause or another the attack began to get very sticky indeed. I think that, on the very broken ground one comes across nowadays, it is difficult to get an attack which has once halted started again – one might even say impossible.

'There were at least three machine-guns attending to us, and the end of it was that we had to go to ground like rabbits until the evening, when we were able to move up again . . .

'I was wounded when I was going up to see what was hanging us up, and I spent the next sixteen hours in a shell hole, until it was dark enough to get back.'

The attack was renewed late in the afternoon, with the 6th King's Shropshire Light Infantry providing a company to reinforce the Ox & Bucks. Colonel Boyle wrote:

'At 6.30pm our barrage came down on Eagle Trench, and Lieutenant Cook collected all men near him, and, with 2nd Lieutenant Tapper, went forward. The enemy surrendered to him, and Lieutenant Cook took a party and bombed along Eagle Trench, meeting with little opposition until about U.23.b.3.o.5, where his bombs gave out, and the enemy bombed him back. He then sent forward some riflemen on the right flank to hold the enemy, whilst he collected all German stick-bombs and formed a block in the trench, which he held. Second Lieutenant Tapper, seeing that this attack was succeeding, pushed forward to Louis Farm . . . Here they linked up with the 6th KSLI and the 12th RB.'

The Casualties

The number of casualties, that is those killed, wounded, missing and taken prisoner, incurred by the British Expeditionary Force in the Third Battle of Ypres is popularly supposed to have been the most grievous of the whole war. This belief is mistaken.

The battle lasted 105 days and the casualty figure was 244,000: that is 2,121 each day on average.

For the Battle of the Somme, which lasted 141 days, the daily rate was 2,950.

For the Battle of Arras and Vimy Ridge, which lasted thirty-nine days, the daily rate was 4,070.

The German offensive from 21 March–30 April 1918, forty-one days, cost 5,848 each day.

The British offensive from 8 August–11 November 1918, ninety-six days, cost 3,645 each day.

Source: John Terraine, *The Smoke and the Fire*, page 46.

They dug in along a line facing a little east of due north to hold the block on the trench, leaving part of the defence in German hands and to their left 59th Brigade established a line facing due east on the other side of the little salient they had not managed to take. On the evening of 21 September they were relieved, having lost three officers killed and nine wounded, forty other ranks killed, 123 wounded and thirty-three missing, probably dead. Willes observed: 'Altogether it was a roughish handling, but with such a quantity of new officers and new men, it is a wonder that things went as well as they did.'

Campaign Chronicle

Eighteen Corps, General Maxse's command, pushed forward from the line between Langemarck and a point forward of St Julien. The shallow Lekkerboterbeek valley was so muddy the thirty tanks of I Tank Brigade faced insurmountable difficulties in getting forward. A tank of D Battalion, making its way up the remains of the St Julien-Poelcappelle Road was described by Major Watson: 'One tank particularly distinguished itself by climbing a barricade of logs, which had been built to block the road a few hundred yards south of Poelcappelle, and slaughtered its defenders.'

This was, perhaps, the single tank said to have reached its objective, Delta House, just to the right of the road, and helped the 51st Division take it: a better performance than Browne allows. The machine was commanded by Lieutenant Symonds of No. 9 Section. The Section lost the first of its tanks to shellfire on leaving St Julien, and the next loss was the second in the column, which slid off the road and blacked the third. That left Symonds as the only support for the Highlanders. The Battalion report says:

'The leading car . . . went on to perform almost superhuman deeds in the 2 miles [3.2km] to Poelcappelle. It surmounted all obstacles, only to find the road become a swamp. By means of continuous ramping the tank was kept in line with the infantry and rendered valuable assistance with its

Eagle Trench: the objective of the Ox & Bucks Light Infantry on 20 September 1917
(Ox & Bucks Archive).

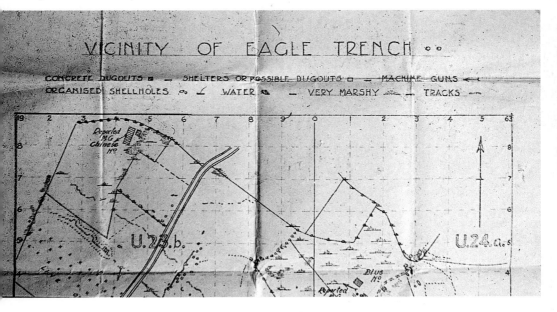

guns, and only on arrival at the outskirts of the village did the engine break down and leave the crew stranded. The tank was held as a strong point till such time as the 51st Division had consolidated. For this action Lieutenant Symonds was awarded the MC and the crew one MM and two Belgian Croix de Guerre.'

The Division had not had an easy time of it as the Germans had built new machine-gun posts along Pheasant Trench, the extension of Eagle Trench. To their right the 58th Division moved east of St Julien finally to secure the strong points on the low ridge: Keerselare, Vancouver, Cluster House, Clifton House and Wurst Farm. General Maxse was satisfied with the day's work, which he described as:

'a really great day for the XVIII Corps, and we have thoroughly proved ourselves. It has in fact been a "devil" of a battle for us all day long, and we have completely defeated the Hun, not only in our original advance of 1,000 yards [0.9km] but in numerous counter-attacks . . .'

He was proud of his men, particularly the volunteers, 'new army', and conscripted units, writing on 21 September:

'Just think of the second-line Post Office Rifles [2/8th London] standing

German aerial photograph of the terrain: autumn 1917 (Kamerad im Westen).

up to the flower of the German Army and mowing them down with machine-guns and rifle fire after themselves being subjected to one half-hour of the most furious enemy shelling . . .'

He was also proud of the success of his own performance in achieving objectives without losses on a scale similar to those incurred by other corps commanders:

'in July I have attained my objectives with fewer casualties than other corps, have used up fewer divs than any other corps, and . . . my divs remain less tired now than most others!

'In this last battle, I put in only two brigades on a front of 3,700 yards [3.3km] — that is I put in only two brigades for my original attack. I had to resist all sorts of advice (to get my own way) but as we came off on my plan I am now "a blue-eyed boy" and listened to with attention — at any rate for the time being!'

To Maxse's right the results of fatigue and inadequate training were evident. Fifth Corps's 55th (1st West Lancashire) Division had lost 135 officers and 3,750 other ranks on 31 July and the replacements, numbering 1,000 inexperienced men, had arrived too late to be trained and had to be left behind. What made matters worse was the attack was expected by the Germans, who took the precaution of sending fresh troops into their front lines and unleashing an artillery barrage and a hail of small arms fire as the British troops assembled before the attack. Nonetheless, the men of 1/4th King's Own (Royal Lancashire) and 1/4th Loyal North Lancashires moved forward into the mist and fire at the appointed hour, only to become seriously mixed. They failed to clear German positions thoroughly and, after they had passed, their enemies emerged from shelters to open fire with machine-guns. The effect was to expose the formations to their right to danger, and although the 9th Division — consisting of the South African and 27th Brigades — eventually attained their objectives, the centre and left of the 55th Division fell short. The 2nd South African Regiment lost half its strength that day, but took the Bremen Redoubt and managed to make the link with the battered 55th Division.

The 12th Royal Scots of 27th Brigade were in support of the 6th KOSB and the 9th Scottish Rifles. Their major engagement was to deal with solid resistance from pillboxes on the Ypres-Roulers railway line and the Potsdam complex of strong points. They succeeded, and Hugh Quigley was inspired to write:

'Thank goodness, that's all over. We had practically a walk-over. I shall never forget that afternoon in Ypres, when every officer and man we met asked us how our division did in the attack. I was proud of it, too, in some kind of perverse delight, not keen on fighting, yet glad to be in it. Even then, among all that sordid mass of ruins we call Ypres, memory and recollection have given a romantic aspect, as some monument worthy of valour and enshrined in our deeds, where our bravest fought to the last and never yielded. It may be a cemetery, a horrible cemetery at that, but an air of nobility blows around it yet.'

On reaching their objectives the successful units — the majority — prepared to meet the expected counter-attacks. German positions were converted to British use and German supplies used to reverse them to face the other way. The communication systems, depending on visual signals by flag and lamp, worked well in the fair weather and were supplemented by pigeons: sixteen pigeons were allocated to each brigade and twelve to each division's forward artillery observers. Ground telephone lines suffered badly from enemy shelling. Two tanks equipped with wireless telegraphy were in the field. The one allocated to I ANZAC Corps was destroyed by a shell as soon as it reached its position close to Glencorse Wood. It was in the air that the radios did their best service.

No longer a bus; now a mobile pigeon loft (Ox & Bucks Archive).

In each corps sector the RFC maintained two-aircraft patrols from the start of the day. Both had wireless, and while one watched for German counter-attacks, the other acted as a contact craft. Signals were sent in a form now standardized to battery receiving stations. Nearly 400 messages were sent on 20 September and about a third of them led to artillery fire being brought to bear on German troops. Substantial efforts were made by the Germans to thrust the British back before nightfall: three *Eingreif* divisions failed.

General Gough wrote cheerfully about the success of the day:

'as is usual in this battle, the Germans counter-attacked fiercely. On the V Corps front they launched no less than six counter-attacks. These were either beaten off, or our supporting troops immediately counter-attacked in their turn and once more drove the Germans out. Their losses were very heavy and we captured over 1,300 prisoners. By the end of the day we had captured all our objectives with the exception of two farms — an average penetration of 1,000 yards [0.9km] along the front of attack. The

Second Army on our right had been equally successful.

'In this attack our aeroplanes co-operated most usefully by flying low and firing on the German infantry. This new form of close co-operation of all arms was now becoming an established practice in all armies, German as well as our own.'

Sir Douglas Haig wrote approvingly of the battle's outcome:

'As the result of this most successful operation the whole of the high ground crossed by the Menin road, for which such desperate fighting had taken place during our previous attacks, passed into our possession. Important positions were won also on the remainder of our front, by which the right of our attack was rendered more secure, and the way opened for the advance of our left.'

Ludendorff's thoughts were mixed. He remarked in general:

'The enemy managed to adapt himself to our method of employing counter-attack divisions. There were no more attacks with unlimited objectives, such as General Nivelle had made in the Aisne-Champagne Battle. He was ready for our counter-attacks and prepared for them by exercising restraint in the exploitation of success. In other directions, of course, this suited us very well.'

Ludendorff continues with an appreciation of what was going on elsewhere, remarking on the terrible strain he was under as the 'affairs in the West' hampered what could be achieved in other theatres of the war. Not only was there fighting near Petrograd to worry about, but the Eleventh Battle of the Isonzo was taking place in north-east Italy and the Austrians, he thought, were in need of support. Indeed, a major effort in Italy might ease pressure on the Western Front. At much the same time David Lloyd George, the British Prime Minister, was entertaining similar ideas about Italy. One event receives scant coverage. On 1 September the Germans had carried out a successful attack on Riga. Of this Ludendorff remarks only that the Germans needed to find ways to damage Russia further and accelerate her dissolution. The scientific precision of the artillery action in that success, planned by Lieutenant Colonel Georg Bruchmüller, lay at the heart of the action and marked a revolution in artillery tactics. It may be what Ludendorff mentioned as 'thorough preparations'. It is after this review, mentioning many other subjects and affairs in other theatres, that Ludendorff returns to the Ypres Salient:

'After a period of profound quiet in the West, which led some to hope the Battle of Flanders was over, another terrific assault was made on our lines on the 20th September. The third bloody act of the battle had begun. The

main force of the attack was directed against the Passchendaele-Gheluvelt line. Obviously the English were trying to gain the high ground between Ypres and the Roulers-Menin line, which affords an extensive view in both directions. These heights were also important for us, as they afforded us ground observation posts and a certain amount of cover from hostile view.

'The enemy's onslaught on the 20th was successful, which proved the superiority of the attack over the defence. Its strength did not consist of the tanks; we found them inconvenient, but put them out of action all the same. The power of the attack lay in the artillery, and in the fact that ours did not do enough damage to the hostile infantry as they were assembling, and, above all, at the actual time of the assault.'

It was clear to everyone that this had been an artillery battle with substantial infantry participation. The cost had been high for the British, with some 20,000

casualties between 20 and 25 September, for what was a modest gain of ground as compared with Fifth Army's achievements on 31 July, which cost 27,000; but that is not to compare like with like. The detail and qualifications appropriate to a judgement are important. The state of the ground, as a result of shellfire and water content not even three weeks of dry weather could correct, precluded a flexible use of tanks. Technical advances in radio communications were still limited. British control of artillery was becoming steadily more sophisticated and flexible. Ludendorff concluded that infantry and artillery alone could succeed and, in the following year, was to come close to proving it. Fortunately for the Allies, so simple a solution was not to be proposed in 1918, for it might well have failed. In the meantime, Plumer and Haig gave orders for more of the same: the next attack was to be on 26 September.

The days from 21 to 25 September were rainless. Various divisions were relieved and in a brisk little action on Sunday 23 September 12th KRRC and 10th Rifle Brigade went into Eagle Trench from both ends and bombed the Germans out. German attacks on Sunday and Tuesday were repulsed.

Wednesday 26 September 1917: Battle of Polygon Wood

Weather: mist; temperature, 68°F (20°C); rainfall, 0.01in (0.5mm)

On 24 September Major General Sir John Monash wrote home:

'You will have heard by now that the campaign for the Passchendaele Ridge (which I foreshadowed in a recent letter) started on the 20th. First ANZAC (which has again resumed the 4th Division) is having the first go, and we (2nd ANZAC) shall come in later. First and 2nd Divisions did the first 'push' most brilliantly; day after tomorrow 4th and 5th Divisions will come through them and do a second push; and early in October, self and

Russell (NZ) expect to capture the Gravenstafel Spur, and later get on to the Passchendaele Ridge proper. . . . The fighting done in this 'push' by the Australians has been most brilliant in every way. . . .

'We have been doing four weeks' re-organization and training in most beautiful rolling country, mostly in beautiful autumn sunshine, and we finished up last Saturday with a splendid review by the Commander-in-Chief . . .

'I dined with him and Lieutenant General Kiggell, chief of general staff, and Major General Butler, deputy-chief of general staff. There were only the four of us present. After each course was served, the mess stewards went out of the room and the doors were locked from the inside, until the Chief gave the sign for the next course. So you may imagine some very important and confidential matters were discussed, about which I need say no more than that there is no question that we are very rapidly wearing down the German military power, and now it is a question of time and weather.'

Haig, encouraged by the success of 20 September, had sent orders and a map for the next phase. Having completed the second step with the capture of Polygon Wood and Zonnebeke, Second Army was to extend its frontage northwards and, with II ANZAC Corps, take the Broodseinde Ridge and then seize the rest of the high ground to protect Fifth Army from the east and south-east when they thrust north-eastwards. In readiness for a possible breakthrough, five cavalry divisions were available, and on the coast Fourth Army would join in the advance. But first they had to have the ridge and, before that, a start-line close enough to adhere to the policy of striking only for attainable objectives.

The fine weather allowed the British to build more wooden roads to bring up supplies and move artillery forward. The frontages for the attack were fixed, with the road to Reutel, along the southern edge of Polygon Wood, marking the dividing line between the Australians to the north and the 33rd Division, looking eastwards down the valley of the Reutelbeek, to the south. On 23 September Crown Prince Rupprecht had written in his diary that he feared the British would soon hold the whole Gheluvelt plateau and he therefore ordered an attack to be undertaken the next day. Fresh troops were required for it, so a day's delay was granted to allow 3rd Bavarian Ersatz Division to be relieved by 50th Reserve Division and for the deployment of twenty heavy and forty-four field batteries to provide artillery support for the assault. During the early hours of 25 September X Corps's 23rd Division was being relieved by the 33rd Division, which was to attack the following day. At 5.15am the German barrage began and fifteen minutes later, in the early morning mist, the attack was launched.

North of the Reutelbeek the front of the 1st Middlesex was driven in and they were forced back to the west of Lone House where, with the intervention of 2nd Argyll and Sutherland Highlanders, they were able to establish a line of defence and push Lewis gunners forward into shell holes to break up German attacks. Some of the Middlesex were holding on to the southern flank of Polygon Wood; others, with the Argylls, were clinging on near Lone House, but it was not possible to regain the original line, and this left the right flank of the ANZACs exposed. South of the Reutelbeek the line had held. The necessity of defending the vulnerable flank of their 5th Division required the 58th Australian Battalion to take up a south-facing position while 5/6th Scottish Rifles of the 33rd Division's 19 Brigade was brought up to head the attack with the 4th Suffolks. Lieutenant Colonel Spens brought the Scottish Rifles up on the night of the 25th/26th:

'The ground in front was new to us, and guides from the front battalions were asked for. The night was dark and the shelling worse than ever. Battalion headquarters had been established near some friendly-looking tanks, which appeared to be on fairly firm ground at L Farm, formerly an

On the alert for a counter-attack: machine-gunners peer across a shattered landscape, in the foreground, a comrade's grave (Taylor Library).

old road running north and south past Fitzclarence Farm. The surrounding ground was a mass of shell holes filled with stinking water and mud and if you fell in you were lost. . . . it seemed safest to keep to the road, so out the party stretched, in Indian file, in the dark, with the guide and the colonel in front. For an hour the party followed the lead. Fires were observed burning fiercely, and as the party drew near, it found itself back at the place from which it had started. The tanks were now a blazing mass of twisted iron. What had gone wrong with the guide? He was obviously lost and had been walking in a circle.'

By daybreak, far from being in a position to attack, all they could achieve was a reinforcement of the existing defence position. The 33rd Division's objectives were not attained till the following day.

In spite of the small setback inflicted by the Germans on the 33rd Division, a 600-yard [0.5-km] loss of ground on a limited front, there was no hesitation in continuing with the attack planned for 26 September. At 5.50am the bombardment crashed down and clouds of dust added to the mist of the morning. Officers leading their men forward had to reply on their compasses to hold their direction. On the right two battalions from 8 Australian Brigade had been given to 15 Brigade to make up for their need to hold a defensive line to the south, and so keen were they to keep up to the barrage that the 59th Battalion suddenly found itself getting mixed up with the newcomers from 29th and 31st Battalions. Germans manning the pillboxes at the south-west corner of the wood held them up for a while, as did another on the 'racecourse' in the centre of the remains of the wood. Here, confused, the 59th paused in the belief this was the first objective. The 57th and 60th Battalions were trying to suppress German fire from the right, but there were a number of well set-up pillboxes in the 33rd Division's sector that needed to be taken. The 31st Battalion attacked pillboxes west of Jerk House and the Germans laid down a heavy fire from Cameron House as well. The progress on this flank slowed.

Private Frank Richards of the 2nd Royal Welch Fusiliers was coming up with his battalion:

'At 8am orders arrived that the Battalion would move off to the assistance of the Australians who had made an attack early in the morning on Polygon Wood. Although the attack was successful they had received heavy casualties and were now hard-pressed themselves. . . . One part of the ground we travelled over was nothing but lakes and boggy ground and the whole of the Battalion were strung out in Indian file walking along a track about 18 inches [45.7cm] wide. We had just got out of this bad ground but were still travelling in file when the enemy opened out with a fierce bombardment. Just in front of me half a dozen men fell on the side of the track; it was like as if a Giant Hand had suddenly swept them to one side. The Battalion had close on a hundred casualties before they were out of that valley. . . .

'We arrived on some rising ground and joined forces with the Australians. I expected to find a wood, but it was undulating land with a tree dotted here and there and little banks running in different directions.'

They had reached Black Watch Corner, and ahead of them an earthen bank was lined with Australians through whom the Fusiliers charged to take position beyond. The shellfire was continuous. Richards was sharing a tin of meat with an Australian officer when a shell plunged into the trench they were sheltering in, killing the man behind him and showering his meal with dirt. He had to open another tin.

Suddenly, in the afternoon, the shelling stopped. The Australian officer, Mr Diamond, ordered stand-to, expecting a German attack. Captain J C Dunn mentioned the incident briefly:

'A commotion on the Australian front, at the west side of Polygon Wood, led an Australian officer to turn his men and HQ details [including Richards] out of their trench to be ready to deal with what he thought was a German infantry attack. They were lying out when the German plane [which had fired on them minutes before], which had only gone as far as Becelaere, came back. It flew on the same course as before, amidst a fusillade. This time it got too low . . . The plane crashed not far from C Company. The pilot was seen to have been shot.'

Richards gives a markedly different account. He reports that Dr Dunn 'temporarily resigned' from the Royal Army Medical Corps and told Richards to get him a rifle, bayonet and ammunition. They then went forward together towards the low bank and as they approached it some Fusiliers who had been holding a position further on began to fall back. Dunn halted them and had them join the line of Australian and British men. No attack came and darkness was falling. Richards was surprised to see the Australian Brigadier come up to sort out his men:

'It was the only time during the whole of the War that I saw a brigadier with the first line of attacking troops. Some brigadiers that I knew never moved from Brigade headquarters. It was also the first time I had been in action with the Australians and I found them very brave men. There was also an excellent spirit of comradeship between officers and men.'

Lewis Gun mounted for anti-aircraft use (Ox & Bucks Archive).

For all that, this flank of Polygon Wood remained in danger. To the left matters had unfolded much more pleasingly for the ANZACs.

An officer of the 53rd (Australian) Battalion wrote a brief account of what appears to have been a textbook assault:

> 'Punctually at zero hour (5.50am) our barrage opened and the Battalion immediately rose and doubled across 'No Man's Land' till reaching about 60 yards [54.8m] short of the barrage, where the men knelt down waiting for it to begin creeping forward. . . . Resistance from 'pillboxes' and strong posts was encountered almost immediately, but in no case was the advance checked. In one case a strong post was encountered and machine-gun fire opened on the attackers. Immediately a CSM [Company Sergeant Major] and about half a dozen men worked around the flanks while a Lewis Gun team opened direct fire on the position drawing the enemy fire off the enveloping parties, who were then easily able to work round, rush the position with bombs and the bayonet, and accounted for the occupants and captured the gun.'

They swept on to the Butte, the mound at the north-eastern end of the wood, and then worked through the dugouts beneath, using hand grenades to overcome what resistance was offered. The cost was two officers and ten men as casualties. The 56th and 55th Battalions came through and the Australians were consolidating their final objective by 8.50am, the 29th Battalion having overcome German pillboxes on Polygonebeek.

The attack of the 4th Australian Division was north of the wood, towards the outskirts of Zonnebeke on the left and Molenaarehoek on the right. In spite of the formidable defences of the German Flanders I Line they had to take, they made excellent progress. The 16th Battalion attacked with the 15th and 14th in support across terrain still sodden and muddy as a result of the destruction of the drainage system by shellfire. From the 16th's left fire from pillboxes gave them difficulties until men of the 14th, led by Captain Albert Jacka, silenced them. As the advance continued some men got too close to the barrage and, fearing death by 'friendly fire' turned back. Jacka steadied them and they were on their final objective, indeed beyond it, by 8am.

On the flanks there was satisfactory progress. The 39th Division south of the Menin road took Tower Hamlets at last, although the boggy ground had broken up their formations at the start of the day. On the Australian left the 3rd Division took Zonnebeke and of their objectives only Hill 40, north-west of the ghost of the village, remained in enemy hands. Again it was boggy ground that slowed the advance. Alongside them the 59th Division took all its objectives but the northernmost formation, the 58th, did not do so well. They lost direction early on and, although they recovered and continued to advance, they could not hold all the ground gained and finished short of Aviatik Farm. Nonetheless, this was a minor setback, for by midmorning the mist had gone, the ground gained had been consolidated, and the German counter-attacks were easily observed and targeted by British guns. Nine counter-attacks were thrown against British lines by the end of the afternoon, and five were halted by the artillery alone before they reached their enemy.

Sir Douglas Haig's December despatch spoke of the 25th September attack:

'parties of German infantry succeeded in entering our lines north of the Menin road. Heavy and confused fighting took place in this area throughout the day, in which English, Scottish and Australian troops (33rd Division and 5th Australian Division) gradually drove the enemy from the limited foothold he had gained.

'The enemy's casualties in these many counter-attacks, as well as in all those subsequently delivered by him on the Ypres front, were consistently very heavy. Our constant resistance reflects the greatest credit on the fighting qualities of our infantry, on the courage and devotion of our airmen, and upon the excellence of our artillery arrangements.'

Campaign Chronicle

The more substantial battle of the next day gets sparse mention, little more than a rehearsal of ground gained and which divisions took it. The narrative is straining to get on to the next step. General Gough recalled that:

> 'After the battle of the 26th I wrote a memorandum to GHQ pointing out that if the left of the attack now remained stationary, I could withdraw a corps and several divisions and send them to Plumer to extend his right. To clear the main ridge was the real and decisive object, and another corps on the right would enable the attack to move forward with greater ease. In fact an attack could thus be made almost due northwards, taking the main German defences in the flank, with its own outer flank well-covered by the corps I suggested sending to Plumer. This proposal, however, never materialized.'

From the German side the situation did not seem at all comfortable. Ludendorff wrote:

> 'the 26th proved a day of heavy fighting, accompanied by every circumstance that could cause us loss. We might be able to stand the loss of ground, but the reduction of our fighting strength was again all the heavier. Once more we were involved in a terrific struggle in the West, and had to prepare for a continuation of the attacks on many parts of the front.
>
> 'October came, and with it one of the hardest months of the war. The world at large . . . saw only Tarnopol, Czernovitz, Riga, and later Osel, Udine, the Tagliamento and the Piave. It did not see my anxiety, nor my deep sympathy with the sufferings of our troops in the West. My mind was in the East and Italy, my heart on the Western Front. . . .
>
> 'The actions in the Third Battle of Flanders had presented the same set-piece characteristics as those in the Second and the fighting at Verdun. The depth of penetration was limited so as to secure immunity from our counter-attacks, and the latter were then broken by the massed fire of artillery.'

In an attempt to thrash out a solution to this problem, Ludendorff visited the front in person.

In discussion with the men on the spot, it was decided the front lines should be slightly strengthened and that, instead of using counter-attack divisions, local counter-attacks should be undertaken. A second-line division, close behind the front line and spread over a wide front, was to be deployed, thus doubling the manpower in forward positions. It was a heavy requirement when other fronts were hungry for troops. Ludendorff's staff was doubtful about the departure from their textbook guidelines for the conduct of the Defensive Battle, but their chief acceded to the requests of the men on the ground. He did, however, take the opportunity of reminding them about the use of artillery:

> 'Another tactical detail which was emphasized everywhere was the value of ground observation for artillery. Only by that means could the attacking hostile infantry be annihilated, particularly after penetrating our front, or fire be concentrated on decisive points of the battlefield.'

The weather for the rest of the month was dry and warm. Sir Douglas Haig was, according to Gough, rather optimistic at the conference of 28 September, even speaking of getting tanks and cavalry forward as the enemy's strength was sapped:

> 'from the strategical point of view the Commander-in-Chief's operations were fully achieving their object; from a tactical outlook, however, his hopeful opinion was not justified when one considered the ground, the weariness of our own men, and the stout hearts which, in spite of all, were still beating under the German tunics.'

4 October 1917: Battle of Broodseinde

Weather: overcast; temperature 60°F (15°C); rainfall, 0.18in (4.6mm)

The first new rain fell on 2 October, 2.7mm. Another 1.2mm fell the next day. The 'real' rain began on 4 October, in the afternoon, and it rained for a week, the temperature dropping as low as 47°F (8°C).

On 2 October Plumer and Gough were in conference with Haig. In response to letters from his generals, the Field Marshal explained that his plans did not assume the opportunity to break through the Germans would necessarily come, but that if it did he wanted to be in a position to take advantage. Haig recorded the meeting in his diary:

> 'I pointed out how favourable the situation was and how necessary it was to have all the necessary means for exploiting any success gained on the 10th [the forthcoming Battle of Poelecappelle which was to secure the Ridge, in fact fought on the 9th], should the situation admit, e.g. if the enemy counter-attacks and is defeated, then reserve brigades must follow after the enemy and take the Passchendaele Ridge at once . . .'

In the First Battle of Ypres Haig himself had been in command here and he was of the opinion the German failure to exploit British exhaustion on 31 October 1914 had cost them the day. Therefore each division was to have a brigade in reserve, ready to move up and with its own mobile artillery consisting of two 60-pounder batteries, two 6-inch howitzer batteries and four field artillery brigades. Careful planning of transportation to move the forces forward was put in hand. Haig allocated two tank battalions to the Second Army and one to the Fifth, saying: 'The firmer ground and better going beyond the shell-torn area, which we hope shortly to reach, will give tanks a better chance, and will permit their employment in large numbers.'

The optimism shown was not entirely self-deception, for hope that the weather would hold was reasonable. These schemes can thus be regarded either as prudent or fantastical: but it is clear neither Plumer nor Gough gave them much chance of becoming a reality. For the time being they concentrated on the next step, while assuring their commander they would put them into effect when the time came.

The principal objective was again that allocated to the ANZACS: the Broodseinde village and ridge. To their right X Corps was reinforced with the 5th Division from the Fifth Army (a fact not mentioned in Gough's memoirs) and, south of the Menin road, the 37th Division of IX Corps was to secure the flank. The Fifth Army, to the ANZAC's left, were attacking Poelcappelle. The artillery plan was changed to confuse the enemy. The Battle of the Menin Road had been preceded by a week-long bombardment, while the Polygon Wood action had only a twenty-four-hour preparatory bombardment. This time the artillery fire was to be laid down at zero hour, when the troops were to advance, but a series of 'practice barrages' were laid down from 27 September onwards. The plan of the barrage was also new. It would begin 150 yards (137m) in front of the jumping-off line and go forward in 100-yard (0.9-km) lifts until an infantry pause line was protected. It would then wander forward 1,000 yards (0.9km) before coming back to cover the advance to the final objective. Second Army had 796 heavy and medium guns and 1,548 field guns and howitzers to provide this barrage.

Second ANZAC Corps, the 3rd Australian and the New Zealand Divisions, came up to fight alongside I ANZAC's 1st and 2nd Divisions, but had to make haste as the interval before the next assault was reduced by two days. The fresh formations replaced Gough's V Corps and extended Plumer's frontage northwards. Sir John Monash, commanding the 3rd Australian Division, wrote home from a dugout close to the Menin Gate in Ypres on 1 October:

'Difficult as it is to convey any idea of the destruction of Ypres, it is simply impossible to describe the life and turmoil in the whole area, from

Traffic passes a shellhole, on the Menin road (Taylor Library).

Poperinghe forward through Vlamertinghe (also destroyed) and Ypres, as far as our present forward position. It is one enormous medley of military activity of every conceivable description, and the traffic on the main roads is simply incredible. . . . streams of men, vehicles, motor lorries, horses, mules, and motors of every description, moving ponderously forward, at a snail's pace, in either direction, hour after hour, all day and all night, day after day, week after week, in a never halting, never ending stream.'

The area south of Polygon Wood had seen two German attacks in the preceding days – 30 September and 1 October – and some hard fighting ensued, but the hostile forces were thrown back with significant casualties. At the same time plans were being brought to maturity for a more substantial assault north of Polygon Wood, scheduled for 3 October. This was then delayed by a day and the German 211th and 212th Infantry Regiments and the 4th Guards Division were given extra time to prepare.

H Battalion, Tank Corps, had come from England only four weeks before: on 3 October, it was sent to the Ypres Salient. Captain D E Hickey was a section commander and he went forward the next day to see how they could get forward from their detraining point at Ouderdoom to go into action for the final assault on Passchendaele Ridge. The reconnaissance was made to discover a route avoiding roads – always a target for enemy artillery as well as a bad place to break down – given the need for supply traffic to move freely. Hickey wrote:

> 'As we trudged along, the awful nature of the salient gradually became apparent. Now the copses and fields gave place to a horrid waterlogged swamp, and the ground was shell-pocked, boggy clay, with not a blade of grass nor a tree that had not been torn to pieces by shellfire. . . .
>
> 'For 2.5 miles [4km] we plodded on across slippery mud, threading our way among the guns, until we came to a spot bearing the rustic name of Valley Cottages. The cottages, if they had ever existed, had been wiped off the face of the earth. At this spot there was a track made of hardwood logs . . . This "corduroy road" . . . marked the original lane, now completely obliterated by shellfire. . . . Here and there at the side of the road were the bodies of pack-mules. They had been taking up shells, and slipping off the greasy track had sunk in the mud. . . . they had to be shot on the spot. It was obvious that tanks could not cross this ground, and even a corduroy road was impossible, for the weight of the tanks would smash it and their tracks would rip it to pieces.
>
> 'It was a dismal day, and a cold bleak drizzle was falling. As we reached the track the drizzle turned to a steady downpour.'

On 4 October, at 5.30am, a German barrage fell on the British lines. As far back as Zouave Wood, near Hellfire Corner on the Menin road close to Ypres, the 1st Australian Division's reserve, 3rd Brigade, had to shelter from shellfire intended for 17th Heavy Battery, Royal Garrison Artillery. For the men waiting to advance the experience had serious implications: it seemed their plan of attack was known to the enemy. The heaviest shelling fell on I ANZAC between Zonnebeke and Polygon Wood: here one in every seven was killed or wounded before the attack even began. W J Harvey was with 24th Battalion, 2nd Australian Division and recalled:

> 'It was hardest on our battalion and on the 21st next to us. We had forty killed, including two of our platoon officers, and taking into account the wounded a third of our men were put out of action. Everyone kept their nerve, although it was a terrible strain to lie there under that sort of fire without being able to do a thing about it, knowing that there was a terrible struggle ahead and that we'd be going into it well under strength. It seemed an eternity before our own guns opened up and we got the order to advance.'

Then, at 6am, the British bombardment smashed down on the German line. Immediately the ANZACs moved forward, out of the German fire, to follow the friendly barrage, taking up their rehearsed formations as they did so. Each

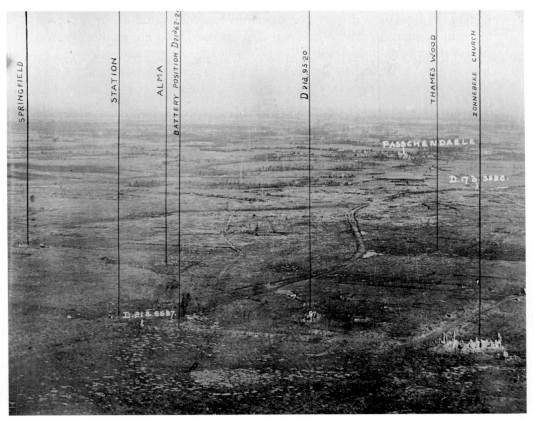

Aerial photograph of the approaches to Passchendaele: so near ... (Taylor Library).

battalion had three companies in front and one in reserve in case of counter-attack. Each company had a platoon in extended line behind the barrage, two platoons following in section columns to mop up any remaining enemy and one platoon in reserve. The dawn was murky with drizzle, and as they moved forward they saw German soldiers staggering out of shell holes immediately the barrage passed: the German 212th and 211th and the 4th Guards had been on the point of assaulting the Australian line. Many had been killed or wounded, some surrendered, others were shot or bayoneted as they fought or fled. In spite of the surprise and defeat of the would-be attackers, the German defensive system still worked efficiently and the ANZACs moved into the routine of firing on, outflanking and bombing pillbox after pillbox. The 1st Division were on the ridge by 8.10am. On their left the 2nd Australian Division cleared out the ruins of Zonnebeke, which were dotted with machine-gun posts and pushed up the Broodseinde Ridge at such a pace they were in danger of their own artillery fire. Once on top they came under fire from German positions in Daisy Wood and the commander on the ground decided to halt short of the final objective and consolidate a better defensive position. It turned out to be the old British line of the winter of 1914 and fragments of khaki uniform were turned up by their spades as they dug in. W J Harvey said:

> 'From the Broodseinde Ridge the whole field was under observation, and as we gazed back over the country we could see quite plainly the movements of our own units on various duties – guns, transport, men, the lot. The ridge was a prize worth having. Hundreds of German prisoners were now struggling back through our lines. By now we felt really quite sorry for them, they were in such abject misery.'

Captain W. Bunning, also of the 24th, remarked on the view from the top of the ridge, a view that was to beguile his commanders into persisting in these attacks long after the weather had broken:

> 'What was really surprising was to look across and see before you the green fields of Belgium. To see actual trees and grass – of course the fields had been churned up a good deal by barrage shells, but as far as we were concerned it was open country. But then to look back to where we'd come from, Ypres – there was total devastation. And then at dawn you could see why our own gunners had such a gruesome time. You could see the flashes of all the guns firing right from Broodseinde to the Menin Gate.'

Second ANZAC was given the task of securing two spurs that jut out north-west from the Broodseinde/Passchendaele Ridge, the Zonnebeke and Gravenstafel Spurs: the first of these separating the streams of the Zonnebeek from the Hanebeek, and the second the Hanebeek from the Stroombeek. The direction of the attack was to the north-east, crossing the north-south defence of the Flanders I Line. On the right, 3rd Australian Division had to use duckboard bridges to cross the Zonnebeek to their assembly points. Their barrage smashed resistance on Hill 40 and the attackers went in with the bayonet. On they went across the Hanebeek, taking out stubborn German resistance from pillboxes and from Abraham Heights, a German field-gun position. On their left the New Zealand Division advanced with equal determination and, reaching their objectives, found they were under fire from Korek, north of Gravenstafel, about 120 yards (110m) further forward: so they took that position as well.

Tanks were in action both north and south of the ANZAC sector. South of Polygon Wood the road to Reutel drops down a shallow slope to cross the Polygonbeek, which flows south to the Reutelbeek. The shell-smashed

German prisoners display a range of moods at Broodseinde.

watercourses had now become wide, muddy marshes, across which the remains of the road offered some sort of causeway. The slopes beyond were well defended with pillboxes and four tanks were allocated to the 21st Division to give them some chance of success. To their left the 7th Division's attack was almost successful, although the objective on the southern flank was not taken and they had to form a defensive flank, the stability of which would depend on how, eventually, the 21st got on.

For three days and nights before the attack, Captain Clement Robertson and his servant, Private Allen, marked out the route for the tanks. They used tape and when, on the morning of 4 October, the mist and drizzle added to the slurry of obscuring mud, Robertson walked ahead of his tanks to show the way. From inside the tank vision was too restricted to allow the driver to follow the markings. They arrived at the assembly place in good time and at 6am forward they went, the captain leading on foot. Down the slope, on through the marsh, where an error would lead to a tank being hopelessly enmired if it left the roadway, and over the bridge they went. Then up the other side to firmer ground, where they could go into action against the machine-gun posts. With them went the 9th King's Own Yorkshire Light Infantry. They took Joist Farm and Juniper Trench and then came under fire from a pillbox east of Reutel, which was dealt with by one of the tanks, but by then Captain Robertson had been killed. Captain Hickey heard about it later in the day and wrote afterwards:

'after our experience of that day, [we] realized only too well what he had had to contend with, and what a wonderful show he put up. Robertson, a Haileyburian, by his gallant action, won the first VC for the Tank Corps. We felt that he had set a standard which we should find it very difficult to live up to.'

On the Fifth Army front Maxse's XVIII Corps sent the 11th Division towards Poelcappelle, supported by ten tanks of D Battalion, 1st Tank Brigade. Major W H L Watson described the events:

'It was determined to clear Poelcappelle as soon as possible, since, while the Germans held it, we were greatly handicapped in attacking either the south-east edge of the Houthulst Forest or the Passchendaele Ridge itself from the north-west. Further, the only two main roads in the neighbourhood passed through the village. . . .
    'The attack was scheduled for 4 October. Marris [commanding No. 10 Company] brought his tanks into St Julien and camouflaged them among the ruins. St Julien, though now still easily within close field-gun range, was now respectably "behind the line". It was only shelled once or twice a night, and during the day on state occasions.'

The attack began at 6am and the tanks moved forward in company with the 9th Lancashire Fusiliers and the 11th Manchesters. Watson reports:

'The attack was incredibly successful. Of Marris's twelve tanks, eleven left St Julien and crawled perilously all night along the destroyed road. At dawn they entered the village with the infantry and cleared it after difficult fighting. One section even found their way along the remains of a track so obliterated by shellfire that it scarcely could be traced on the aeroplane photographs, and "bolted" the enemy from a number of strong points.'

The tanks pulled back as the day wore on, and German shelling and counter-attacks regained them the northern end of the village. Pleasing as the tanks' performance had been, the job was unfinished.

Monash was delighted. He jotted a hasty letter: 'We have had a magnificent success . . . A fine bag of prisoners is pouring in. All are most elated, particularly the fine feat of pulling off so big a job with only three days for our local preparation.'

After the 3rd Australian Division had been relieved by the 66th Division on the morning of 7 October, Monash wrote again, at greater length, looking forward to the next operation:

'Great happenings are possible in the very near future, as the enemy is terribly disorganized, and it is doubtful if his railway facilities are good enough to enable him to re-establish himself before our next two blows, which will follow very shortly and will be very severe. My next objective will be Passchendaele, unless the 66th succeed in getting so far in the next battle. . . . Our success [on 4 October] was complete and unqualified. Over 1,050 prisoners and much material and guns. Well over 1,000 dead enemy counted, and many hundreds buried and out of reach. We got absolutely astride of the main ridge. Both corps and army declare there has been no finer feat in the war.'

Ludendorff made this observation:

'The infantry battle commenced on the morning of the 4th. It was extraordinarily severe, and again we only came through it with enormous loss. It was evident the idea of holding the front line more densely, adopted at my last visit to the front in September, was not the remedy. I now followed my own judgement without asking for further outside opinions, and recommended the Fourth Army to form an advanced zone, that is to say, a narrow strip between the enemy's front line and the line which our troops were to hold by mobile defence. The enemy would have to cross this strip in making his attack, and our artillery would have time to get onto him before he could reach our main line of resistance. The great difficulty lay in withdrawing the garrison of the advanced zone in case of attack, and in bringing the artillery barrage back to our own line.'

He admitted there was some puzzlement about the definition of the advanced zone and that Fourth Army were not enthusiastic about complying with his wishes. Indeed, the concept has much in common with the heroic, honourable but ultimately fatal role of the 'forlorn hope' in seventeenth century warfare: a force one was prepared to sacrifice.

The delight of the British and Empire commanders at this time is easy to understand, but it was still raining. Sir Douglas Haig sent Brigadier General Charteris to see General Plumer and urge the immediate extension of current operations, skipping the planned interval until 10 October, but the Second Army commander injected a certain level of caution. He had himself been brought up short by the commander of I ANZAC, Sir William Birdwood, who had declined to push his men eastward to take a spur beyond Broodseinde on the grounds his men had already taken serious casualties and the necessary artillery support was lacking until guns had made the next move forward. This was repeated to Charteris, and the presence of German reserve divisions, eight immediately to the rear of the battle sector and another seven further back in Belgium, and the imminence of German counter-attacks added to the argument. In the afternoon of 4 October Haig, Plumer and Gough all met in Cassel, where the Commander-in-Chief had moved to be close to events, and the suggestion that the pace of the operations should be increased was discussed. Haig's diary records:

> 'In order not to miss any chance of following up our success if the enemy were really demoralised, I met Generals Plumer and Gough with their staff officers in my house in Cassel at 3pm. Plumer stated that in his opinion we had only up-to-date fought the leading troops of the enemy's divisions on his front. Charteris, who was present, thought that from the number of German regiments represented among the prisoners all divisions had been seriously engaged and that there were few more available reserves . . .
>
> 'After full discussion I decided that the next attack should be made two days earlier than already arranged, provided Anthoine [French General] could also accelerate his preparation.
>
> 'At 4pm I saw the latter . . . Finally it was found only possible to advance the attack by one day.
>
> 'Rain fell heavily this afternoon as I took a walk.'

The British appreciation of German tactics was misled by the capture of documents on 4 October in which the arrangements adopted after Ludendorff's visit, which were now to be abandoned on his orders, were taken to be an enduring policy. Haig's despatch said:

> 'The enemy had suffered severely, as was evidenced by the number of prisoners in our hands, by the number of his dead on the battlefield, by the costly failure of his repeated counter-attacks, and by the symptoms of confusion and discouragement in his ranks.
>
> 'In this connection, documents captured in the course of the battle of the 4th October throw an interesting light upon the success of the measures taken by us to meet the enemy's new system of defence by counter-attack. These documents show that the German Higher Command had already recognised the failure of their methods, and were endeavouring to revert to something approximating to their old practice of holding their forward positions in strength.'

In this we now know Haig and his staff were mistaken, and perhaps rather optimistic in assuming the enemy's behaviour would continue unmodified in the face of the cost incurred on 4 October.

On Friday 5 October, with the temperature standing at 52°F (10°C), 0.12in (3.1mm) of rain fell. The next three days, with the temperature remaining much the same and cloud-covered skies, 0.08in (2.1mm), 0.4in (10.4mm) and 0.5in (14.6mm) were the totals: 1.2in (30.2mm) in all.

Up on the Poelcappelle Road Major Watson of D Battalion, Tank Corps, went with a colleague to inspect the route his men would have to take in the next attack:

'On the 6th, Cooper and I made a little expedition up the Poelcappelle Road. It was in desperate condition, and we felt a most profound respect for the drivers of No. 10 Company. The enemy gunners had shelled it with accuracy. There were great holes that compelled us to take to the mud at the side. In places the surface had been blown away, so the road could not be distinguished from the treacherous riddled waste through which it ran. To leave the road was obviously certain disaster for a tank. Other companies had used it, and at intervals derelict tanks which had slipped off the road or received direct hits were sinking rapidly in mud. I could not help remembering that the enemy must be well aware of the route which so many tanks had followed into battle.'

Exactly what happened between the Commander-in-Chief and the army commanders in the two days before the next stage of the battle is disputed. That there was resistance at a senior level to carrying out an attack on 9 October is clear from Monash's letter of 15 October. He says:

'I am inclined to believe that the plan [to attack on 9 and again on 12 October] was fully justified, and would have succeeded in normal weather conditions. It could only have succeeded, however, in the hands of first-class fighting divisions whose staff work was accurate, scientific and speedy.'

He continued to offer the evidence of how his 3rd Australian and the New Zealand Divisions had performed before the 4 October attack and stated his opinion that they could have repeated that with preparation time of only forty-eight hours:

'But the Higher Command decided to allow us only twenty-four hours, and even under these circumstances with normal weather conditions, we might have succeeded.

'However, a number of vital factors intervened, and I personally used every endeavour to secure from the corps and army commanders a twenty-four hours' postponement. The Chief, however, decided that every hour's postponement gave the enemy breathing time, and that it was worth taking the chance of achieving the final objective for this stage of the Flanders battle.'

He tells his correspondent that his corps commander, Lieutenant General Sir Alexander Godley, and his army commander, General Plumer, were both the recipients of his requests for a delay, but that 'the Chief', presumably, Sir Douglas Haig, decided otherwise. He gives no precise dates, so he might have been advocating delay after the failed attack of 9 October – it is not clear. It is reported in the *Official History* that a conference took place at GHQ on the evening of 7 October attended by both army commanders and the Commander-in-Chief, at which Haig expressed his hopes of completing the conquest of the Passchendaele Ridge before winter. In his despatches, written the following December, Haig rehearses the arguments for and against continuing the assault, and attributes the decision to proceed to considerations of giving support to his Allies on other fronts. Monash's plea for a day's pause is not mentioned.

All of the above is thrown into question by the Australian scholars, Robin Prior and Trevor Wilson. They state: 'no contemporary record of the conference can be found, despite the existence of files which contain every other conference between Haig, Gough, and Plumer mentioned in the *Official History*.'

Their view is supported by the absence of a reference to such a meeting in Haig's diary entry for 7 October. In that he says: 'In view of the heavy rain today, and the possibility of the ground on Tuesday [9th] being too wet to admit of our men going forward beyond the "limited objective" I decided to delay issuing an order to collect wagons until tomorrow . . .'

And so how this decision – possibly the most crucial in the entire history of the campaign – was taken is under question. That proceeding to attack again so soon was queried, Monash makes clear. That he understood Haig to have rejected the idea of a pause is likely. One additional fragment of information comes from Haig's diary entry for 8 October, in which he records a conversation with Plumer in which the latter said II ANZAC Corps had specifically asked there should be no postponement: that is, that Monash's immediate superior had made a request expressly contrary to what Monash advocated. Haig also remarks:

'Owing to rain yesterday mud was very bad, and so only enough guns have been pushed forward to cover tomorrow's attack, but there are not enough to cover exploitation! It is therefore evident that my decision yesterday not to concentrate rolling stock was correct . . .

'Gough telephoned Kiggell as to postponement. He said Cavan was against it, but Maxse wanted to postpone. I ordered them to carry on.'

What we also know is the 9 October battle took place and that Haig, supported by at least some of his senior commanders, expressly refused to sanction any delay.

The day before Sir Douglas wrote to his wife about the conditions, which he described as: 'bright and clear with a high wind which is drying the ground nicely. But yesterday's rain made the mud bad beyond Ypres in the low ground, and stopped all the guns we wanted getting forward, but we have enough for tomorrow's attack.'

9 October 1917: Battle of Poelcappelle

Weather: clear skies; temperature, 53°F (11°C); rainfall, nil

The objective on 9 October was for Second Army to clear the Passchendaele Ridge and for Fifth Army to advance east of Poelcappelle to take the German Flanders I position that ran through Spriet, halfway to Westroosebeke on the road due north of Passchendaele village. Second Lieutenant Ernest Parker of the 2nd Royal Fusiliers had his mind on more immediate problems:

Poelcappelle to the Ridge: a map hand-corrected after 6 July, 1917 (Tank museum).

Campaign Chronicle

'On the eve of 9 October the Battalion left Boesinghe by platoons. Gleaming in the rain, the waterproof sheets and the shrapnel helmets of the troops could be picked out in the darkness as we hurried over the canal bridge to follow the guides along newly made fascine roads leading to the positions taped for our assembly before the attack of tomorrow.'

Although the unit halted and officers settled in shell holes to sleep, Parker was aware they were not in the correct position, so he cast about in the dark to locate the other companies:

'During my wanderings I was struck several times by descending fragments of shells which rang sharply against the steel of my shrapnel helmet without doing any damage. . . . I went on and finally learnt where we should be. With this information I returned to my platoon and moved them off. As they climbed out of their shell holes our preliminary bombardment opened up [at 5.20am] with the crushing violence of a thunderstorm. At the same time day began to break and from all points of the compass the shining bayonets of the attack thrust themselves from innumerable holes in the earth. The men of the 2nd Royals in long files of platoons began their advance towards the enemy, cut off from sight by a long wall of smoke rising from the shell bursts of the creeping barrage.

'Behind me the platoon struggled round the lips of shell craters, wholly unable to form into line. Several times I attempted to shout individually into each man's ear to make them form a line, but all I received in reply were bewildered noddings showing that my voice was inaudible in the storm of shelling. To make sure of our direction I stopped now and then to take a compass bearing, but after a time the whole attack had drifted to the right, leaving a gap on the left flank which I did my best to fill without losing touch with the rest of the Battalion, who seemed to be drifting too far to the right.'

On reaching the top of a rise in the ground, Parker could see the long, straight lines of the Guards approaching the edge of the Houlthust Forest. The barrage halted, and they took shelter in shell holes. Parker immediately decided to reorganize his platoon, but as he stood up to do so a bullet smashed through his right wrist, ending his part in the battle and, indeed, the war.

The rest of the attack on this, the left flank of Fifth Army, attained most of its objectives, but to their right, at Poelcappelle itself, there were problems. The assault on the village ruins was planned as a joint tank and infantry operation of a type at which Maxse's XVIII Corps was becoming adept. D Battalion provided eight tanks for the purpose. Watson wrote:

Campaign Chronicle

'Two sections of my tanks — Talbot's and Skinner's — had moved forward once more from the Canal, and were safely camouflaged in St Julien by dawn on the 8th. All the tank commanders had reconnoitred the road . . . The attack was to be made at 5.20am on the 9th. The tanks were ordered to enter Poelcappelle with the infantry and drive the enemy out of the houses which they still held.'

Watson himself was detained by duties in the rear and attempted to come up by car after dusk, but in the dark they had two minor crashes and Watson discovered his driver could not see in bad light. So he abandoned the vehicle and slogged forward in the rain into Ypres. As he did so the rain ceased and a pale moon looked down on the ghostly, ruined town. It began to rain again. Watson hitched a lift in an empty ambulance and stayed with it until a traffic jam stopped it:

'I wormed my way through the transport, and, passing the big guns on the near side of the crest which the enemy had held for so many years, I splashed down the track into St Julien. I only stumbled into one shell hole, but I fell over a dead mule in trying to avoid its brother.'

Almost as soon as he got there, German shelling began to fall all around. Undeterred, the tank crews went methodically about the business of getting ready to move off and at about 10pm seven were on the road; one had crashed so deep into a ruined house it could not be extracted. The rain stopped again and the moon broke through the cloud from time to time:

'Very slowly the seven tanks picked their way to Poelcappelle. The strain

Ypres from the ramparts (Taylor Library).

was appalling. A mistake by the leading tanks, and the road might be blocked. A slip – and the tank would lurch off into the mud. The road after the rain would have been difficult enough in safety by daylight. Now it was a dark night, and, just to remind the tanks of the coming battle, the enemy threw over a shell or two.

'One tank tried to cross a tree trunk at the wrong angle. The trunk slipped between the tracks and the tank turned suddenly. The mischief was done. For half an hour S. did his best, but on the narrow slippery road he could not swing his tank sufficiently to climb the trunk correctly. In utter despair he at last drove his tank into the mud, so that the three tanks behind him could pass.'

The shelling increased. All approaches to Poelcappelle were being plastered with shellfire:

'In front of each tank the officer was plunging through the shell holes and the mud, trying hard not to think of the shells. The first driver, cursing the darkness, peered ahead or put his ear to the slip, so that he could hear the instructions of his commander above the roar of the engine. The corporal "on the brakes" sat stiffly beside the driver. One man crouched in each sponson, grasping the lever of his secondary gear, and listening for the signals of the driver, tapped on the engine-cover. The gunners sprawled listlessly, with too much time for thought, but hearing none of the shells. . . .

'Suddenly a shell crashed into the third tank, just as it was passing a derelict. The two tanks in front went on. Behind, four tanks were stopped. The next tank was hit on a track.

'It was a massacre. The tanks could not turn, even if they had wished.'

The two leading tanks struggled on towards Poelcappelle. A huge crater blocked the way and as the leading machine paused to find a way round it was hit and burst into flames. The crew scrambled out. The second tank turned back and ditched as it tried to weave through the blockage to the rear. Watson was waiting anxiously in St Julien:

'The weary night had passed with its fears, and standing in front of the ruin we looked down the road. It was bitterly cold, and tragedy hung over the stricken grey country like a mist. First a bunch of wounded came, and then in the distance we saw a tank officer with his orderly. His head was bandaged and he walked in little jerks, as if he was a puppet on a string.'

They sat the shocked man down, gave him tea, and extracted the news. Watson sent a runner to order the crews staying with their tanks to come in and they tramped the long road back to base, bitterly grieving their failure and the loss of their comrades.

The infantry attack on Poelcappelle failed. The 11th Division's 33rd Brigade was part of the 5.20am assault. The 6th Green Howards and the 9th West Yorkshire Regiment moved to the left of the village. As soon as the Green Howards came up to the fork in the road by the Brewery on the far side, they came under fire. They took various pillboxes, but could not hold them and the West Yorks found themselves enfiladed from the village. The 8th Duke of Wellington's came up to help consolidate, but the advance achieved had been trivial without tanks or effective artillery support to deal with the strong points.

To their right, the attack on the Passchendaele Ridge was faring no better. Attempting to advance astride the Mosselmarkt road to the left of Passchendaele, the 49th Division, serving in II ANZAC Corps, was faced with the crossing of the Ravebeek: now a sea of mud some 30-50 yards (27.5--45m) wide and waist-deep in places. On the left they made enough progress to come under fire from strong points at Bellevue, but on the right they made none at all, finding the barbed wire deep and intact. The 66th Division, also part of II ANZAC, ended the day with only the first objective secured, although men of

Fatigue party of the Irish Guards taking duckboards up to the front, 10 October 1917 (Taylor Library).

the Lancashire Fusiliers pushed on to take the second, even sending patrols forward in the direction of Passchendaele village. The patrols never came back, but men of the 2/8th and 3/5th Lancashire Fusiliers were identified among the bodies found there when it finally fell to the Canadians. It was necessary to create a defensive line on the left to link with the 49th and, seeing the movement but unaware of what was actually being done, the men holding the second objective fell back to the first. To their right I ANZAC were covering the flank of the 66th, although their 10th Battalion sent a company to raid Celtic Wood, forward of the line, as a diversion. What became of many of those men remains a mystery: forty are known to have been lost. The attempts to move the artillery forward having failed before the attack, Passchendaele was at the extreme range of the British guns and thus the German artillery beyond was able to fire undisturbed. Clearly the chances of moving British artillery would be just as poor in the days to come.

The progress in the north had been satisfactory, and that in the centre contributed to the total of ground gained, but on the flank of Passchendaele Ridge, beyond the moat of mud at its foot, gains had been trivial and losses painful. Even Brigadier General Charteris, noted for his optimism and eagerness to press on, wrote:

> 'I was out all yesterday at the attack. It was the saddest day of the year. We did fairly well but only fairly well. It was not the enemy but mud which prevented us doing better. There is now no chance of complete success here this year. We must still fight on for a few weeks, but there is no purpose in it now as far as Flanders is concerned.'

Sir Douglas Haig, writing in his diary, was much more cheerful:

> 'The results were very successful . . . The ground was so bad that eight hours were taken in marching to forming up points: troops in consequence late and barrage started before the troops were ready. Notwithstanding this the 66th Division advanced without barrage and took all objectives — 49th gained all except a small piece on the left.'

He also wrote briefly of the action in his despatch, mentioning the few gains but none of the failed efforts of II ANZAC and went on to say:

> 'Though the condition of the ground continued to deteriorate, the weather after this was unsettled rather than persistently wet, and progress had not yet become impossible. I accordingly decided to press on while circumstances still permitted, and arrangements were made for a renewal of the attack on the 12th October.'

Campaign Chronicle

The rain continued, with 0.09in (2.5mm) on 10 October and 0.19in (4.9mm) the next day and the temperature dropped below 50°F (10°C). Captain Hickey's tanks had been moved up to Voormezeele, but had played no part in the fighting. He was sent with two of them to a position near Birr Crossroad:

'There seemed to be no immediate prospect of storming the Passchendaele Ridge with our tanks. Any plan for using them as fighting weapons appeared to have been abandoned. In an endeavour to find a job for tanks, my two were being sent forward to be used experimentally as tractors for hauling guns and supply sledges.

'Very soon after our arrival at Birr X-Rd we had a chance to show what we could do. A lorry had gone off the road . . . one of [my tanks] succeeded in pulling the lorry on to the road again. Similarly, a 6-inch howitzer was unditched at Birr X-Rd itself.'

Other ordnance was not so lucky. Two guns near Maple Copse were too far away from the hard surface and the same applied to a gun stuck in Sanctuary Wood. While they were there Brigadier General Courage and some staff officers came to visit. After conferring with the colonel and the company commander, they made to leave by way of a duckboard track towards the Menin road:

'The path led across the Bellewarde-beek, which was little more than a ditch filled with water. The duckboards were slippery. I was almost at the end of the procession, and the general was well ahead. Suddenly his foot slipped and he lost his balance. Looking up I saw the distinguished officer with his two legs in the air, coming down in a sitting position in the mud. His cane flew out of his hand and was rescued by the brigade major. I have a mental picture of a red-tabbed staff officer making several unsuccessful attempts to restore the stick to the general, who, floundering in the mud, was more concerned with regaining his feet than recovering his lost cane.'

Up on the St Julien-Poelcappelle Road the tanks that had blocked the way were still there, and had to be moved to allow the free movement of supplies and, perhaps, more tanks. D G Browne wrote of this:

'A party under the chief engineer of the 1st Brigade began the work at once. It had to be done at night, and then under conditions of extreme danger, for the Germans knew perfectly well what was happening, and shelled the village and the road ferociously. One by one the tanks, filled not only with their own dead but with the bodies of wounded infantrymen who had crawled in from that tormented street to die, were blown up by heavy charges of gun-cotton. Within a week the ghastly road was clear again, except for the human debris which accumulated always there.'

In the evening of 11 October, as the rain fell, General Gough telephoned his colleague, General Plumer, to say he thought the attack should be postponed. Plumer consulted his corps commanders and 'phoned back at 8pm to say they considered it best for the attack to be carried out.'

12 October 1917: First Battle of Passchendaele – ANZACS and British Flounder in Mud and Blood on Passchendaele Ridge

Weather: heavy cloud; temperature, 55°F (12°C); rainfall, 0.3in (7.9mm)

The ANZACs – the New Zealand Division on the left and the 3rd Australian on the right – set off from their assembly points 5 miles (8km) away from the front line at 6pm on 11 October. By the time Plumer returned Gough's telephone call they had already been on the move for at least two hours.

Sergeant Travis, a New Zealander, was nicknamed 'King of No Man's Land' because of his skill and courage in reconnoitring the German positions. His, and other reports, contributed the details given in the divisional history. It recounts that the field batteries had been unable to move, as had the heavy batteries, so they lacked counter-battery cover and a barrage of any solidity behind which to make their advance. What was more, from the Gravenstafel Spur the German pillboxes and newly strung barbed wire could clearly be seen, and the forward liaison officers repeated requests for heavy artillery fire on those features throughout 11 October. Nothing happened until late afternoon, as light was fading, all energies having been devoted to futile efforts to shift the guns forward.

Gunner B O Stokes, 13th Battery, New Zealand Field Artillery, told what that was like:

'C and D guns went forward first, and didn't they have a time getting them through the sea of mud and slush! They had to have eight horse-teams to do the job. . . . a sound of a shell coming over told us it was going to land very near. We crouched to the earth, and the shell landed only 3 yards [2.7m] away. . . . there lay four of our boys dead. . . . You can't imagine how we felt. The shelling didn't cease for another half-hour. Shelling. Shelling. Shelling. . . . The wind and rain lashing down. The horses screaming and rearing and plunging down into the mud as the shells exploded all around us.'

It was not until 5pm that they reached the new position and they had to leave two guns behind, leaving them only four. They spent the night sitting on boxes in a half-smashed pillbox because there was too much water on the floor to permit them to lie down.

The assault began at 5.25am. The 2nd Otago Regiment led the way for the 2nd New Zealand Brigade, with the 1st Otago following to take over once the first objective had been taken, and in reserve was the 2nd Canterbury Regiment. They were astride the road from Gravenstafel with their right at Marsh Bottom. Private W Smith was serving with the Machine-Gun Company:

'We made a bad "blue" in sticking to that main . . . road. It certainly looked the best part to get a footing on – covered with inches of mud, of course, but with a fairly firm footing underneath. I suppose Fritz had anticipated this. As we started up the road we were caught in enfilade fire from the big pillboxes in the low ground to our right. People were dropping all the way. Then, as we turned the corner on top of the rise, we saw this great bank of wire ahead, maybe 100 yards [91.4m] away. A rat couldn't have got through that. The bombardment should have cut the wire but it hadn't even dented it. Not that we could get near it anyway, for it was positively spitting fire. . . . More than half of us fell.'

But the Otagos did try to get through the wire. They had a go at cutting it, crawling under it, climbing it. Incredibly, some of them managed to overcome the first belt. The 1st Otagos came up to help. On the right two big pillboxes had been causing terrible damage and Second Lieutenant A R Cockerell, now having been commander of 8th Company for a matter of minutes, saw they had to be dealt with. In the confusion he found himself alone, but still went forward towards the trench in front of the first fortification. Forty Germans in it had shot away all their ammunition, so they surrendered. Those men attempting to emerge from the pillbox were bayoneted in series by Cockerell and so the rest inside surrendered too. Now assisted by a Lewis gun-toting Private G Harris, they went for the next blockhouse. That, too, had no more ammunition and two officers and thirty men were made prisoner. Men of the 3rd Australian Division arrived and together they planned to advance, but they were unable to communicate with their commanders to the rear and co-ordinate with the artillery, so they stayed where they were.

The 3rd Australian Division was badly hit by enemy shelling just as they moved forward but still managed to subdue three machine-gun posts and push on with the railway to their right and up the road to Passchendaele. Here they

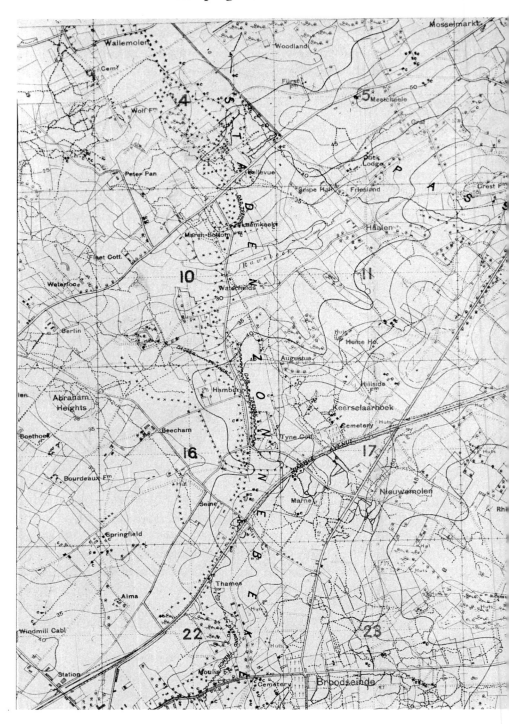

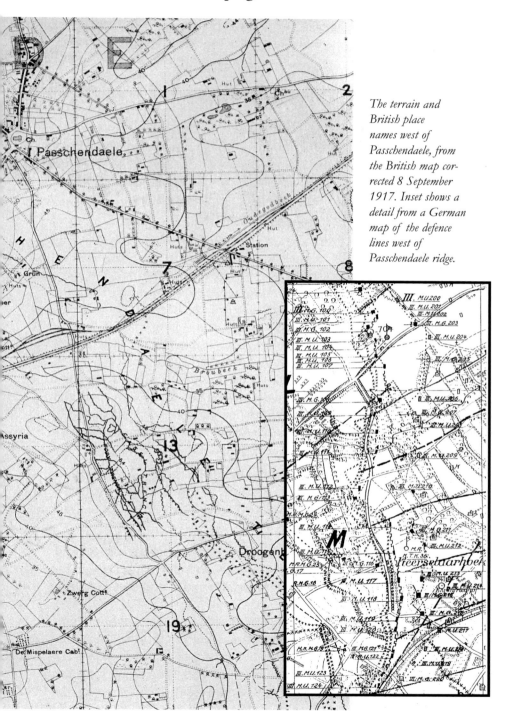

The terrain and British place names west of Passchendaele, from the British map corrected 8 September 1917. Inset shows a detail from a German map of the defence lines west of Passchendaele ridge.

found wounded men of the 66th Division still huddled in shell holes. The got almost as far as Crest Farm on the outskirts of the village and even sent patrols into it, but they were by now too few to hold the position and at 3pm they pulled back. To their left the 10th Brigade were struggling across the bog of the Ravebeek and, although they took Waterfields, they could not make further progress because of the fire from Bellevue and, at 3.30pm they were almost back at their start line.

The Fifth Army made some small progress, having fewer water hazards to surmount. Hugh Quigley of the 12 Royal Scots was with 26 Brigade, 9th Division in the advance towards Banff House on the New Zealanders' left. The brigade made little more than 100 yards' (91.4m) progress during the day. Quigley wrote a surprisingly cheerful letter home from hospital:

'I just want to tell you about the last affair. Our division had the pleasing task of making a bold bid for Passchendaele: of course, the officers told us the usual tale, "a soft job", and I reckon it might have been easy enough if we had had a decent start. But none of us knew where to go when the barrage began, whether half-right or half-left: a vague memory of following shell-bursts as long as the smoke was black, and halting when it changed to white. It was all the same to me: I was knocked out before I left the first objective, a ghastly breast-work littered with German corpses. . . .

'Apart from that, the whole affair appeared rather good fun. You know how excited one becomes in the midst of great danger. I forgot absolutely that shells were meant to kill and not to provide elaborate lighting effects, looked at the barrage, ours and the Germans', as something provided for our entertainment . . .'

General Monash was frustrated and angry, but his letter about the First Battle of Passchendaele was restrained. It is dated 15 October, and includes the passages about asking for a delay mentioned above. Of the events of 12 October he said:

'Just in the degree that the battle of 4 October was brilliantly successful, so were the operations of 12 October deeply disappointing, although the 3rd Australian Division did magnificently under the most adverse circumstances.

'It is bad to cultivate the habit of criticism of higher authority and, therefore, I do so now with some hesitation, but chiefly to enable you to get a correct picture of what the situation was. . . .

'Considerable rain began to set in on 6 October. The ground was in a deplorable condition by the night of 8 October, and, in consequence, the

66th and 45th Divisions who had taken up the role of the 3rd Australian and the New Zealand Divisions, failed to accomplish more than about quarter of a mile [400m] of their projected advance. Even in the face of this the Higher Command insisted on going on, and insisted, further, that the uncompleted objectives of this fourth phase should be added to the objectives of our fifth phase; so that it amounted to this that Russell [NZ commander] and I were asked to make an advance of $1^3/_4$ miles [2.8km].

'The weather grew steadily worse on 10 and 11 October. There was no flying and no photographing, no definite information of the German redispositions, no effective bombardment, no opportunity of replenishing our ammunition dumps; and the whole country from Zonnebeke forward to the limits of our previous captures was literally a sea of mud, in most places waist deep. Even in spite of all these difficulties, I might have succeeded in accomplishing the goal aimed at but, most unfortunately, the division on my left (the New Zealanders) had in the first stage of their advance to cross the Ravebeek, which not only proved physically impossible, but the banks of it had been strongly wired on the enemy's side. Consequently, the New Zealand Division could obtain no footing upon the Bellevue Spur, and the left flank of my advance was, therefore, fully exposed to the enfilade fire of a large number of concrete forts scattered over the spur.

'At the end of the day's operations we had accomplished only about another three-quarters of a mile [1,200m] of our advance, being pulled up by the exhaustion of our men within 1,000 yards [0.9km] of the village. My casualties have been rather heavy . . .

'It has now been decided to persist in the plan and troops from another Dominion are going to attempt it, but on this occasion ample time will be allowed for proper preparations.'

In a letter of 18 October Monash allowed his measured tone to slip, revealing a passion some would have found surprising. The matter under discussion was not military so much as political. The Australian Prime Minister, William Hughes, was dealing with the consequences of having failed to introduce conscription to supplement the ranks of the Australian Imperial Force, the volunteer army permitted to serve overseas. The absence of his voice at the highest levels in London was seen by Monash as a serious problem, and he wrote:

'Our men are being put into the hottest fighting and are being sacrificed in hair-brained ventures, like Bullecourt and Passchendaele, and there is no one in the War Cabinet to lift a voice in protest. It all arises from the fact that Australia is not represented in the War Cabinet, owing to Hughes, for political reasons, having been unable to come to England. So Australian interests are suffering badly, and Australia is not getting anything like the recognition it deserves.'

One additional observation is made about the recent battle in this letter. Having given his family a succinct account of how battlefield casualties were treated and evacuated, he remarks: 'During the battle of 12 October the work was very heavy. The average "carry" from the front line [to the regimental aid-posts] was over 4,000 yards [3.65km], through a heavy morass, and each stretcher took sixteen bearers, in four relays of four men in each – instead of two men as normally.'

Ludendorff did not regard the two most recent battles as victories, and worried about the influence they were having on his freedom of operation elsewhere:

'There were further severe engagements on the 9th and 12th October. The line held better than on the 4th, although in some places the enemy penetrated to a considerable distance. The wastage in the big actions of the Fourth Battle of Flanders was extraordinarily high. In the West we began to be short of troops. The two divisions that had been held in readiness in the East, and were already on their way to Italy, were diverted to Flanders. The attack on Osel [in the Gulf of Riga], at any rate, had commenced, but the Italian operation could not be started before the 22nd, and the weather held it up until the 24th. These days were the culminating point of the crisis.'

Haig's despatch was muted in its tone and nothing was said about the stalled assaults along the Ravebeek:

'Our attack, launched at 5.25am on the 12th October between the Ypres-Roulers Railway and Houthulst Forest, made progress along the spurs and higher ground; but the valleys of the streams which run westward from the main ridge were found to be impassable. It was therefore determined not to persist in the attack, and the advance towards our more distant objectives was cancelled.'

And in his diary the comment is simply: 'Owing to the rain and bad state of the ground, General Plumer decided that it was best not to continue the attack on the front of his Army.'

Comment on these remarks seems unnecessary.

The United States of America

The USA was keen to stand aloof from the war, but was inexorably drawn in. Both sides wooed the industrial giant, but financially the USA sided with the Allies early on by engaging in trade and extending massive credit. By March 1917, for example, Britain owed the bankers J P Morgan $4 billion and the American economy had grown by 60 per cent. The German ambassador in Washington was sent home in early February as the result of unrestricted submarine warfare being resumed; the first casualty came on 3 February with the sinking of the American ship *Housatonic* off the Scilly Isles. On 24 February the American ambassador in London, Walter Page, exposed the Germans to his government as having attempted to bribe the Mexicans to invade the USA and to approach the Japanese with a view to getting them to join the Germans. On 2 April 1917 President Woodrow Wilson addressed Congress and proposed a declaration of war on Germany, using the words 'keeping the world safe for democracy.' The declaration was signed four days later.

Haig, as well as Ludendorff, had plans further afield to consider. The French were planning an assault on the Aisne front to take place on 22 October and the preparations for what was to be known as the Battle of Cambrai were well advanced. This was to be undertaken by General Sir Julian Byng's Third Army and almost the entire tank force available to the British. Haig wrote:

'By this time the persistent continuation of wet weather had left no further room for hope that the condition of the ground would improve sufficiently to enable us to capture the remainder of the ridge this year. By limited attacks made during intervals of better weather, however, it would still be possible to progress as far as Passchendaele, and in view of other projects which I had in view it was desirable to maintain the pressure on the Flanders front for a few weeks longer.

'To maintain his defence on this front the enemy had been obliged to reduce the garrison of certain other parts of his line to a degree which justified the expectation that a sudden attack at a point where he did not expect it might attain a considerable local success. The front for such an attempt had been selected, and plans had already been made. But certain preparations and movements of troops required time to complete, and the 20th November has been fixed as the earliest date for the attack.'

Another conference was held on Saturday 13 October and Haig noted in his diary:

'I held a conference at Cassel at noon with Generals Plumer, Gough, their staff officers, Kiggell, Nash, Birch, Charteris, Davidson . . . I said that our immediate objective was the mass of high ground around Passchendaele. Once this was taken the rest of the ridge would fall more easily. The Canadians would join the Second Army at once for next attack . . . We all agreed that our attack should only be launched when there is a fair prospect of fine weather. When ground is dry no opposition which the enemy has put up has been able to stop them.'

On 13 October another 0.4in (10.7mm) of rain fell and the temperature remained low. Then on the 14th the rain held off, as it did on the 15th as well. The rainfall for the next week totalled 0.5in (14.2mm), but there was one day with no rain at all. People cheered up a bit, but the going underfoot remained awful.

The ANZACs were relieved by the Canadian Corps, commanded by Lieutenant General Sir Arthur Currie, on 18 October. The Canadians had fought here before, in April 1916 when gas was used by the Germans for the first time on this front. The landscape bore little relation to that of eighteen months before. The trees had gone, the farms had gone, the streams had gone: only the mounding up of the hills and the depressions of the little valleys bore witness to what once had been. The Steenbeek was now a morass half a mile (800m) wide and the low ground in front of Passchendaele was a lake of mud. In his diary Currie noted: 'Battlefield looks bad'. An inspection of the artillery available to the Australians, which the Canadians were to take over, was made by Brigadier General E W B Morrison in person. Of the 250 heavy guns alleged to be there, only 227 could be located and of those 89 were out of action. Of 306 18-pounder field artillery pieces more than half were out of action. Further, the difficulty of moving guns at all had led to considerable bunching so that there were four great gun batteries, so to speak, just asking to be shelled by the enemy. To move these guns, and to bring up more, new roads were needed and the ground was in a shocking state. Haig's diary note of 13 October included the observation that one of the light railway engines had sunk in halfway up its boiler, thrusting the track deep into the boggy soil.

Observing the ant-like bustle behind British lines, the Germans made use of their recently developed gas-shelling techniques. They had introduced a solid chemical that dispersed in the air as a powder that ordinary gas masks could not keep out. This 'Blue Cross' – diphenylchloroarsene – caused the victim to sneeze, retch and vomit and therefore to pull off his gas mask. It was then followed with dichlorethylsulphide, 'Yellow Cross' or 'Yperite', commonly known as mustard gas. The effect of mustard gas was to burn the skin or, if inhaled, the lungs. It dissolved in water, which meant it could be washed off the skin but also that it endured in puddles and diving into a shell hole for cover from fire might well lead to being immobilized by an all-engulfing skin-rash.

Gunner Frank Ferguson was an American serving with the Canadians in 1st Canadian Siege Battery. He recalled going up to the front:

'though St Jean, and after half an hour of swimming through the mud and trying to walk on the road . . . we got to the guns.

'The mud hereabouts is chronic; and I'll bet a cookie that every kid born in this Godforsaken neck of the woods had web toes like a duck. There is one consolation attached to being up here and that is that the "Old Man" won't ask us to dig him a dugout. At least not unless he wants to use it as a bathtub, as a hole dug here will fill with water almost as soon as it is dug.'

The next day Ferguson experienced an air attack:

'I heard a terrible din overhead, and looked up to see a fleet of about ten Gothas coming through the clouds dropping bombs by the ton. And to make the scene more harrowing, they were heading in my direction. A machine-gunner sat out on the wing of each plane sweeping the ground below, while from the bottom of the planes were dropping those lovely "eggs" which, to my mind, are the worst thing this war has brought out.'

Currie's first proposal was for the first of his three attacks to take place on 24 October, but the difficulties with roads and guns led him to change that to 29 October. Haig was not pleased as the French attack at Malmaison was scheduled for the 23rd. Plumer then became involved and a limited attack by the Fifth Army was therefore arranged for 22 October and the Canadian assaults were to start on the 26th, followed by further attacks on, provisionally, 30 October and 6 November.

22 October 1917: Fifth Army Attacks

Weather: overcast; temperature 56°F (13°C); rainfall, 0.12in (3.2mm)

At 5.35am a three-division attack was made beyond Poelcappelle and up towards the Houthulst Forest, with the French attacking on the left. The Germans, by an order of 11 October, had adopted Ludendorff's defensive arrangements with a lightly held *Vorfeld* or forefield and, some 880 yards (800m) back, a strong, main line of resistance. The idea was that the scattered forefield defenders should, in the case of a serious assault, retreat before the British barrage so a German counter-barrage could be let loose on the attackers.

On the right the XVIII Corps' 18th Division first made use of a 'Chinese' attack. General Maxse had written about the idea in a letter of 25 September. He had been training 100 men from the Cyclist Corps to make 'sham attacks by "pole targets" and painted figures which rise and fall with a string.' The ruse distracted the Germans from the 8th Norfolks' advance on the Brewery, which they took. At 7.30 the 10th Essex passed through the Norfolks and proceeded to take Noble's Farm, Meunier House and Tracas Farm, which was more than had been asked of them. Maxse was delighted. On 24 October he wrote:

> 'The XVIIIth are again "blue-eyed boys" in consequence of being the only ones to capture all their objectives on the 22nd and to hold them definitely. They did even more and advanced their front beyond what was demanded. I never know how long the "blue-eyed" phase may last? Sometimes only for a day!'

To their left the 34th Division made reasonable progress, with one curious incident marking the advance of the 15th Royal Scots of 101 Brigade between the Ypres-Staden railway and the Watervlietbeek. The attack had begun at 5.35am and as the 15th went forward with B Company on the left and A Company on the right, a small group of the latter, an officer and thirteen men, were approached by about 100 Germans who demanded their surrender. This was not to the Royal Scots' taste and they opened fire. Only one of the enemy was seen to regain his lines. A strong German counter-attack late in the day pushed the left of the division back to Egypt House. Further left, the 35th Division was thrusting up towards the forest and first objectives were taken straightforwardly, but resistance stiffened as they went further and counter-attacks pushed them back and even, on the extreme left, broke through, forcing a retirement to the original line. The change in German defensive tactics was demonstrable, but the British use of the artillery barrage was more effective than the defenders expected: they were so close behind it the forefield troops had no time to pull back before the attack was on them. Further, British use of artillery to break up counter-attacks was effective once again.

Between Tuesday, 23 October and Thursday, 25 October it was cold

Campaign Chronicle

(48°F/9°C) and wet. The rainfall totalled 0.6in (16.2mm), making any movement a severe challenge and living conditions atrocious.

D E Hickey of H Battalion, Tank Corps, was still doing what he could near the Menin road. From their base at Voormezele he and his men went forward and back every day. He wrote:

> 'From forward in the salient on our way back to our dugout each evening at dusk, we used to pass the men going up to the firing line. They marched in single file along the side of the Menin road. Their sallow faces haunted me. For many it would be their last journey.
>
> 'About 21 October, after seventeen days in the salient, we hoped to be sent to a rest camp at a small seaside town.
>
> 'We were looking forward to the end of our fruitless labours, floundering in the mud around Ypres. Then there was a sudden reversal of plan.
>
> 'Two tanks were to take part in an attack against Polderhoek Chateau, on the Passchendaele Ridge.'

The location Hickey gives is misleading. The position of the objective was south of Polygon Wood and the Reutelbeek and overlooking, to its south, the marsh that had been the Scherriabeek and, beyond on the Menin road, Gheluvelt. Hickey describes the planned approach, along the Menin road and then, before Gheluvelt, turning north, presumably along the line of the road that then kinks eastwards towards the Château. The mission was to be undertaken by tanks commanded by Brown and Glanville, and the section would be led by Gerrard:

> 'It would be essential for Gerrard to lead his tanks on foot, to prevent their being ditched or losing direction once they were off the road.
>
> 'There was a conference of officers, including some of the staff, to discuss the plan of attack, Gerrard, of course, being present. The colonel said he felt confident that any of his officers would be willing, like Captain Robertson, to make the supreme sacrifice, in

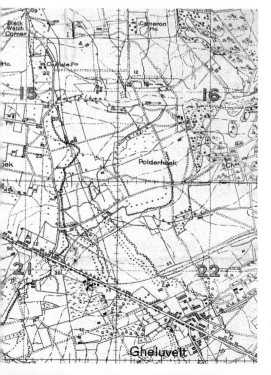

Detail from the Veldhoek Map: Polderhoek Château, north of Gheluvelt (Tank museum).

order to secure the success of the attack.

'When the conference ended the plan of attack had been arranged; but the date and hour had not yet been fixed. The colonel shook hands with Gerrard as though in final goodbye, promising that his kit would be looked after.'

The three officers made a reconnaissance of the terrain over which they would have to go and found it in fearful state. The road was so severely smashed they doubted they would even be able to negotiate that, let alone turn off it. Late in the night of Tuesday, 23 October, Gerrard was summoned to be told the enterprise would be undertaken at daybreak on the 25th and that he was under orders to lead his tanks from outside. Hickey did his best to be optimistic, but both men knew how slight Gerrard's chances of survival were. Then Hickey was sent for: he was to take a party out at 6am to work on the repair of the road between Hooge Dump and the 'crater beyond Clapham Junction' to ease the way for the tanks. He told Gerrard of his probably fatal assignment and his friend became visibly more cheerful, telling him of two major craters that needed filling, one at Hooge Dump and the other beyond Clapham Junction.

The next morning Hickey took twenty-six NCOs and men and two junior officers out to Birr Crossroad and divided them into two parties. One was to begin at Hooge, the other at Clapham Junction. He went with the Hooge group to get them started, and the other party moved off and was quickly swallowed up in the traffic. When Hickey later tried to contact them, his runner could not find them. It soon became clear they were lost somewhere or other. Hickey

Polderhoek Château: Gerrard's objective had ceased to exist by October 1917 (Taylor Library).

went beyond Clapham Junction:

> 'The road here was deserted. There was not a living soul to be seen. . . . I passed a hand sticking up. Its owner had evidently been buried by a shell. I have since been told that this hand remained unburied because the troops going up into the line regarded it with superstitious reverence. They believed if they touched it, no harm would come to them. At the point I reached there was a water-filled crater stretching almost across the road. I presumed this was the crump to which Gerrard had referred. Five or six tanks could have sunk in it easily. Floating on the surface of the water were several dead bodies. As I gazed forward across a black expanse of mud where no life was visible, the desolation of the scene reminded me of a cold grey sea and deserted shore.'

Further searching proved fruitless and then he had to shelter from a massive British barrage, which stopped both his watches. Hickey returned to his camp where he learned the working party had failed to see the British front line and had walked on into the Germans who immediately offered surrender. But, when they saw the tank men were armed only with picks and shovels, they tried to kill them instead. A fight broke out in which grenades thrown were grabbed up and hurled back at the Germans, but only one wounded man got away to report, while thirteen men were made prisoner. The presence of tanks was, by now, known to the enemy. The attack was cancelled.

Gerrard, who had been moving his tanks forward through the drab and dreary countryside, was ordered to turn back. As he retraced his path, he told Hickey, the colours were bright and cheerful and the beauties of nature revealed themselves on every hand.

The artillery barrages continued through this period, and on Thursday evening the Canadian 4th Division's 46th Battalion moved close to the line held by the 50th, south of the Ravebeek, while the 3rd Division readied itself to the north of the former rivulet: the bog it had become had to be avoided. This put the 4th Division with its right on the railway and Broodseinde-Passchendaele road, where the 3rd Australian Division had attacked, and the 3rd with its right straddling the Gravenstafel-Mosselmarkt road, where the New Zealanders had fought so valiantly.

26 October 1917: Second Battle of Passchendaele, First Phase – Canadians Reach Dry Ground

Weather: overcast skies; temperature, 48°F (9°C), rainfall, 0.3in (7.8mm)

Campaign Chronicle

The attacks began at 5.40am. On the extreme right the 7th Division, astride and south of the Menin road, and the 5th Division to their left had to contend with the two little streams, or rather the mud lakes that lay in their place, south and north of the Menin road at Gheluvelt. Where the shallow valleys were the attacks failed with considerable loss, but on the higher, dryer ground, some temporary success was achieved with the 2nd Border Regiment coming close to Gheluvelt, the 8th and 9th Devons almost reaching the church there, and the 15th Warwicks taking Polderhoek Château. It did not last. Because of German counter-attacks or because of being exposed in a salient without flank support, they were all back at their starting lines by the end of the day. Their most valuable contribution had been to distract, to some extent, from the Canadian activity in the centre.

Private R Le Brun was serving with the 16th Machine-Gun Company, 4th Canadian Division and was to give covering fire to the attack:

'The infantry attacked early in the morning of 26 October. We had been ordered to fire 500 rounds every twenty minutes throughout the previous night at targets in front. We were right out in front of the line, and the mud was so deep in our shell holes that we had to put at least six boxes of ammunition underneath us – 303 ammo with 1,000 rounds to a box – just to stand on to get out of the mud. We had to keep on filling our belts with ammo. Whenever we did that, we put our groundsheets across to

Private R Le Brun, pictured nearest the camera, ready to give covering fire to the Canadian attack (IWM CO2246).

cover the shell holes while we loaded up. At dawn the infantry went on past us, and we elevated our sights to cover them.'

The 4th Canadian Division attacked with one battalion, the 46th (South Saskatchewan), astride the Passchendaele road with the 18th Australian Battalion on its right. They seized their objectives but then came under heavy fire from Laamkeek, on the far side of the Ravebeek. Fire also came in from Decline Copse, straddling the railway cutting halfway between the point at which the road crossed it to the south, and Vienna Cottages to the north-east. Neither the Canadians nor the Australians had been given exclusive responsibility for taking it, the railway being the dividing line between the two forces. As a result it remained uncleared, full of Germans, and spitting machine-gun fire. The 46th suffered 70 per cent casualties amongst the 420 men who carried out the attack and they were forced to pull back.

On the other side of the Ravebeek mudbath the 9 Canadian Brigade was attacking the same objectives as the New Zealanders. On the left, close to the Mosselmarkt road, the 43rd (Cameron Highlanders of Canada) Battalion managed at last to seize the Bellevue pillbox complex, but could make no further progress against German shellfire. Below, to their right, the 58th (Central Ontario) Battalion had run into trouble from the Laamkeek cluster of strong points. Lieutenant Robert Shankland of the 43rd, fortunately for his comrades, had got together men from other companies to reinforce his own platoon as well as two detachments of the 9th Machine-Gun Company. With this small private army he defended a position on the Bellevue Spur to the north of the road. This gave the 52nd (Manitoba) Battalion the opportunity to get up to Shankland's position and then, methodically, to work across the spur southwards, taking out one pillbox after another until, by mid-afternoon, all the Bellevue and Laamkeek defences were in Canadian hands. Three Victoria Crosses were awarded for achievements on that day. In addition to Lieutenant Shankland, Captain C P J O'Kelly and Private T W Holmes received the award.

Further north, the Fifth Army was also in action with the 63rd (Royal Naval) Division on the right, and to their left, the 58th, 57th and 50th Divisions. Gains were trivial and losses heavy, but, like their brothers on the southern flank, these troops diluted German resistance to the Canadian assault.

General Gough wrote, wearily:

'On the 26th all three Armies attacked again, but it rained heavily during the night and the ground in front of the Fifth Army was becoming almost impossible, and very little progress was made either by us or by the Second Army. The state of the ground had been frightful since the 1st

August, but by now it was getting absolutely impossible. Men of the strongest physique could hardly move forward at all and became easy victims to the enemy's snipers. Stumbling forward as best they could, their rifles also soon became so caked and clogged with mud as to be useless.'

Sir Douglas Haig was a good deal more cheerful about things. Of the Canadian advance along the Passchendaele Ridge he said they had 'established themselves securely on the small hill south of Passchendaele', and of the attack north of the Ravebeek, he said they 'had gained practically the whole of their objectives'. His determinedly rosy view was applied to the fighting on the flanks as well, and he went on to speak of the French and Belgian operations to the left of the British:

> 'The operations of our Allies on this day were limited to establishing bridgeheads across the floods of the St Jansbeek [the stream north of Bixscheote, into which the Steenbeek flows]. This was successfully accomplished, in spite of considerable opposition. Next day the French continued their advance in concert with Belgian troops, who crossed the Yser opposite Knockehoek, and captured Aschhoop, Kippe, and Merkem. The southern end of the Blankaart Lake was reached the same day, and early on the 28th October French and Belgian troops completed the capture of the whole Merkem peninsula.'

The apparent success of his allies on the left seems to have encouraged hopes that, with just one more thrust, the long-awaited result might be obtained. His diary for 26 October reports another plea from Gough for a cessation of operations:

> 'In the evening General Gough communicated with General Kiggell CGS that he found the ground on his front so very bad that he recommended delaying further operations until frost set in! . . . In my opinion today's operations at the decisive point (Passchendaele) had been so successful that I was entirely opposed to any idea of abandoning the operations till frost set in. If wet continues, a day or two's delay may be advisable before we launch the next attack.'

Unmentioned in the despatch of December 1917, quite reasonably, is the other event of 26 October: the decision to help the Italians in the aftermath of the German and Austrian success at Caporetto, by sending two British divisions from the Western Front. General Lord Cavan, then of XIV Corps in the Fifth Army, was to be in command of a force comprised initially of the 23rd and 41st Divisions of X Corps. Another three were to follow in November.

27 October 1917: Second Battle of Passchendaele, First Phase – Canadians Consolidate

Weather: half cloud; temperature, 49°F (10°C); rainfall, nil

Field Marshal Haig's idea of how things were up on the Passchendaele Ridge was seriously flawed. The Germans were still in possession of the vital Decline Copse position. The Canadian 46th Battalion had been reinforced with the 44th (Winnipeg) and the 47th (British Colombia) Battalions, but the general position was unchanged. At about midnight 26/27 October a messenger arrived at the headquarters of the 47th in Seine dugout, to report that Decline Copse had been taken, but two hours later an irate Australian officer turned up to say it had not: he had scouted the position and found it rigid with Germans. The general confusion is reported in the 44th's regimental history:

> 'Stretcher bearers work doggedly in the almost hopeless task of caring for the countless wounded who mingle with the dead in advanced positions. Parties of men lose direction in the darkness and wander to and fro in the mud, trying to find their units. The toll of killed and wounded mounts steadily under the everlasting bombardment of enemy guns. Overhead the great enemy bombing planes roar back and forth.'

In the morning the Copse was attacked and taken and a line pushed eastwards to deal with a number of enemy pillboxes. It was not an outcome the Germans were content to accept, for the following evening they mounted a vigorous attack just as the 85th Battalion were relieving the 44th. The Canadians were pushed out of the Copse and counter-attacked at once, the 44th on the right of the railway embankment and the 85th on the left, as described in the 44th's Regimental History:

> 'Captain Martyn, leading elements of the 44th, reaches the eastern side of the copse alone. A party of the enemy crawls towards him. The 44th officer is in a quandary as to what to do. He calls to the 44th men behind him. Sergeant Swayne and a Lewis gun crew rush forward; only the gunner, Private Lawrence, gets through; he has his gun – but no ammunition. Corporal Hughes essays to reach the post with ammunition; he is shot through and through; with a dying effort he hurls two "pans" [magazines] forward. Pushing the officer aside, Lawrence now gets into action with his Lewis gun, mowing down the steadily advancing enemy.'

His action, and that of the unfortunate corporal, tipped the balance. Another gun was got up and the firepower of the machine-guns drove the Germans back.

Sunday, 28 October was relatively dry with only 0.05in (1.3mm) of rain, but it was cold. The temperature fell to 41°F (5°C) and while Monday was dry, it was only a little warmer. Canadian activity was intense. The next phase of the battle was planned for 30 October: but before then the supply system had to be overhauled and tracks of corduroy roads, fascine-based bridges, and duckboards had to be laid so the mule-trains could move. Each brigade was allotted a train of 250 beasts to haul supplies to the front: mechanized transport was out of the question in the conditions. The supply trains had to move by night and the losses from animals straying off the roads and sinking in the mud were many.

Tuesday 30 October 1917: Second Battle of Passchendaele, Second Phase – Crest Farm and Meetcheele in Canadian Hands

Weather: clear with showers; temperature 44°F (6°C); rainfall, 0.09in (2.3mm)

The Canadians now had to take the Blue Line, some 600-700 yards (550-640m) beyond the Red Line objective of four days earlier. On the right, Crest Farm would have to fall. It was a well fortified German position on a spur jutting out south-west of Passchendaele above the Ravebeek. On the left, the line would have to be advanced to embrace the hamlet of Meetcheele and the area north-west of it. There was no need to reposition the artillery to achieve this and the renovated supply arrangements ensured sufficient ammunition.

On the Canadians' left, Fifth Army also attacked, if reluctantly. Gough noted:

> 'The Fifth Army had, however, to take part in one more attack. On the 30th October . . . we attacked with part of two divisions, but being in the low ground and operating in the valleys of the small streams that run westwards off the ridge, we could not get far forward – an advance of 300 yards [275m] or so being the limit of the day's objectives.'

The Canadian *Official History* says the attack began at 5.50am, in clear but cold and windy weather. While we have the temperature and rainfall data, we do not know the wind speed and therefore cannot calculate the wind-chill factor, but if the wind was blowing at 24mph (38.5kph) the perceived temperature would have been 28°F (-2.3°C).

On the ridge the 4th Canadian Division attacked with 12 Brigade: the 85th

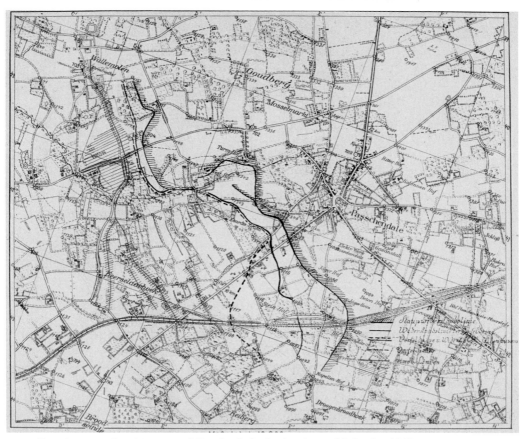

Bavarian map of positions west of Passchendaele: the situation on 20 October 1917
(Bayerische Hauptstaats Archiv, Munich).

General classification of ground map dated November 1917 showing the Passchendaele ridge running north to south. Passchendaele is in square 6. The dark shading indicates waterlogged ground.
(Zonnebeke 28NE1).

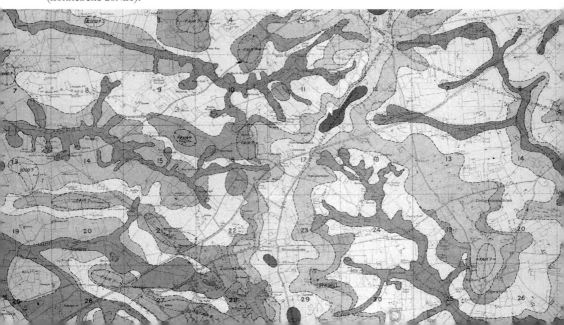

Campaign Chronicle

(Nova Scotia Highlanders), 78th (Winnipeg Grenadiers) and 72nd (Seaforth Highlanders) Battalions. The 78th was on the right, east of the road to Passchendaele, and Private J Pickard was a signaller with the battalion. His commanding officer decided that, in spite of the poor chances of success, they would try to establish effective telegraph communications, so Pickard was, with six others, loaded with equipment when he moved forward:

> 'The bombardment was murderous – ours and the Germans' – and they weren't only flinging over shells, they were simply belting machine-gun fire for all they were worth. . . . off we went with the first wave of infantry and started stringing out the wire. . . . it was utterly useless. We could see the wire we were stringing was being chopped to pieces as fast as we laid it.'

Soon only Pickard and Corporal Sims were left unharmed. They had no choice but to go forward, for their CO would not have welcomed them back at their starting point:

> 'The shells were falling thick and fast and by some sort of capillary action the holes they made filled up with water as you looked at them – or as you lay in them, for the only way we could move was to dodge from one hole to another, hoping that lightning really didn't strike twice in the same place. Sims and I were separated. I splashed and wallowed through the mud, hoping I was going in the right direction, but none too sure.'

After a pause in a hole miraculously furnished with a little willow-bush, into which a dud shell fell as he smoked a cigarette, Pickard hurried on:

> 'I got out of there like a bat out of hell and made for where the boys were digging in, linking up a row of wet shell holes to make a new front line. They'd done well. They'd got far ahead. I reported to a major and explained what had happened to the communications department. He greeted me with open arms, for his runner had just been wounded and he had a report to send back to Battalion HQ. Would I volunteer to go back? Would I! The Germans were massing for a counter-attack and the shelling and machine-gun fire was wicked. I would have volunteered to walk across the floors of Hell barefooted to get out of that, so I started back to HQ. It was in a pillbox we called Hamburg House.'

They had all done well. On the right the 85th Battalion took Vienna Cottage, Tiber and Grün, but lost half their strength in doing so. The 78th secured the centre and, on the right, the 72nd captured Crest Farm and sent patrols forward into the village, which the Germans appeared to be abandoning. They had encircled the position with A Company on the higher ground to the west and B Company coming up from the south. Lance Corporal Irwin, a Lewis gunner, observed three silent machine-guns on the crest of the slope, waiting to enfilade A Company's lines when they got into position. Irwin got behind the enemy and took out all three, firing his Lewis gun from the shoulder.

Pickard was doing his service as a runner:

> 'I was back and forward to the line as acting-runner, and every time we'd got a bit nearer Passchendaele. They stopped eventually at the foot of a lane leading into the village. You could tell it had been a lane by the ruined cottages on either side, and you could see the church just beyond them. It was a place they called Crest Farm. They had to fight hard to get it and the place was thick with bodies. But we took it, and we held the line.'

The 3rd Canadian Division had started operations during the previous night when Princess Patricia's Canadian Light Infantry had taken Snipe Hall, a particularly dangerous pillbox on the edge of the Ravebeek swamp, below Bellevue. They then pushed on through the slime to take Duck Lodge, but the hail of German fire pouring down the valley prevented further progress and inflicted serious casualties, particularly among their junior officers, almost all of whom had been lost within an hour. The PPCLI then seized the Meetcheele crossroads position, an action during which two VCs were won in the fights for the pillboxes, and dug in. To the left of the main road, the assault was made by the 49th (Edmonton) Battalion and they took Fürst Farm after heavy fighting. Their advance had almost been stalled by a machine-gun position when Private Cecil Kinross shed all unnecessary equipment, keeping only his rifle and ammunition pouches, and charged. He killed the six men there and destroyed the gun. To their left the 5th Canadian Mounted Rifles struggled through the morass of Woodland to take Source and Vapour Farms, which they then held against counter-attacks, using carrier pigeons to report back. Their progress was hampered by the impossible task given to the 63rd and 58th Divisions of XVIII Corps on either side of the Lekkerboterbeek. The German counter-barrage was dropped 100 yards (91.4m) behind the British creeping barrage, right amongst the advancing troops. The casualties were immense, particularly in the Artists Rifles (28/London) Battalion.

The next week was relatively warm and dry, with temperatures around 49°F (10°C) and a total rainfall of 0.03in (0.9mm). Currie had agreed with Plumer twelve days earlier that a seven-day pause should take place at the Blue Line, which by and large, was now in their hands. The 1st and 2nd Canadian

Divisions were brought up to relieve the 3rd and 4th and the hand-over was complete by 5 November. Two steps remained to be completed: first, the taking of the village, and second, the securing of the main ridge to the east.

Tuesday 6 November 1917: Second Battle of Passchendaele, Third Phase – Passchendaele Falls to the Canadians

Weather: overcast; temperature 52°F (11°C); rainfall, 0.039in (1mm)

At 6am the assaults began again. Away to the extreme right the 5th Division was in action south of Polygon Wood in the area of Polderhoek Château, where the front was still stalled. It remained so on this day as well, though the 1st Devons and 1st Duke of Cornwall's Light Infantry did all they could before the enemy put down a massive barrage, from which they had to pull back. Between the 5th and the Canadians, I ANZAC, IX and VIII Corps made simulated attacks to keep the Germans interested in something other than Passchendaele.

The 2nd Division formed the Canadian right with the 27th (City of Winnipeg), 31st (Alberta) and 28th (North-West) Battalions attacking the village itself. They followed so close behind the barrage that the counter-barrage of the enemy fell to the rear of the attackers. Within an hour they had enveloped the village and were clearing the remaining fortifications. Corporal H C Baker was serving with the 28th Battalion and recalled:

> 'The buildings had been pounded and mixed with the earth, and the shell-exploded bodies were so thickly strewn that a fellow couldn't step without stepping on corruption. Our opponents were fighting a rearguard action which resulted in a massacre for both sides. Our boys were falling like ninepins, but it was even worse for them. If they stood up to surrender they were mown down by their own machine-gun fire aimed from their rear at us; if they leapfrogged back they were caught in our barrage.'

By 9am the village was secured.

The 1st Division moved up the road towards Mosselmarkt with surprising ease. The blockhouse fell by 7.45am and the 1st (Western Ontario) and 2nd (Eastern Ontario) Battalions made the position secure. To their left the 3rd (Toronto) Battalion had a much harder time, coming under heavy fire from Vine Cottage, but it was overcome in time for the German counter-attack at 9.30am to be suppressed.

Haig wrote briefly, but enthusiastically, about the day in his diary:

> 'The operations were completely successful. Passchendaele was taken, as

also were Mosselmarkt and Goudberg. The whole position had been most methodically fortified. Yet our troops succeeded in capturing all their objectives early in the day with small loss – "under 700 men"!'

For the next three days the rain continued, 0.22in (5.6mm) in all. The temperature dropped as low as 44°F (7°C). The 1st Canadian Division made ready for a final push. General Plumer left for Italy on 9 November, after handing over command of the Second Army to General Sir Henry Rawlinson.

Saturday 10 November 1917: Second Battle of Passchendaele, Final Phase – Canadians Secure the High Ground

Weather: cloudy; temperature, 50°F (10°C); rainfall, 0.06in (1.6mm)

The purpose of the day's action was to secure all the high ground north of the village. The task was that of the 1st Canadian Division on the right and the 1st British Division on the left. The Canadians did well on their narrow front, in spite of their exposure to shellfire, and gained their objectives by 7.45am. The British did not succeed.

The 1st Division's 3 Brigade attacked with the 1st South Wales Borderers on the right and the 2nd Munsters on the left, but as they went forward their own barrage was falling short in the centre, and the 1st SWB veered right to avoid it. As a result, Goudberg Copse was left in enemy hands with the Munsters north of it. But while the 1st SWB made contact with the Canadians and dug in, the Munsters tackled Void Farm, Veal Cottages and Vat Cottages. By 6.45 they had them. They waited a while, and then decided independently to press on to the main ridge, stopping at 7.30am to clear their rifles of the clinging mud. Soon after, they saw the Germans massing for a counter-attack, and sent up an SOS flare. They were well forward of the position they were expected to occupy. The British barrage fell amongst them.

Back the Munsters came, contesting ground all the way. They held for a while at Void Farm, reduced to throwing balls of mud at their enemies. They were lucky the Germans mistook them for grenades. At 8.30am the Germans had them out of the farm and struggling back to their own line. The 1st SWB, in the meantime, had been forced to withdraw as well, and the progress made by the 1st Division that day was none at all. The Munsters lost three-quarters of their strength, and the SWB over half. The northern end of the ridge remained German.

What had been the early objective in a vast, sweeping campaign that would carry the Allies deep into Belgium had still not been achieved in full. The look-out from which the Ypres Salient could be surveyed was shared between enemies.

Haig's comments, in his despatch, on these final phases of the campaign were brief:

'on the 6th November Canadian troops . . . renewed their attack and captured the village of Passchendaele, together with the high ground immediately to the north and north-west. Sharp fighting took place for the possession of 'pillboxes' in the northern end of the village, around Mosselmarkt, and on the Goudberg Spur. All objectives were gained at an early hour, and at 8.30am a hostile counter-attack north of Passchendaele was beaten off.

'Over 400 prisoners were captured during this most successful attack, by which for the second time within the year the Canadian troops achieved a record of uninterrupted success. Four days later, in extremely unfavourable weather, British and Canadian troops . . . attacked northwards from Passchendaele and Goudberg, and captured further ground on the main ridge, after heavy fighting.'

Ludendorff was not so brief:

'On the 26th and 30th October and 6th and 10th November the fighting was again of the severest description. The enemy charged like a wild bull against the iron wall which kept him from our submarine bases. He threw his weight against Houthulst Forest, Poelcappelle, Passchendaele, Beccelaere, Gheluvelt and Zandvoorde. He dented it in many places, and it seemed as if he must knock it down. But it held, although a faint tremor ran through its foundations.

'The impressions I continuously received were very terrible. In a tactical sense, everything possible had been done. The advance zone was good. The effectiveness of our artillery had considerably improved. Behind almost every division in the front line there was another in support; and we still had reserves in the third line. We knew the enemy suffered heavily. But we also knew he was amazingly strong and, what was equally important, had an extraordinarily stubborn will.'

He went on to say that Lloyd George was the steel behind the determination to prevail and that it was impossible to know how long this would go on. He concludes, rather desperately, 'The enemy must tire some time.' It was fortunate he did not know just how tired his enemy was.

The newcomer to the scene, Sir Henry Rawlinson, was not impressed with his inheritance. He wrote:

'Nothing we can hope to do can make the line now held a really satisfactory defensive position. We must therefore be prepared to withdraw from it, if the Germans show signs of a serious and sustained offensive on this front, or if an attack elsewhere necessitates the withdrawal of more troops from the front of the Second Army.'

If, then, this was a victory, it was hollow at its core. In the long run, however, it was not without value.

Aftermath

O n 21 March 1918 the Germans launched Operation Michael against Bapaume and Péronne, and on 9 April (the anniversary of the Battle of Vimy Ridge and Arras) Operation Georgette on the River Lys, immediately south of the Ypres Salient. On 15 April 1918 General Plumer, who had only returned from Italy to resume his command of the Second Army on 17 March, gave the order to withdraw from the Passchendaele Ridge and fall back on positions close to Ypres itself. To those who had suffered so much to take the position from the Germans their victory must have seemed hollow indeed. To those interested in winning the war this event took its place on a broader canvas.

The Context

The Third Battle of Ypres can be studied either in isolation, which is interesting but not informative for students of the First World War as a whole, but it can also be examined in context: that is, as a major passage in the long and distressing story of one of the costliest wars known. It is a tautology to state that its reputation as one of the most ghastly battles of that war can only be assessed in the larger context, but this is so frequently neglected that it has to be said.

The experience of 1916 on the Somme had been one of repeated efforts to overcome German trench lines. The battles of early 1917 were similar, and the heroic but largely unsuccessful assault on Bullecourt demonstrated that the new German defences of the so-called Hindenburg Line, which dominated the British front to the south, were formidable. The Battle of the Messines Ridge was again an attack against long-established, entrenched positions. The Third Battle of Ypres was not. The terrain did not allow trenches to be dug without the risk of flooding, and the German lines were principally composed, as both British and German memoirs show, of pillboxes and shell hole-based lines between them.

Aftermath

The battles that came after Passchendaele again depart from the trench warfare of the earlier years. Only two weeks after the end of Third Ypres, the British attacked at Cambrai. The artillery bombardment was limited to avoid giving notice of the assault and to avoid rendering the terrain impassable to tanks. The tanks themselves fought as groups of machines with infantry support, instead of being used as mobile pillboxes to give infantry covering fire or suppress threatening strong points. The tanks worked in groups of three. The first machine rolled over the enemy wire and turned left, opening fire on the front trench. The second tank followed to drop its fascine into the front trench, cross over, and fire on the second trench. The third tank dropped its fascine into the second trench and covered the first tank's advance to drop a fascine into the third trench, when all three were free to advance and engage strong points to the rear while the infantry cleared the trenches and prepared to occupy the ground beyond them. By this means the break-in was made. It was not transformed into a breakthrough because the necessary reserves to follow up were not available and those that were ready were cavalry, lacking the breadth of abilities and the power to hold ground that was needed. However, the possibility of a new era in warfare was demonstrated.

Territorial Gains

Contemporary reports frequently cite an advance of so many yards on a given frontage as an indicator of achievement. Within a restricted area, for example, a particular battlefield, this may offer some basis for comparing one attack with another. The concept has been extended by calculating the number of casualties incurred in the acquisition of a given area of ground. For example, 15,375 casualties for 3.5 square miles (5.6 square kilometres) of territory in the battle that gained Polygon Wood (4,400 a square mile/1.6k square kilometres) compared with 2,200 a square mile in the Menin road battle. This is a suspect approach, as it assumes that all areas are of equal military value – an error Horatio did not make in selecting a bridge as the best ground for the defence of Rome.

It was not a demonstration the Germans chose to follow. Their success in the sophisticated use of artillery at Riga, under Bruchmüller, and the combination of a similar artillery programme commanded by Lieutenant

Aftermath

General Richard von Berendt, plus the use of specially trained attacking infantry units, led by such men as Lieutenant Erwin Rommel (at Caporetto), persuaded the German High Command they had found the solution to winning the war. In an attempt to disrupt the Allies before the Americans were present in significant numbers, Operation Michael was launched against the British on 21 March 1918 with the intention of breaking in south of Cambrai and rolling up the line northwards. The resistance they met redirected their thrust towards Amiens, but they outran their supply lines and reserves and were stopped by 5 April. A fresh thrust south of Ypres was made in Operation Georgette on 9 April but that, too, was halted, after a bitter and close-run battle, three weeks later. It was during this period that Plumer withdrew from the Passchendaele Ridge in order to shorten the line on that front and release forces to deal with the incursion: a manoeuvre that succeeded. Two further assaults, this time against the French east of Paris, were attempted and, with vital American help, were also defeated by late June.

The French and Americans struck back to pinch out the Soissons/Reims Salient in July, but the first demonstration of a truly effective combination of artillery, infantry, air and armoured arms was given by a force commanded by General Monash at Le Hamel on 4 July. In Gary Sheffield's words, 'the BEF's weapons system had reached maturity.' It was followed by the Battle of Amiens

Australian Troops advance, making their way forward over a duckboard track, October 1917 (Taylor Library).

on 8 August, in which the combined arms operated on a much greater scale, inflicting such losses on the Germans that Ludendorff described it as the 'black day of the German Army'. The battle was halted on 10 August, and over the coming weeks a series of battles, each of a duration limited by the logistic capabilities of the BEF, rolled the Germans back to the Belgian border, breaking into and through the Hindenburg Line on the way: an achievement built on the experiences of 1917. Sir Douglas Haig presided over the victory. It should be noted the daily casualty rate suffered in this period of success was 72 per cent greater than during Third Ypres.

Passchendaele was, then, a part – even a major part – of a chain of developments that took warfare from mobile conflict of Victorian simplicity, through the stalemate of trench warfare, to a form of mobile warfare of a sophistication undreamed-of only four years earlier.

A Flawed Plan?

In considering the wisdom of a plan, it is necessary to take into account what the planners actually knew and what the planners believed to be the case. It is also necessary to recall that military enterprise is not an exact science and that an emotional element is a vital component of effective leadership.

The underlying intention of the plan for the Third Battle of Ypres was the occupation of the Belgian coast and the neutralization of the German submarine installations at Bruges, Ostend and Zeebrugge. On 1 January 1915 the battleship *Formidable* had been sunk in the English Channel by a German submarine, and cross-Channel shipping was at risk from U-boat operations thereafter. On 2 February 1917 the Germans had resumed unrestricted submarine warfare, with the risk of bringing the Americans into the war, but in the hope of inflicting such damage on British supply shipping as to force their enemies to sue for peace. The shortest route to the Western Approaches was through the English Channel and while the larger, deep-water U-boats were based in the Baltic, the small inshore boats – just as much a threat as ships approached harbour – had to be stopped: either by destruction of their bases in Belgium or by the stopping-up of the narrows at Dover. The First Sea Lord, Admiral Sir John Jellicoe, was deeply concerned, expressing fears to the American Admiral William S Sims when he came to London in April in striking terms: 'It is impossible for us to go on with the War if losses [to U-boats] like this continue.' His views were challenged by Lloyd George but Jellicoe stuck to them and influenced discussions by the War Cabinet. In May 1917 Haig took the interesting decision to alleviate reliance on shipping to some extent by making hay on land won from the Germans. By the time 1918 came and the possibility of resuming the campaign in the Ypres Salient might have been considered, the introduction of the convoy system had frustrated U-boat attacks sufficiently to abate the pressure for the Army to close the submarine bases: although they still seemed enough of a threat to justify the Zeebrugge and Ostend raids by the Royal Navy.

An additional reason for a campaign in Flanders was that Belgium, occupied almost in its entirety, was a major asset the Germans were loathe to lose: it would be a valuable bargaining counter in a peace negotiation, as well as offering a high road to an eastbound invader. The experience of crossing the same country westbound in 1914 lent credence to this view, and Ludendorff remarked in his memorandum of 14 September 1917: 'We should only be absolutely safe . . . if we were in military occupation of the whole of Belgium and held the coast of Flanders.' Suggestions that this sector was of small importance do not conform to the opinions of the opposing sides at the time, and the view that it was necessary to wear the enemy down before a decisive blow could succeed was also commonly held at that time. This, then, was a front the Germans would be obliged to defend with determination, even if at high cost.

It is also easy to forget that the objective was not the Passchendaele Ridge alone. The high ground curves up around Ypres along the Menin road and Gheluvelt Plateau, through Broodseinde and Passchendaele and on round to the east, to end at the Merckem Peninsula (the capture of which on 28 October Haig celebrated), overlooking Dixmude. From these hills the entire German communication system in Belgium would be threatened: a possibility to which both sides were very much alive. Further, while the hills were daunting to attack, they were difficult to defend because the construction of works similar to the Hindenburg Line was, as we have seen, impossible.

By the time the final decision to undertake the battle in the Ypres Salient had to be taken, the situation had changed considerably. The French Army was on the point of collapse and the future of the Russian alliance was questionable. The pressure on Haig to take up the full burden of the conflict on the Western Front was huge.

If the weather had been that of an average year, would the plan have succeeded? Such questions cannot be answered with certainty, but can help to concentrate the mind. In the case of this campaign, it is possible to doubt that normal weather would have guaranteed success. The allocation of the task to Gough and the Fifth Army when Plumer and the Second Army not only knew the ground thoroughly, but had just scored a great victory at Messines, was probably Haig's most serious mistake. Indeed, John Terraine puts forward the case for reversing the order of the objectives: having taken the Messines Ridge, the Gheluvelt Plateau should have been next, then the Passchendaele Ridge and so on, which Plumer could well have handled. Alternatively, one could consider going further, making the Houthulst Forest and Dixmunde the first objective and outflanking the German positions on the Passchendaele Ridge. After all, the most impressive progress was consistently made by the French and the Fifth Army's left. The argument thus devolves to one about how best to carry out the plan, rather than about the plan itself.

Should It Have Been Stopped?

It is argued the campaign was pursued too long and that halting would have spared hundreds of lives. The difficulty is to determine where a defensible stopping place might have been. Indeed, Tim Harington wrote in his memoirs:

> 'I asked, in my *Life of Lord Plumer*, if anyone could suggest a line on which we could have stopped; I have never seen a reply. I had personally reconnoitred all that ground under the most appalling conditions and I feel sure that if he had been with me on the Gravenstafel Ridge, the most violent critic of Passchendaele would not have voted for staying there for the winter, or even for any more minutes than necessary.'

The limiting factor, as demonstrated the following year, is the ability of the Army to supply itself and to reposition its fighting components to continue the battle. The difficulty is to apply this logic to a situation in real-life as opposed to an academic study, fully furnished with the benefits of hindsight. Further, it seemed in late October that one last little effort could decide the issue and bring the whole of the ridge under British control: the Canadians paid for the error, although they achieved a notable success. However, the incomplete British occupation of the ridge was never challenged directly, and all the subsequent German effort was directed to fronts further south, which suggests the actual stopping place was at least secure in practice.

In his popular book, *The War in Outline, 1914 – 1918* (Faber and Faber, 1937) Liddell Hart wrote:

> 'Shortly after the battle had been brought to a close, one of Haig's principal coadjutors paid a visit to the battle-front — his first visit. Growing increasingly uneasy as the car approached the fringe of the swamp-like area, he was still well short of the real fighting line when he burst into tears, crying: "Good God, did we really send men to fight in that?"'

Aftermath

Quite apart from the probability the story is an invention, it suggests the British commanders were ignorant of the state of the ground. It is clear from the contemporary records quoted in this work that the knowledge of conditions was detailed and accurate. The decision to continue with the campaign in spite of these conditions was not the product of ignorance, nor was it made in defiance of the difficulties the troops faced. It was reached in the belief that it was the right decision to make.

What Went Wrong?

The most important factor in turning the campaign into a paradigm of the horrors of war was the unusual weather. That 1917 was unusual is beyond doubt, but it was not so outlandishly strange as to be impossible to contemplate in advance. It was coupled with the particular geology of the region, which was certainly known long before the war, but that again had to be coupled with the new brutality of the artillery barrage. Both in terms of quality and quantity, artillery had been revolutionized since the outbreak of the war, and the combination of these factors produced the fearful conditions on the ground that caused so much hardship and loss.

That was not enough, of itself, to create the particular difficulties the British campaign ran into. The new German defence system — itself a product of the terrain — demanded new tactics from the attackers. The speed with which the British changed their approach is demonstrated by the mistaken attempt of the Germans to introduce yet newer defensive tactics during October, only to find they had made their situation even worse. What the British did not exploit effectively, even when a successful demonstration had been made before their very eyes, was the power of the tank: nor did they understand soon enough the limitations of the weapon.

In 1937, relying to a large extent on the writings of British military historians, Heinz Guderian produced an extensive study of the development of tank warfare, which was to become the foundation of German Panzer warfare in the Second World War. In *Achtung — Panzer!* he wrote:

'It is no good sending armour into an attack over ground where it can have no real hope of making progress. It is every bit as wrong to lay down a preparatory bombardment which reduces the terrain to a lunar landscape, where even the most effective modern machines — not to mention horse-drawn vehicles — will end up getting stuck. If the tanks are to keep on the move they must be spared the problem of having to

156

overcome broken terrain when they are on the attack. . . . for the tanks, at least, we must take account of the conformation of the ground and the nature of the surface. If the going for the tanks does not happen to suit the infantry and artillery, it may be necessary to direct the attack of the armour along an axis which runs obliquely to that of the infantry. The main thing is for the tanks to get at the enemy.'

The actions at the Cockcroft and Springfield are not mentioned by Guderian, who dismisses the whole campaign as a mistaken undertaking and, relying on the British historians, asserts that the tanks were consistently misused. He contrasts this with the attack at Cambrai, which he says conformed to the criteria set out in Colonel Ernest Swinton's paper of February 1916: 'Three essential preconditions were laid down for the success of an attack by tanks: suitable ground, employment *en masse* and surprise.'

While Guderian was correct in his conclusions, he was at fault on the full facts of the employment of tanks in the Ypres Salient, as, indeed, was D G Browne who, as we have seen, wrote off tank operations at Poelcappelle as futile when W H L Watson, a fellow officer in the Tank Brigade, was saying the very opposite. What is clear is that the Tank Corps was, wrongly, regarded as suitable for disbandment by many people in October 1917 and it was the outstanding performance at Cambrai that saved them. Contrasting the two battles showed the way forward to the Allies and left the Germans too far behind to develop their own armoured vehicles in time.

Was It Worth It?

Seen on its own as an isolated, closed phase of warfare, as even recent studies do, the campaign appears to have been marginally more to the material advantage of the Germans than of the British. The attempt to break through to take the U-boat bases had been frustrated and serious losses had been inflicted on the Allies. The cost to the Germans was, as they reported, severe, if a little lighter than that they had inflicted on their enemies. The information gathered by the intelligence section of the American Expeditionary Force on the time served in the salient by various German divisions, and shown in the Order of Battle appendix, demonstrates some remarkably high levels of loss in very short periods.

The effect on the morale of the British and Dominion forces surprises modern commentators: no sign of unrest, as amongst the French after the Chemin des Dames, can be detected. This appears to disappoint the critics! Writing of Haig, John Keegan claims 'at Passchendaele he had tipped the survivors into the slough of despond,' but he offers no evidence to counter the accepted view that British and Empire troops, in spite of the horrors, remained doggedly tolerant of their fate. But Keegan's view itself should be seen in context: in a text of some 450 pages, this remark appears at the end of the passage treating this battle (on page 395). That passage, the complete history of Passchendaele, occupies only eleven pages; while the complete history of 1918 occupies only about fifty pages, and the index reveals that Haig is unmentioned in that section.

Casualties Figures for Third Ypres

As has been noted, exact, comparable figures for casualties for all forces engaged are not available. The following figures for losses between 31 July – 10 November 1917 in the Ypres Salient are probably reasonably close to reality.

British

Total, 244,897, of which 170,534 were incurred in the named battles.
Subtotals of the 238,313 reported in operational summaries:
Killed, 35,831. Wounded, 172,994. Missing, 29,488.
Total Western Front, 1917, 817,790.

French

Total (8 July – 31 October), 8,525.
Total Western Front, 1917, 569,000.

German

Total, approximately 230,000.
Total Western Front, 1917, 883,979.

In its contribution to the Allied learning process, the battle was valuable. The futility of massive artillery bombardment was made clear and the need for developments through the work of men such as Brigadier General H H Tudor was underlined. Improvements in communications on the battlefield were also given greater support, and in 1918 radio was widely in use. Infantry tactics received a fierce test and the new organization at platoon level was confirmed as effective. In spite of this, in their *Passchendaele*, Robin Prior and Trevor Wilson, clinging to the narrow view, are prepared to claim: 'the Flanders offensive of 1917 . . . appeared at the last to be just one more sorry episode in

An appeal to save ammunition — assuming one survived the war to care about heavier taxation
(Taylor Library).

a war of anguished incidents, unrelated to each other and lacking discernible consequences or achievements.'

In the context of the war being waged by the Allies, it is hard to see that there was an alternative. The Germans were still in occupation of great tracts of French territory. The French had suffered a terrible set-back, had been obliged to sack their commander-in-chief, and to turn to another general to rebuild morale, and persuade the French Army to fight on. Haig had to take the

Aftermath

offensive. The choice of where to do so can be questioned, but, again, what were the alternatives? Further south the British front faced the massive defences of the Hindenburg Line, and the Battle of Arras had made it obvious a yet heavier cost would be incurred if that became the objective, and the resources to undertake the Cambrai attack, or one like it, were not yet available. What is inevitable must be accepted, and if Haig is blamed for accepting this course with optimism, what would have been the outcome if he had been pessimistic?

John Terraine, writing in the journal *Stand To!* before either Keegan or Prior and Wilson, had put forward a view that — perhaps because it makes for dull headlines — is often neglected. He points out that Haig thought about the necessary stages of war as early as 1909 and listed them as follows:

1: The manoeuvre for position
2: The first clash of battle
3: The wearing-out fight
4: The decisive blow

And of stage three Terrain quotes Haig's own words:

'losses will necessarily be heavy on both sides, for in it the price of victory is paid . . . In former battles this stage of the conflict has rarely lasted more than a few days, and had often been completed in a few hours. When armies of millions are engaged, with the resources of great Empires behind them, it will inevitably be long . . . To this stage belong the great engagements of 1916 and 1917 which wore down the strength of the German Armies.'

And it was this stage that Haig, and Terraine, assert was a necessary precondition for the eventual victory.

Siegfried Sassoon wrote a frequently-quoted epitaph: 'I died in Hell. (They called it Passchendaele.)' He might better have taken heed of General William Tecumseh Sherman's observation, 'War is Hell' and written instead: 'I died in War.'

Firm conclusions are hard to reach and alternative arguments can validly be made. But it is clear that to dismiss Haig and his generals as fools would be not merely frivolous but irresponsible; and failure to consider the Third Battle of Ypres in the context of the war as a whole yields no insights.

Biographical Notes

Birdwood, Lieutenant General Sir William (1865–1951). Birdwood was a professional cavalry soldier and protégé of Lord Kitchener, which did not endear him to Haig. He was given command of the Australian Imperial Force in 1915 and led them at Gallipoli, on the Somme in 1916 and at Ypres he commanded I ANZAC Corps. In May 1918 Monash succeeded him and Birdwood took command of the Fifth Army.

Byng, General Sir Julian (1862–1935). Byng was in command of the Cavalry Corps in 1915 when he was sent to organize the successful withdrawal from Gallipoli. He returned to the Western Front to command the Canadian Corps. In June 1917 he assumed command of the Third Army and planned the Battle of Cambrai. He was Governor-General of Canada from 1921–26.

Cavan, Frederick Rudolph Lambart, tenth Earl of (1865–1946). Cavan took command of the newly formed Guards Division in August 1915. He was promoted head of XIV Corps in December and led them on the Somme, when the first use of tanks was made in September 1916, and at Ypres the following year. He was sent to Italy in October 1917 where he was eventually given command of the Italian Tenth Army.

Charteris, Brigadier General John (1877–1946). As senior intelligence officer on Haig's staff, Charteris was responsible for the assessments of German strength and intentions that influenced the battles of Arras and Messines, as well as Third Ypres. Both Gough and Plumer regarded his reports as being more designed to tell Haig what he wanted to hear than to reflect the facts. He was not liked by his colleagues and after Passchendaele he was removed, becoming a deputy director of transportation.

Currie, Lieutenant General Sir Arthur William (1875–1933). Currie succeeded Byng in command of the Canadian Corps and led his countrymen at Third Ypres. He showed his skill and independence of mind in the attack at Lens in August 1917, ordered as a distraction from Ypres, but under Currie ending as the successful seizure of Hill 70. He resisted Haig's pressure to hurry into action against Passchendaele and ensured that preparations were thorough.

Elles, Brigadier General H J (1880–1945). Elles was on Haig's staff when he was sent to report on trails with the tracked vehicles, which were developed as tanks. He commanded the 'Armoured Car Section of the Motor Machine-Gun Service': the first name given to the tank formation, before it became the 'Heavy Section, Machine-Gun Corps', and finally the 'Tank Corps'. The Battle of Cambrai demonstrated the truth of Elles's assertion the tanks should be used 'to operate on good going in the van of the battle.'

Godley, Sir Alexander John (1967–1957). Godley was Commander-in-Chief of the New Zealand Expeditionary Force as well as commander of II ANZAC Corps. His style of headquarters-based control was unsuited to the conditions of Gallipoli and he contributed to the failure at Sari Bair. In Flanders his formation fought at Messines, and then at Passchendaele, where he ignored Monash's advice to make thorough preparations for attack. He took over XXII Corps in 1918, fighting successfully under French command, and then III Corps, which fought well in the battles of August 1918.

Gough, General Sir Hubert de la Poer (1870–1963). Gough became the youngest British Army commander of the war, having led a cavalry brigade and then a division in 1914, and an infantry division and then a corps in 1915. His impressive performance led to his being given command of the Reserve Army, intended for use after the 'breakthrough', in May 1916. As commander of the Fifth Army he won the Battle of the Ancre in November 1916. The aggressive vigour he showed led to the Fifth Army being chosen to spearhead the Flanders campaign in 1917. Gough's handling of the Fifth Army against the German assault of March 1918 showed him to be a master of 'open' warfare, but the massive retreat required a scapegoat and he suffered accordingly.

Haig, Field Marshal Sir Douglas (1861–1928). Haig commanded I Corps of the BEF in 1914 and played a minor part in operations until the First Battle of Ypres in October/November, when his coolness under immense pressure was essential to success. He was made Commander-in-Chief of the BEF in December 1915 and presided over the terrible losses on the Somme on 1 June 1916, when he failed to press his advice to modify plans on the field commander, Rawlinson. Haig remained committed to securing victory on the Western Front, but clung to the questionable objective of a breakthrough. After Third Ypres he was obliged to take over a greatly lengthened front line without matching reinforcements and the Fifth Army was almost broken in consequence. Haig remained steady under the pressures of retreat and then presided over the vindication of the new weapons systems in the victory of 1918.

Biographical Notes

Jacob, Lieutenant General Sir Claud William (1863–1948). Jacob commanded II Corps, later Fifth Army, under Gough from August 1916. He was charged with the capture of the Gheluvelt Plateau on 31 July 1917 and, in spite of his confidence, failed in a succession of costly fights. He oversaw the withdrawal of the British from Passchendaele Ridge in April 1918 and the advance over the same terrain that autumn.

Kiggell, Lieutenant General Sir Launcelot Edward (1862–1954). At the end of 1915 Kiggell became chief of staff to Haig and served him through the great battles of the Somme and Third Ypres, only to be retired as a sop to politicians after that expensive campaign. The story that he burst into tears when he saw the battlefield, saying 'Good God! Did we really send men to fight in that?' is without reliable foundation.

Kuhl, General Herman von (1856–?). Kuhl was chief staff officer to Prince Rupprecht's Army Group, having held the equivalent post under the same commander in the Sixth Army. He was influential in the decision to withdraw to the Hindenburg Line in 1917 and he argued for the evacuation of the Messines Ridge, but local commanders prevailed with their protests that they could hold it. After Third Ypres he advocated an attack south of the salient and, although his plan was diluted by other offensives, it came close to success.

Lloyd George, David (1863–1945). Becoming Liberal minister of munitions in May 1915, Lloyd George increased production sufficiently to satisfy the greed of the guns on the Western Front and in June 1916 he became Minister of War. In December 1916 he became Prime Minister. He hankered after ways to avoid continued conflict in France and found temptation in making military deals with the Allies without consulting his own generals. He was at pains, in his memoirs, to blacken Haig's name.

Ludendorff, General Erich (1865–1937). Before the war Ludendorff was head of the Aufmarschabteilung, the general staff unit responsible for mobilization. After taking part in the invasion of France, he was made chief of staff to Hindenburg on the Eastern Front, a highly successful working relationship. After German failure at Verdun, these men became the supreme command and the retreat to the Hindenburg Line was planned. Under his direction the German Army held firm on all fronts through 1917. Ludendorff attempted to end the war in 1918 with a series of violent attacks, but the effort could not be sustained and systematic use of modern weapons by the Allies defeated his forces later that year.

Maxse, Lieutenant General Sir Ivor (1862–1958). Maxse commanded the 18th (Eastern) Division in the Battle of the Somme and was one of the few successful generals on the first day. He was promoted to lead XVIII Corps in 1917 in Third Ypres and showed himself receptive to new ideas. In 1918 his corps retreated so swiftly that it lost contact with XIX Corps on his left. Maxse was part of the board of enquiry into the March retreat, which blamed poor training as a contributory factor. He was then made inspector-general of training, a job he performed to a standard that assured him a high reputation as one of the greatest trainers of troops of the time.

Monash, Major General Sir John (1865–1931). Monash was perhaps unique in numbering both Haig and Lloyd George amongst his admirers. A civil engineer and businessman from Australia, he became a master of combined operations, using tanks, artillery, aircraft, machine-gunners and infantry in a co-ordinated fashion with the intention, in the ideal, of allowing the foot to occupy ground cleared by the others. His approach was demonstrated at Hamel in July 1918: an operation recognised as a classic. He commanded the 4th Infantry Brigade at Gallipoli, 3rd Australian Division at Ypres and became GOC Australian Corps in May 1918.

Plumer, Lieutenant General Sir Herbert Charles Onslow (1857–1932). Plumer joined the 65th Foot (York and Lancaster Regiment) in 1876. In the Boer War he took part in the relief of Mafeking and became a column commander during the guerrilla phase of the war. In February 1915 he took command of V Corps in the Ypres Salient and of Second Army later that year. Second Army remained in that sector in the following, relatively quiet, two years. During Third Ypres he faithfully carried out Haig's orders for continued attacks, even when Gough was demanding delay. In 1918 he withdrew from Passchendaele Ridge in time to allow German shelling to fall on empty trenches and then masterminded a flexible defence. After the war he became Governor of Malta and then High Commissioner for Palestine.

Rawlinson, Lieutenant General Sir Henry Seymour (1864–1925). Rawlinson joined the King's Royal Rifles in 1884, and transferred to the Coldstream Guards in 1892. He was besieged in Ladysmith at the outbreak of the Boer War and later became a column commander. In 1914 he commanded IV Corps in Belgium and at the First Battle of Ypres. He took over the command of the First Army from Haig at the end of 1915 and he was then charged with the creation of the Fourth Army, principally from the volunteers raised by Lord Kitchener's famous appeal. He commanded this army in the Battle of the Somme in 1916, where what success he enjoyed was at enormous cost. He took over the remnants of Gough's Fifth Army after the retreat of spring 1918 and, with the crack Australian and Canadian contingents under his command, had a great victory in the Battle of Amiens.

Rupprecht of Bavaria, Field Marshal Crown Prince (1869–1955). Prince Rupprecht was a professional soldier and, in 1914, commanded the

Biographical Notes

German Sixth Army on the Lorraine front, where he defeated the French Second Army. His force was immediately moved to the other wing of the attack and fought in the First Battle of Ypres, narrowly failing to break the British under Haig. In August 1916 he became commander of an army group, which added the Second and Fourth armies to his own. In 1917 Rupprecht's group endured the repeated blows of British attacks at Messines, Ypres and Cambrai, replying with operations Michael and Georgette in 1918.

Watts, Lieutenant General Herbert Edward (1858–?). Watts fought at Ypres in command of the 21st Brigade in 1914. In 1916 he led the 7th Division in one of the few successes on the first day of the Battle of the Somme. In 1917 he formed and commanded XIX Corps at Third Ypres and then, with great skill, as part of the Fifth Army in the retreat of March 1918. In September 1918 they were advancing once more in the Ypres sector.

Frank Hurley, the Australian photographer best known for his pictures of Shackleton's Antarctic expedition, could not avoid creating a work of art in this portrayal of Garter Point, 24 October 1917 (Taylor Library).

Orders of Battle

BEF

Commander-in-Chief, Field Marshal Sir Douglas Haig
Second Army, General Sir Herbert Plumer
Fourth Army, General Sir Henry Rawlinson
Fifth Army, General Sir Hubert Gough

I Corps, Lieutenant General Sir Arthur Holland
II Corps, Lieutenant General Sir Claud Jacob
V Corps, Lieutenant General Sir Edward Fanshawe
IX Corps, Lieutenant General Sir Alexander Gordon
X Corps, Lieutenant General Sir Thomas Morland
XIII Corps, Lieutenant General Sir William McCracken
XIV Corps, Lieutenant General Earl of Cavan
XV Corps, Lieutenant General Sir John du Cane
XVIII Corps, Lieutenant General Sir Ivor Maxse
XIX Corps, Lieutenant General H E Watts
Canadian Corps, Lieutenant General Sir Arthur Currie
I ANZAC Corps, Lieutenant General Sir William Birdwood
II ANZAC Corps, Lieutenant General Sir Alexander Godley

Guards Division, Major General G P T Fielding
   1st Guards Brigade: 2nd Grenadier Gds, 2nd Coldstream Gds, 3rd
   Coldstream Gds, 1st Irish Gds.
   2nd Guards Brigade: 3rd Grenadier Gds, 1st Coldstream Gds, 1st Scots
   Gds, 2nd Irish Gds.
   3rd Guards Brigade: 1st Grenadier Gds, 4th Grenadier Gds, 2nd Scots Gds,
   Welsh Gds.
   Pioneers: 4th Coldstream Gds.

1st Division, Major General E P Strickland

Orders of Battle

1st Brigade: 10th Gloucester, 1st Black Watch, 8th Royal Berkshire, 1st Camerons.

2nd Brigade: 2nd Sussex, 1st Loyal North Lancashire, 1st Northamptonshire, 2nd Kings Royal Rifle Corps.

3rd Brigade: 1st South Wales Borderers, 1st Gloucester, 2nd Welsh, 2nd Munster Fusiliers.

Pioneers: 1/6th Welsh.

3rd Division, Major General C J Deverell

8th Brigade: 2nd Royal Scots, 8th East Yorks, 1st Royal Scots Fusiliers, 7th Kings Shropshire Light Infantry.

9th Brigade: 1st Northumberland Fusiliers, 4th Royal Fusiliers, 13th King's, 12th West Yorks.

76th Brigade: 8th King's Own, 2nd Suffolk, 10th Welsh Fusiliers, 1st Gordons.

Pioneers: 20th Kings Royal Rifle Corps.

4th Division, Major General T G Matheson

10th Brigade: 1st Royal Warwick, 2nd Seaforth, 1st Irish Fusiliers, 2nd Royal Dublin Fusiliers.

11th Brigade: 1st Somerset Light Infantry, 1st East Lancashire, 1st Hampshire, 1st Rifle Brigade.

12th Brigade: 1st King's Own, 2nd Lancashire Fusiliers, 2nd Essex, 2nd Duke of Wellington's.

Pioneers: 21st West Yorks.

5th Division, Major General R B Stephens

13th Brigade: 2nd Kings Own Scottish Borderers, 1st Royal Warwick, 14th Royal Warwick, 15th Royal Warwick.

15th Brigade: 1st Norfolk, 1st Bedford, 1st Cheshire, 16th Royal Warwick.

95th Brigade: 1st Devon, 1st East Surrey, 1st Duke of Cornwall's Light Infantry, 12th Gloucester.

Pioneers: 6th Argyll & Sutherland.

7th Division, Major General T H Shoubridge

20th Brigade: 8th Devon, 9th Devon, 2nd Border Regiment, 2nd Gordons.

22nd Brigade: 2nd Royal Warwick, 2nd Royal Irish, 1st Royal Welsh Fusileers, 20th Manchester.

91st Brigade: 2nd Queen's, 1st South Staffords, 21st Manchester, 22nd Manchester.

Pioneers: 24th Manchester.

Orders of Battle

8th Division, Major General W C G Heneker
  23rd Brigade: 2nd Devon, 2nd West Yorks, 2nd Middlesex, 2nd Scottish Rifles.
  24th Brigade: 1st Worcester, 1st Sherwood Foresters, 2nd Northampton, 2nd East Lancs.
  25th Brigade: 2nd Lincoln, 2nd Royal Berkshire, 1st Royal Irish Rifles, 2nd Rifle Brigade.
  Pioneers: 22nd Durham Light Infantry.

9th (Scottish) Division, Major General H T Lukin
  26th Brigade: 8th Black Watch, 7th Seaforth, 5th Camerons, 10th Argyll & Sutherland.
  27th Brigade: 11th Royal Scots, 12th Royal Scots, 6th King's Own Scottish Borderers, 9th Scottish Rifles.
  South African Brigade: 1st Regiment (Cape Province), 3rd Regiment (Transvaal & Rhodesia), 2nd Rifle Brigade.
  Pioneers: 9th Seaforth.

11th Division, Major General H R Davies
  32nd Brigade: 9th West Yorks, 6th Green Howards, 8th Duke of Wellington's, 6th York and Lanc.
  33rd Brigade: 6th Lincoln, 6th Border Regiment, 7th South Staffords, 9th Sherwood Foresters.
  34th Brigade: 8th Northumberland Fusiliers, 9th Lancashire Fusiliers, 5th Dorset, 11th Manchester.
  Pioneers: 6th East Yorks.

14th (Light) Division, Major General V A Couper
  41st Brigade: 7th King's Royal Rifle Corps, 8th King's Royal Rifle Corps, 7th Rifle Brigade, 8th Rifle Brigade.
  42nd Brigade: 5th Ox and Bucks Light Infantry, 5th King's Shropshire Light Infantry, 9th King's Royal Rifle Corps, 9th Rifle Brigade.
  43rd Brigade: 6th Somerset Light Infantry, 6th Duke of Cornwall's Light Infantry, 6th King's Own Yorkshire Light Infantry, 10th Durham Light Infantry.
  Pioneers: 11th King's.

15th (Scottish) Division, Major General H F Thuillier
  44th Brigade: 9th Black Watch, 8th Seaforth Highlanders, 8/10th Gordon Highlanders, 7th Cameron Highlanders.
  45th Brigade: 13th Royal Scots, 6/7th Royal Scots Fusiliers, 6th Cameron Highlanders, 11th Argyll & Sutherland Highlanders.

46th Brigade: 10th Scottish Rifles, 7/8th King's Own Scottish Borderers, 10/11th Highland Light Infantry, 12th Highland Light Infantry.
Pioneers: 9th Gordon Highlanders.

16th (Irish) Division, Major General W B Hickie.
47th Brigade: 6th Royal Irish Regiment, 6th Connaught Rangers, 7th Leinster, 8th Royal Munster Fusiliers.
48th Brigade: 7th Royal Irish Rifles, 1st Royal Munster Fusiliers, 8th Royal Dublin Fusiliers, 9th Royal Dublin Fusiliers.
49th Brigade: 7th Royal Inniskilling Fusiliers, 8th Royal Inniskilling Fusiliers, 7th Royal Irish Fusiliers, 8th Royal Irish Fusiliers.
Pioneers: 11th Hampshire.

17th (Northern) Division, Major General P R Robertson.
50th Brigade: 10th West Yorkshire, 7th East Yorkshire, 7th Green Howards, 6th Dorset.
51st Brigade: 7th Lincoln, 7th Border Regiment, 8th South Staffords, 10th Sherwood Foresters.
52nd Brigade: 9th Northumberland Fusiliers, 10th Lancashire Fusiliers, 9th Duke of Wellington's Regiment, 12th Manchester.
Pioneers: 7th Yorkshire and Lancashire.

18th (Eastern) Division, Major General R P Lee.
53rd Brigade: 8th Norfolk, 8th Suffolk, 10th Essex, 6th Royal Berkshire.
54th Brigade: 11th Royal Fusiliers, 7th Bedford, 6th Northampton, 12th Middlesex.
55th Brigade: 7th Queens, 7th Buffs, 8th East Surrey, 7th Royal West Kent.
Pioneers: 8th Royal Sussex.

19th (Western) Division, Major General C D Shute acting to 19 June, Major General G T M Bridges wounded 20 September, Brigadier General W P Monkhouse acting to 22 September, Major General G D Jeffreys.
56th Brigade: 7th King's Own, 7th East Lancashire, 7th South Lancashire, 7th Loyal North Lancashire.
57th Brigade: 10th Royal Warwick, 8th Gloster, 10th Worcester, 8th North Staffordshire.
58th Brigade: 9th Cheshire, 9th Royal Welsh Fusiliers, 6th Wiltshire.
Pioneers: 5th South Wales Borderers.

20th (Light) Division, Major General W Douglas Smith.
59th Brigade: 10th King's Royal Rifle Corps, 11th King's Royal Rifle Corps, 10th Rifle Brigade, 11th Rifle Brigade.

Orders of Battle

60th Brigade: 6th Oxfordshire & Buckinghamshire Light Infantry, 6th King's Shropshire Light Infantry, 12th King's Royal Rifle Corps, 12th Rifle Brigade.
61st Brigade: 12th King's, 7th Somerset Light Infantry, 7th Duke of Cornwall's Light Infantry, 7th King's Own Yorkshire Light Infantry.
Pioneers: 11th Durham Light Infantry.

21st Division, Major General D G M Campbell.
62nd Brigade: 12th Northumberland Fusiliers, 13th Northumberland Fusiliers, 12th Durham Light Infantry, 13th Durham Light Infantry.
64th Brigade: 1st East Yorks, 9th King's Own Yorkshire Light Infantry, 10th King's Own Yorkshire Light Infantry, 15th Durham Light Infantry.
110th Brigade: 6th Leicester, 7th Leicester, 8th Leicester, 9th Leicester.
Pioneers: 14th Northumberland Fusiliers.

23rd Division, Major General J M Babington.
68th Brigade: 10th Northumberland Fusiliers, 11th Northumberland Fusiliers, 12th Durham Light Infantry, 13th Durham Light Infantry.
69th Brigade: 11th West Yorks, 8th Green Howards, 9th Green Howards, 10th Duke of Wellington's Regiment.
70th Brigade: 11th Sherwood Foresters, 8th King's Own Yorkshire Light Infantry, 8th Yorkshire and Lancashire, 9th Yorkshire and Lancashire.
Pioneers: 9th South Staffords.

24th Division, Major General L J Bols.
17th Brigade: 8th Buffs, 1st Royal Fusiliers, 12th Royal Fusiliers, 3rd Rifle Brigade.
72nd Brigade: 8th Queen's, 9th East Surrey, 8th Royal West Kent, 1st North Staffords.
73rd Brigade: 9th Royal Sussex, 7th Northampton, 13th Middlesex, 2nd Leinster.
Pioneers: 12th Sherwood Foresters.

25th Division, Major General E G T Bainbridge.
7th Brigade: 10th Cheshire, 3rd Worcester, 8th Loyal North Lancashire, 1st Wiltshire.
4th Brigade: 11th Lancashire Fusiliers, 13th Cheshire, 9th Loyal North Lancashire, 2nd Royal Irish Rifles.
75th Brigade: 11th Cheshire, 8th Border Regiment, 2nd South Lancashire, 8th South Lancashire.
Pioneers: 6th South Wales Borderers.

29th Division, Major General Sir B de Lisle.

Orders of Battle

86th Brigade: 2nd Royal Fusiliers, 1st Lancashire Fusiliers, 16th Middlesex, 1st Royal Dublin Fusiliers.
87th Brigade: 2nd South Wales Borderers, 1st King's Own Scottish Borderers, 1st Royal Inniskilling Fusiliers, 1st Border Regiment.
88th Brigade: 4th Worcester, 1st Essex, 2nd Hampshire, Royal Newfoundland Regiment.
Pioneers: 2nd Monmouth.

30th Division, Major General W de L Williams.
21st Brigade: 18th King's, 2nd Green Howards, 2nd Wiltshire, 19th Manchester.
89th Brigade: 17th King's, 19th King's, 20th King's, 2nd Bedford.
90th Brigade: 2nd Royal Scots Fusiliers, 16th Manchester, 17th Manchester, 18th Manchester.
Pioneers: 11th South Lancashire.

33rd Division, Major General P R Wood.
19th Brigade: 20th Royal Fusiliers, 2nd Royal Welsh Fusiliers, 1st Scottish Rifles, 5/6th Scottish Rifles.
98th Brigade: 4th King's, 4th Suffolk, 1st Middlesex, 2nd Argyll & Sutherland Highlanders.
100th Brigade: 1st Queen's, 2nd Worcester, 16th King's Royal Rifle Corps, 1/9th Highland Light Infantry.
Pioneers: 18th Middlesex.

34th Division.
101st Brigade: 15th Royal Scots, 16th Royal Scots, 10th Lincoln, 11th Suffolk.
102nd Brigade: 20th Northumberland Fusiliers, 21st Northumberland Fusiliers, 22nd Northumberland Fusiliers, 23rd Northumberland Fusiliers.
103rd Brigade: 24/27th Northumberland Fusiliers, 25th Northumberland Fusiliers, 26th Northumberland Fusiliers, 9th Northumberland Fusiliers.
Pioneers: 18th Northumberland Fusiliers.

35th Division.
104th Brigade: 17th Lancashire Fusiliers, 18th Lancashire Fusiliers, 20th Lancashire Fusiliers, 23rd Manchester.
105th Brigade: 15th Cheshire, 16th Cheshire, 14th Gloster, 15th Sherwood Foresters.
106th Brigade: 17th Royal Scots, 17th West Yorks, 19th Durham Light Infantry, 18th Highland Light Infantry.
Pioneers: 19th Northumberland Fusiliers.

Orders of Battle

36th (Ulster) Division, Major General O S W Nugent.

    107th Brigade: 8th Royal Irish Rifles, 9th Royal Irish Rifles, 10th Royal Irish Rifles, 15th Royal Irish Rifles.

    108th Brigade: 11th Royal Irish Rifles, 12th Royal Irish Rifles, 13th Royal Irish Rifles, 9th Royal Irish Rifles.

    109th Brigade: 9th Royal Inniskilling Fusiliers, 10th Royal Inniskilling Fusiliers, 11th Royal Inniskilling Fusiliers, 14th Royal Irish Rifles.

    Pioneers: 16th Royal Irish Rifles.

37th Division, Major General H Bruce Williams.

    110th Brigade: 8th Leicester, 7th Leicester, 6th Leicester, 9th Leicester.

    111th Brigade: 10th Royal Fusiliers, 13th Royal Fusiliers, 18th King's Royal Rifle Corps, 13th Rifle Brigade.

    112th Brigade: 11th Royal Warwick, 6th Bedford, 8th East Lancashire, 10th Loyal North Lancashire.

    Pioneers: 9th North Stafford.

38th (Welsh) Division, Major General C G Blackader.

    113th Brigade: 13th Royal Welsh Fusiliers, 14th Royal Welsh Fusiliers, 15th Royal Welsh Fusiliers, 16th Royal Welsh Fusiliers.

    114th Brigade: 10th Welsh, 13th Welsh, 14th Welsh, 15th Welsh.

    115th Brigade: 10th South Wales Borderers, 11th South Wales Borderers, 17th Royal Welsh Fusiliers, 16th Welsh.

    Pioneers: 19th Welsh.

39th Division, Major General G J Cuthbert to 20 August, Major General E Feetham,

    116th Brigade: 11th Royal Sussex, 12th Royal Sussex, 13th Royal Sussex, 14th Hampshire.

    117th Brigade: 16th Sherwood Foresters, 17th Sherwood Foresters, 17th King's Royal Rifle Corps, 16th Rifle Regiment.

    118th Brigade: 1/6th Cheshire, 1/1st Cambridgeshire, 1/1st Hertfordshire, 4/5th Black Watch.

    Pioneers: 13th Gloster.

41st Division, Major General S T B Lawford.

    112nd Brigade: 12th East Surrey, 15th Hampshire, 11th Royal West Kent, 18th King's Royal Rifle Corps.

    123rd Brigade: 11th Queen's, 10th Royal West Kent, 23rd Middlesex, 20th Durham Light Infantry.

    124th Brigade: 10th Queen's, 26th Royal Fusiliers, 32nd Royal Fusiliers, 21st King's Royal Rifle Corps.

Orders of Battle

Pioneers: 19th Middlesex.

42nd Division.
125th Brigade: 5th Lancashire Fusiliers, 6th Lancashire Fusiliers, 7th Lancashire Fusiliers, 8th Lancashire Fusiliers.
126th Brigade: 4th East Lancashire, 5th East Lancashire, 9th Manchester, 10th Manchester.
127th Brigade: 5th Manchester, 6th Manchester, 7th Manchester, 8th Manchester.
Pioneers: None.

47th (1/2nd London) Division (TF), Major General Sir George Gorringe.
140th Brigade: 1/6th London (City of London), 1/8th London (Post Office Rifles), 1.7th London (City of London), 1/15th London (CS Rifles).
141st Brigade: 1/17th London (Poplar & Stepney Rifles), 1/19th London (St Pancras), 1/20th London (Blackheath & Woolwich), 1/18th London (London Irish Rifles).
142nd Brigade: 1/21st London (1st Surrey Rifles), 1/23rd London, 1/22nd London (The Queen's), 1/24th London (The Queen's).
Pioneers: 1/4th Royal Welsh Fusiliers.

48th (1st South Midland) Division, Major General R Fanshawe.
143rd Brigade: 1/5h Royal Warwick, 1/6th Royal Warwick, 1/7th Royal Warwick, 1/8th Royal Warwick.
144th Brigade: 1/4th Gloster, 1/6th Gloster, 1/7th Worcester, 1/8th Worcester.
145th Brigade: 1/5th Gloster, 1/4th Oxfordshire & Buckinghamshire Light Infantry, 1/1st Buckingham, 1/4th Royal Berkshire.
Pioneers: 1/5th Royal Sussex.

49th (1st West Riding) Division (TF), Major General E M Percival.
146th Brigade: 1/5th West Yorkshire, 1/6th Wes Yorkshire, 1/7th West Yorkshire, 1/8th West Yorkshire.
147th Brigade: 1/4th Duke of Wellington's, 1/5th Duke of Wellington's, 1/6th Duke of Wellington's, 1/7th Duke of Wellington's.
148th Brigade: 1/4th King's Own Yorkshire Light Infantry, 1/5th King's Own Yorkshire Light Infantry, 1/4th Yorkshire & Lancashire, 1/5th Yorkshire and Lancashire.
Pioneers: 19th Lancashire Fusiliers.

50th (Northumbrian) Division (TF), Major General P S Wilkinson.
149th Brigade: 1/4th Northumberland Fusiliers, 1/5th Northumberland

Fusiliers, 1/6th Northumberland Fusiliers, 1/7th Northumberland Fusiliers.
150th Brigade: 1/4th East Yorkshire, 1/4th Green Howards, 1/5th Green
Howards, 1/5th Durham Light Infantry.
151st Brigade: 1/5th Border Regiment, 1/6th Durham Light Infantry, 1/8th
Durham Light Infantry, 1/9th Durham Light Infantry.
Pioneers: 1/7th Durham Light Infantry.

51st (Highland) Division, Major General G M Harper.
152nd Brigade: 1/5th Seaforth Highlanders, 1/6th Seaforth Highlanders,
1/6th Gordon Highlanders, 1/8th Argyll & Sutherland Highlanders.
153rd Brigade: 1/6th Black Watch, 1/7th Black Watch, 1/5th Gordon
Highlanders, 1/7th Gordon Highlanders.
154th Brigade: 1/9th Royal Scots, 1/4th Seaforth Highlanders, 1/4th Gordon
Highlanders, 1/7th Argyll & Sutherland Highlanders.
Pioneers: 1/8th Royal Scots.

55th (1st West Lancashire) Division, Major General H S Jeudwine.
164th Brigade: 1/4th King's Liverpool, 1/8th (Irish) King's Liverpool, 2/5th
Lancashire Fusiliers, 1/4th Loyal North Lancashire.
165th Brigade: 1/5th King's Liverpool, 1/6th King's Liverpool, 1/7th King's
Liverpool, 1/9th King's Liverpool.
166th Brigade: 1/10th King's Own (Royal Lancaster), 1/10th (Scottish)
King's Liverpool, 1/5th South Lancashire, 1/5th Loyal North Lancashire.
Pioneers: 1/4th South Lancashire.

56th (1st London) Division, Major General F A Dudgeon.
167th Brigade: 1/1st London (Royal Fusiliers), 1/3rd London (RF), 1/7th
Middlesex, 1/8th Middlesex.
168th Brigade: 1/4th London (RF), 1/12th London (Rangers), 1/13th
London (Kensington), 1/14th London (London Scottish).
169th Brigade: 1/2nd London (RF), 1/5th London (London Rifle Brigade),
1/9th London (QVR), 1/16th London (QWR).
Pioneers: 1/5th Cheshire.

57th (2nd West Lancashire) Division, Major General R W R Barnes.
170th Brigade: 2/5th King's Own (Royal Lancaster), 2/4th Loyal North
Lancashire, 2/5th Loyal North Lancashire, 4/5th Loyal North Lancashire.
171st Brigade: 2/5th King's Liverpool, 2/6th King's Liverpool, 2/7th King's
Liverpool, 2/8th King's Liverpool.
172nd Brigade: 2/9th King's Liverpool, 2/10th King's Liverpool, 2/4th South
Lancashire, 2/5th South Lancashire.
Pioneers: 2/5th Loyal North Lancashire.

Orders of Battle

58th (2/1st London) Division, Major General H D Fanshawe to 6 October, Major General A B E Cator.
173rd Brigade: 2/1st London, 2/2nd London, 2/3rd London, 2/4th London.
174th Brigade: 2/5th London, 2/6th London, 2/7th London, 2/8th London.
175th Brigade: 2/9th London, 2/10th London, 2/11th London, 2/12th London.
Pioneers: None.

59th (2nd North Midland) Division, Major General C F Romer.
176th Brigade: 2/5th South Staffordshire, 2/6th South Staffordshire, 2/5th South Staffordshire, 2/6th South Staffordshire.
177th Brigade: 2/4th Lincoln, 2/5th Lincoln, 2/4th Leicester, 2/5th Leicester.
178th Brigade: 2/5th Sherwood Foresters, 2/6th Sherwood Foresters, 2/7th Sherwood Foresters, 2/8th Sherwood Foresters.
Pioneers: None.

61st (2nd South Midland) Division, Major General C J Mackenzie.
182nd Brigade: 2/5th Royal Warwick, 2/6th Royal Warwick, 2/7th Royal Warwick, 2/8th Royal Warwick.
183rd Brigade: 2/4th Gloster, 2/6th Gloster, 2/7th Worcestershire, 2/8th Worcestershire.
184th Brigade: 2/5th Gloster, 2/4th Oxfordshire & Buckinghamshire Light infantry, 2/1st Buckingham, 2/4th Royal Berkshire.
Pioneers: 1/5th Duke of Cornwall's Light Infantry.

63rd (Royal Naval) Division, Major General C E Lawrie.
188th Brigade: Anson Battalion, Howe Battalion, 1/Royal Marine Battalion, 2/Royal Marine Battalion.
189th Brigade: Hood Battalion, Nelson Battalion, Hawke Battalion, Drake Battalion.
190th Brigade: 1st Honourable Artillery Company, 7th Royal Fusiliers, 4th Bedford, 10th Royal Dublin Fusiliers.
Pioneers: 14th Worcestershire.

66th (2nd East Lancashire) Division, Major General Hon. H A Lawrence.
197th Brigade: 3/5th Lancashire Fusiliers, 2/6th Lancashire Fusiliers, 2/7th Lancashire Fusiliers, 2/8th Lancashire Fusiliers.
198th Brigade: 2/4th East Lancashire, 2/5th East Lancashire, 2/9th Manchester, 2/10th Manchester.
199th Brigade: 2/5th Manchester, 2/6th Manchester, 2/7th Manchester, 2/8th Manchester.

Orders of Battle

Pioneers: 10th Duke of Cornwall's Light Infantry.

1st Canadian Division, Major General A C Macdonell.
  1st Brigade: 1st (Ontario) Battalion, 2nd (East Ontario) Battalion, 3rd Battalion (Toronto Regiment), 4th Battalion.
  2nd Brigade: 5th (Western Cavalry) Battalion, 7th Battalion (1st British Columbia), 8th Battalion (90th Rifle), 10th Battalion.
  3rd Brigade: 13th Battalion (Royal Highlanders), 14th Battalion (Royal Montreal Regiment), 15th Battalion (48th Highlanders), 16th Battalion (Canadian Scottish).
  Pioneers: 1st Canadian Pioneer Battalion.

2nd Canadian Division, Major General H E Burstall.
  4th Brigade: 18th (West Ontario) Battalion, 19th (Central Ontario) Battalion, 20th (Central Ontario) Battalion, 21st (East Ontario) Battalion.
  5th Brigade: 22nd (Canadian Français) Battalion, 24th Battalion (Victoria Rifles), 25th Battalion (Nova Scotia Rifles), 26th (New Brunswick) Battalion.
  6th Brigade: 27th (City of Winnipeg) Battalion, 28th (North-West) Battalion, 29th (Vancouver) Battalion, 31st (Alberta) Battalion.
  Pioneers: 2nd Canadian Pioneer Battalion.

3rd Canadian Division, Major General L J Lipsett.
  7th Brigade: Princess Patricia's Canadian Light Infantry, Royal Canadian Regiment, 42nd Battalion (Royal Highlanders), 49th (Edmonton) Battalion.
  8th Brigade: 1st Canadian Mounted Rifles, 2nd Canadian Mounted Rifles, 4th Canadian Mounted Rifles, 5th Canadian Mounted Rifles.
  9th Brigade: 43rd Battalion (Cameron Highlanders), 52nd (New Ontario) Battalion, 58th Battalion, 60th Battalion (Victoria Rifles).
  Pioneers: 3rd Canadian Pioneer Battalion.

4th Canadian Division, Major General D Watson.
  10th Brigade: 44th Battalion, 46th (South Saskatchewan) Battalion, 47th (British Columbia) Battalion, 50th (Calgary) Battalion.
  11th Brigade: 54th (Kootenay) Battalion, 75th (Mississauga) Battalion, 87th Battalion (Canadian Grenadier Guards), 102nd Battalion.
  12th Brigade: 38th (Ottawa) Battalion, 72nd Battalion (Seaforth Highlanders), 73rd Battalion (Royal Highlanders), 78th Battalion (Winnipeg Grenadiers).
  Pioneers: 67th Canadian Pioneer Battalion.

1st Australian Division, Major General H B Walker.

Orders of Battle

1st (New South Wales) Brigade: 1st Battalion, 2nd Battalion, 3rd Battalion, 4th Battalion.

2nd (Victoria) Brigade: 5th Battalion, 6th Battalion, 7th Battalion 8th Battalion.

9th (Queensland) Brigade: 9th (Queensland) Battalion, 10th (South Australia) Battalion, 11th (Western Australia) Battalion, 12th (South & Western Australia, Tasmania) Battalion.

Pioneers: 1st Australian Pioneer Battalion.

2nd Australian Division, Major General N M Smyth.

5th (New South Wales) Brigade: 17th Battalion, 18th Battalion, 19th Battalion, 20th Battalion.

6th (Victoria) Brigade: 21st Battalion, 22nd Battalion, 23rd Battalion, 24th Battalion.

7th Brigade: 25th (Queensland) Battalion, 26th (Queensland, Tasmania) Battalion, 27th (South Australia) Battalion, 28th (Western Australia) Battalion.

Pioneers: 2nd Australian Pioneer Battalion.

3rd Australian Division, Major General Sir John Monash.

9th Brigade: 33rd Battalion, 34th Battalion, 35th Battalion, 36th Battalion.

10th Brigade: 37th Battalion, 38th Battalion, 39th Battalion, 40th Battalion.

11th Brigade: 41st Battalion, 42nd Battalion, 43rd Battalion, 44th Battalion.

Pioneers: 3rd Australian Pioneer Battalion.

4th Australian Division, Major General W Holmes killed 2 July, Brigadier General C Rosenthal acting to 16 July, Major General E G Morgan-Sinclair.

4th Brigade: 13th (New South Wales) Battalion, 14th (Victoria) Battalion, 15th (Queensland, Tasmania) Battalion, 16th (South and Western Australia) Battalion.

12th Brigade: 45th (New South Wales) Battalion, 46th (Victoria) Battalion, 47th (Queensland, Tasmania) Battalion, 48th (South and Western Australia) Battalion.

13th Brigade: 49th (Queensland) Battalion, 50th (South Australia) battalion, 51st (Western Australia) Battalion, 52nd (South and Western Australia, Tasmania) Battalion.

Pioneers: 4th Australian Pioneer Battalion.

5th Australian Division, Major General J Talbot Hobbs.

8th Brigade: 29th (Victoria) Battalion, 30th (New South Wales) Battalion, 31st (Queensland) Battalion, 32nd (South and Western Australia) Battalion.

14th (New South Wales) Brigade: 53rd Battalion, 54th Battalion, 55th

Battalion, 56th Battalion.

15th (Victoria) Brigade: 57th Battalion, 58th Battalion, 59th Battalion, 60th Battalion.

Pioneers: 5th Australian Pioneer Battalion.

New Zealand Division, Major General Sir Arthur Russell
1st New Zealand Brigade: 1/Auckland, 1/Canterbury, 1/Otago, 1/Wellington.
2nd New Zealand Brigade: 2/Auckland, 2/Canterbury, 2/Otago, 2/Wellington.
3rd New Zealand (Rifle) Brigade: 1/New Zealand Rifle Brigade, 2/New Zealand Rifle Brigade, 3/New Zealand Rifle Brigade, 4/New Zealand Rifle Brigade.

Pioneers: New Zealand Pioneer Battalion.

German Army

Commander-in-Chief, Chief Quartermaster-General Erich Ludendorff.
Northern Army Group, Field Marshal Crown Prince Rupprecht of Bavaria.
Fourth Army, General Sixt von Arnim.
Chief of Staff, Colonel von Lossberg.

At 31 July 1917:
North Group (Belgian coast): Marine Corps.
3rd Naval Division (1, 2 and 3 Marine Regiments).

Dixmude Group (Noordschoote to Ypres–Staden Railway).
Front division: 111th Division (73 Fusilier Regiment, 76 and 164 Regiments), relieved 30–31 July. Sixteenth October–4 November, Poelcappelle.
Counter-attack division: 2nd Guard Reserve (71, 82 and 94 Reserve Regiments), Bixschoote, relieved 8 August. Tenth–late September W of Passchendaele.

Ypres Group (Bellewarde Lake to Ypres–Staden Railway).
Front divisions, 38th (94, 95 and 96 Regiments), Hooge, relieved 1 August, 19 November–early December, near Passchendaele. Two Hundred and Thirty-Fifth (454, 455 and 456 Regiments), E of Wieltje, relieved 1 August. Third Guard (Gd. Fusilier and Lehr Regiments, 9 Grenadier Regiment), Pilkem to 5 August, 7 October to early November, NE of Zonnebeke.
Counter-attack divisions, 221st (41 and 60 Reserve Regiments, 1 Reserve Ersatz Regiment), to 3 August near Zonnebeke. Fiftieth Reserve (229, 230 and 231 Reserve Regiments), to 10 August, St Julien, 20 September–3

Orders of Battle

October near Gheluvelt.

Wyschaete Group (River Lys to Bellewarde Lake).
Front divisions: 16th (28, 29 and 68 Regiments), at Warneton, 1–12 October
near Zonnebeke. Eighteenth Reserve (31, 84 and 86 Regiments), W of
Houthem to 8 August, 20–29 October, Menin road. Tenth Bavarian (16
Bavarian, 6 and 8 Bavarian Reserve Regiments), Ypres–Comines Canal to
12 August. Twenty-Second Reserve (71, 82 and 94 Reserve Regiments),
relieved 31 July, September at Passchendaele. Sixth Bavarian Reserve (16,
17 and 20 Bavarian Reserve Regiments), relieved 30 July.
Counter-attack divisions: 207th (98, 209 and 213 Reserve regiments), July–8
October, Zandvoorde. Twelfth (23, 62 and 63 Regiments), 1–20 August, E
of Kleine Zillebeke. One Hundred and Nineteenth (46, 58 and 46 Reserve
Regiments), to 15 October.

Lille Group: not engaged.

Group of Northern Armies Reserve: 3rd Reserve Division (2 and 49 Reserve
regiments, 34 Fusilier Regiment), to 18 August, Freezenberg sector, 23–28
September Polygon Wood. Seventy-ninth Reserve Division (261, 262 and
263 Reserve Regiments), to 16 August, Langemarck.
Ghent Group: 23rd Reserve Division (100 Reserve Grenadier Regiment, 102
Reserve Regiment, 392 Regiment), 10 July–early August, Pilkem,
September near Passchendaele. Ninth Reserve Division (6 and 9 Reserve
Regiments, 395 Regiment), 10 August–25 September, Menin road. Fifth
Bavarian Division (1, 19 and 21 Bavarian Regiments), 10–24 August S of St
Julien.

After 31 July 1917, also engaged:

Bavarian Ersatz Division (4 and 15 Bavarian Reserve Regiments, 28 Ersatz
Regiment), 1–25 September.
   1st Bavarian Reserve Division (1, 2 and 3 Bavarian Reserve Regiments),
   Zandvoorde, 8 October–11 February 1918.
   2nd Guard Reserve Division (71, 82 and 94 Reserve Regiments), 31 July–9
   August, 10–30 September.
   4th Guard Division (5 Ft Regiment, 5 Grenadier Regiment, 93 Reserve
   Regiment), 27 September–7 October.
   4th Division (14, 49 and 140 Regiments), 1–24 November.
   4th Bavarian Division (5 Bavarian, 5 Bavarian Reserve and 9 Bavarian
   Regiments), 26 September–27 October.
   5th Bavarian Reserve Division (10, 7 and 13 Bavarian Reserve Regiments),

Orders of Battle

12 October–November.

6th Bavarian Division (10, 6 and 13 Bavarian Regiments), 29 September–8 October.

7th Division (26, 163 and 393 Regiments), 29 October–January 1918.

8th Division (72, 93 and 153 Regiments), 4 October–20 January 1918.

8th Bavarian Reserve Division (18, 19, 22 and 23 Bavarian Reserve Regiments), 26 October–24 January 1918 at Dixmude.

9th Reserve Division (6 and 19 Reserve Regiments, 395 Regiment), 10 August–25 September, Menin road.

9th Bavarian Reserve Division (11 and 14 Bavarian Reserve Regiments, 3 Bavarian Ersatz Regiment), in reserve 9–16 August, 17–20 August at Langemarck.

10th Ersatz Division (369, 370 and 371 Regiments), 24 September–7 October, Poelcappelle.

11th Reserve Division (10 Reserve Regiment, 22 and 156 Regiments), November–January, Passchendaele.

11th Bavarian Division (13 Bavarian Reserve Regiment, 3 and 22 Regiments), 22–27 October, Passchendaele.

12th Division (23, 62 and 63 Regiments), 1–20 August, Menin road.

12th Reserve Division (22, 38 and 51 Regiments), 8–20 August, Langemarck and St Julien.

15th Division (69, 160 and 389 Regiments), 7 October–13 November, N of Menin road.

16th Bavarian Division (8, 11 and 14 Bavarian Regiments) 20–21 September, N of Lys.

17th Division (75 Regiment, 89 Grenadier Regiment, 90 Fusilier Regiment), 9 June to 27 July, Hooge. Twenty-fourth–twenty-eighth September, Polygon Wood.

17th Reserve Division (16 and 162 Regiments, 78 Reserve Regiment) 18 November–January 1918.

18th Division (31 and 85 Regiments, 86 Fusilier Regiment), 16 September–14 October, Mangelaere.

19th Reserve Division (73, 78 and 92 Reserve Regiments), 24 September–5 October, Polygon Wood.

20th Division (77, 79 and 92 Regiments) 27 September–early October, N of Zonnebeke.

24th Division (133, 139 and 179 Regiments), October, W of Gheluvelt.

25th Division (115 Body Guard Infantry Regiment, 116 and 117 Body Infantry Regiments), mid-end September, N of Zandvoorde, mid

November–February 1918, near Passchendaele.

26th Division (119 Grenadier Regiment, 121 and 125 Regiments), 16 August–4 September, N of Langemarck.

26th Reserve Division (119 and 121 Reserve Regiments, 180 Regiment) 19 August–16 September, N of Langemarck, 17–23 October N of Ypres–Staden railway, mid November–February 1918, Merckem.

27th Division (123 Grenadier Regiment, 120 and 124 Regiments), mid-August–12 September SE of St Julien, 11 October–11 November, near Ypres–Roulers railway.

32nd Division (102, 177 and 103 Regiments), mid-June–early September, Menin road.

34th Division (67, 30 and 145 Regiments), 7–24 August, Menin road.

35th Division (141, 61 and 176 Regiments), 22 October–22 January 1918, Houthulst Forest.

36th Division (5 Grenadier Regiment, 175 and 128 Regiments), 10–23 September, Poelcappelle.

39th Division (126, 132 and 172 Regiments), October, Passchendaele.

40th Division (104, 181 and 134 Regiments), 31 July–1 August near Steenstraat.

41st Division (18, 148 and 152 Regiments), 12 November–14 January 1918, Houthoulst Forest.

44th Reserve Division (205, 206 and 208 Reserve Regiments), 10–31 November, N of Passchendaele.

45th Reserve Division (210, 211 and 212 Reserve Regiments) 22 September–12 October, Zonnebeke and Polygon Wood.

49th Reserve Division (225, 226 and 228 Reserve Regiments) Steenstraat, withdrawn 28 July, end October–21 November, Menin road.

52nd Reserve Division (238, 239 and 240 Reserve Regiments), 31 July–11 August, Menin road.

54th Division (84, 27 and 90 Reserve Regiments), 5–19 August.

54th Reserve Division (246, 247 and 248 Reserve Regiments), 29 October–March 1918, Dixmude.

58th Division (106 and 107 Regiments, 103 Reserve Regiment), 17–24 October and 31 October–end November, Houthoulst Forest.

121st Division (60 Regiment, 7 and 56 Reserve Regiments), 19 August–21 September, Ypres–Roulers railway.

183rd Division (184, 418 and 440 Reserve Regiments), 15–20 August, near St Julien.

185th Division (65, 161 and 28 Regiments), 6 November–December,

Houthoulst Forest.

187th   Division (187, 188 and 189 Regiments), 30 September–12 October, Poelcappelle.

195th   Division (6 and 8 Jäger Regiments, 233 Reserve Regiment), 3–12 October, Passchendaele.

199th   Division (114 and 357 Reserve Regiments, 237 Reserve Regiment), 10 November–February 1918, N of Passchendaele.

204th   Division (413 and 414 Regiments, 120 Reserve Regiment), end August–13 September, SE of Poelcappelle, mid-November–end February 1918, N of Poelcappelle.

208th   Division (25 and 185 Regiments, 65 Reserve Regiment), end August–29 September, Langemarck.

214th   Division (50,358 and 363 Regiments), early August–17 August, near Bixschoote.

220th   Division (190 Regiment, 55 and 99 Reserve Regiments), early October–15 October, E of Zonnebeke.

227th   Division (417, 441 and 477 Regiments), 8–15 October, N of Poelcappelle.

231st   Division (442, 443 and 444 Regiments).

233rd   Division (448, 449 and 450 Regiments), withdrawn 30 July, 5–12 October, SE of Zonnebeke.

234th   Division (451, 452 and 453 Regiments), early–end September, St Julien and Zonnebeke.

236th   Division (457, 458 and 459 Regiments), 18–28 September, Polygon Wood and Zonnebeke.

238th   Division (463, 464 and 465 Regiments) 13–30 October, SW of Passchendaele.

239th   Division (466, 467 and 468 Regiments), 23 October–24 November, NE of Poelcappelle.

240th   Division (469, 470 and 471 Regiments), 9–13 October, between Ypres–Staden railway and Poelcappelle.

Campaign Glossary

ANZAC — Australian and New Zealand Army Corps. Also used of a soldier from either of those countries.

Battalion, — British Fighting strength in 1917, sixteen officers and 660 other ranks. War establishment, 1914: thirty officers, 977 men, nine riding horses, twenty-six draught horses, eight heavy draught horses, nine pack horses, two machine guns, sixteen carts and wagons including travelling kitchens and nine bicycles.

Bowie knife — A heavy single-edged hunting sheath knife named after James Bowie (1799-1836), the American soldier and pioneer.

Brigade, Infantry, British — War establishment, 1914: Headquarters, four officers and twenty-three men, four battalions, thus 120 officers and 3,908 men.

Caporetto, Battle of — German reinforcements allowed the Austro–Hungarian Army to share in inflicting a catastrophic defeat on the Italians between 24 October and 30 December 1917, breaking the whole of their defensive line in the east and driving them back to the River Piave, while inflicting 320,000 casualties on them. Another 140,000 Italian casualties were incurred holding the new line.

CGS — Chief of General Staff.

Chinese attack — A sham attack. Used by General Maxse's Cyclist Corps using painted figures raised by means of a string.

CO — Commanding Officer.

Company, British — War establishment 1914: six officers and 221 men.

Corduroy road — A road or track made of cords or lengths of wood laid at right angles to the direction taken.

Croix du Guerre — French decoration for gallantry.

Crump — Slang for shell-burst.

CSM — Company Sergeant Major.

Division, British — War establishment, 1914: Headquarters, fifteen officers, 67 men, three infantry brigades, two field artillery brigades, i.e. sixty-nine officers, 2,316 men, 594 riding horses and 1,650 draught horses, fifty-four 18-pounder guns, one field artillery howitzer brigade of twenty-two officers, 733 men, 700 horses and eighteen 4.5-inch howitzers, one heavy artillery battery with six officers, 192 men, 140 horses, four 60-pounder guns. In addition, two field companies of twelve officers and 422 men, a signal company, a cavalry squadron and various ancillary units to make a total of 585 officers and 17,488 men.

Dressing station – Advanced and main dressing stations were the two units linking the chain of medical services between the front-line regimental aid post and the clearing hospital in the rear, from which a casualty would be passed to a stationary or general hospital and thence to a convalescent depot.

Duckboard – A flooring or pathway for trenches or over boggy surfaces, made of wooden slats.

Eingreiff – Intervention. Used to describe German counter-attack divisions.

Enfilade – Fire on an adversary's flank.

Fascines – Large bundles of wood used to form causeways over ditches or trenches.

Gas – Various kinds of gas were used. Tear-gas, lachrymatory gas, was used first, but poison gas, chlorine, was introduced by the Germans in 1915. A more powerful type, chloropirin, called 'Green Cross I' by the Germans, came in 1916 when the Allies also began to use cyanogen compounds which killed if delivered in concentrated doses but were otherwise temporary in their immobilizing effect. Phosgene was sued by both sides from 1915; it was capable of killing forty-eight hours after exposure, which the victim might not even have noticed. A yet more powerful variant, trichloromethylchloroformate or diphosgene was introduced in 1916. Mustard gas, dichlorethylsulphide, caused blisters and burning of the skin and could damage the respiratory system fatally; the Germans called it 'Yellow Cross'. Sternutators caused sneezing, retching and vomiting and thus made victims remove their masks when it was administered as a powder that could not be excluded. Of this type diphenylchlorarsene was called 'Blue Cross' by the Germans.

GHQ – General Headquarters.

GOC – General Officer Commanding.

Gothas – German bomber aircraft.

Guntrail – The part of the gun carriage that rests on the ground when ready to fire.

Campaign Glossary

Howitzer — A gun that fires at angles up to and above 45 degrees to drop shells behind obstacles.

Indian file — Single file.

Knobkerries — Clubs.

KOSB — King's Own Scottish Borderers.

KRRC — King's Royal Rifle Corps.

KSLI — King's Shropshire Light Infantry.

Lewis gun — Light air-cooled machine gun using the same .303 ammunition as the British rifle. The invention of the American Colonel Isaac Newton Lewis.

MC — Military Cross.

Mebus — A pillbox; a German concrete shelter, sometimes with loopholes, and with an entrance door at the rear. Short for *Mannschafts Eisenbeton Understände.*

Mills bomb — British hand-grenade.

Minenwerfer — German trench mortar.

MM — Military Medal.

Motor lorry — Truck.

NCO — Non-commissioned officer; corporal, sergeant and the like.

New Army — Lord Kitchener appealed for volunteers early in the war from whom new units were formed.

NZ — New Zealand.

Osprey — Code word for a tank, as in 'osprey operations'.

Padre — An army chaplain.

Pillbox — A concrete shelter.

Platoon, British — The quarter of an infantry company, containing four sections.

PPCLI — Princess Patricia's Canadian Light Infantry.

RB — Rifle Brigade.

Respirator — Gas mask.

RFC — The Royal Flying Corps. It became the Royal Air Force, an independent arm of the services, on 1 April 1918.

Setts — Cobbles, road paving.

Sponson — The projecting gun-pod on each side of a British heavy tank.

Stokes mortar — A portable trench mortar designed by Sir Wilfred Stokes in 1915. Made in 3- and 4-inch calibres, it had a light bipod mount and used a base-plate to absord recoil.

SWB — South Wales Borderers.

Tank, Male and Female — Male tanks were armed with two 6-pounder naval guns and four machine guns, while Female tanks carried six machine guns.

VC — Victoria Cross, the highest British award for valour.

Very light — A flare for signalling or illumination fired from a hand-held pistol. Named after the inventor, Samuel W. Very.

Wind Chill — The effect of wind on the human body is to increase the heat loss and thus make the perceived temperature lower than the true temperature. Thus, 44°F (6°C) becomes 36°F (2°C) in a 12mph (19kph) wind, 28°F (-2.3°C) in a 24mph (38.5kph) wind and 22°F (-5.2°C) in a 34mph (55kph) wind.

Woodbines — A brand of cigarette.

Mark IV Tank at Westhoek, September 1917 (Taylor Library).

Sources and Bibliography

For the text of this work published sources have been used and they are included in the bibliography. Maps are based on, or are reproductions of, materials found in the archives of the Tank Museum, Bovington, the In Flanders Fields museum, Ieper, and the Bayerisches Hauptstaatsarchiv, Müchen, to which I am very grateful.

Establishing the facts relating to the Third Battle of Ypres has been very much more difficult than I had anticipated, and even now uncertainties remain. Those of which I am aware are noted in the text. Edmond's *Official History* was written after the Second World War and an account of the undertaking is given by Tim Travers in Chapter 8 of his book *The Killing Ground*. It suggests the published material is the result of a compromise struck between various commentators, including General Gough. It does not agree at all times with other accounts and the version offered here is as close as I have been able to come to a credible history. I have relied heavily on Chris McCarthy's *Passchendaele: The Day-by-Day Account* for hard, factual information, and on Robin Prior and Trevor Wilson's *Passchendaele, the Untold Story* for narrative to set against that given in the *Official History*.

Adam-Smith, Patsy, *The ANZACs*, Thomas Nelson Australia, 1978.

Anon., *Histories of Two Hundred and Fifty-One Divisions of the German Army which participated in the War (1914–1918)* , Chaumont, GHQ, AEF, 1919, reprinted London Stamp Exchange, 1989.

Anon., *Ieper en de Frontstreek*, Sint-Niklaas, A G Claus, no date.

Anon., *Ypres and the Battles for Ypres*, London, Michelin, 1919, reprinted Naval & Military Press.

Sources and Bibliography

Arthur, Max (ed), *Forgotten Voices of the Great War*, London, Ebury Press, 2002.

Ashurst, George, *My Bit*, Ramsbury, Crowood Press, 1987.

Baker-Carr, C D, *From Chauffeur to Brigadier*, London, Ernest Benn, 1930.

Banks, Arthur, *A Military Atlas of the First World War*, London, Heinemann, 1975 and Leo Cooper 1989.

Barton, Peter, Peter Doyle and Johan Vandewalle, *Beneath Flanders Fields, the Tunnellers' War 1914–1918*, Staplehurst, Spellmount, 2004.

Baynes, John, *Far from a Donkey*, London, Brassey's, 1995.

Beckett, Ian F W, *The Great War 1914–1918*, Harlow, Longman, 2001.

Boraston, J H (ed), *Sir Douglas Haig's Despatches*, London, J M Dent, 1919, reprinted Uckfield, Naval & Military Press, 2001.

Browne, D G, *The Tank in Action*, London and Edinburgh, William Blackwood, 1920.

Cave, Nigel, *Passchendaele, the Fight for the Village*, Barnsley, Pen & Sword, 1997.

Cave, Nigel, *Polygon Wood*, Barnsley, Pen & Sword, 1999.

Colville, J R, *Man of Valour*, London, Collins, 1972.

Cutlack, F M (ed), *War Letters of General Monash*, Sydney, Angus and Robertson, 1935.

Doyle, Peter, *Geology of the Western Front, 1914–1918*, London, The Geologists' Association, 1998.

Doyle, Peter, F Bostyn, Peter Barton and Johan Vandewalle, 'The Underground War, 1914–18: Geology of the Beecham Dugout, Passchendaele,' *Proceeding of the Geologists' Association* 112:263–274, 2001.

Dunn, C J, *The War the Infantry Knew*, P S King, 1938 and London, Abacus, 1994.

Edmonds, Sir James E, *Military Operations France and Belgium, Volume II*, London, HMSO, 1948.

Fletcher, David, *Tanks and Trenches*, Stroud, Sutton, 1994.

Fosten, D S V, and R J Marrion, *The German Army 1914–18*, London, Osprey, 1978.

Sources and Bibliography

Gough, Sir Hubert, *The Fifth Army*, London, Hodder and Stoughton, 1931.

Gough, Sir Hubert, *Soldiering On*, London, Arthur Barker, 1954.

Gray, Randal, with Christopher Argyll, *Chronicle of the First World War*, New York and Oxford, Facts on File, 1990.

Griffith, Paddy, *Battle Tactics of the Western Front*, New Haven and London, Yale University Press, 1994.

Guderian, Heinz, *Achtung–Panzer!* , London, Arms and Armour, 1992.

Harington, Charles, *Tim Harington Looks Back*, London, John Murray, 1940.

Haythornthwaite, Philip J., *The World War One Source Book*, London, Arms and Armour, 1992.

Hickey, D E, *Rolling into Action*, London, Hutchinson, 1933.

Lawson, Eric and Jane, *The First Air Campaign*, Conshohoken, Combined Books, 1996.

Lomas, David, *First Ypres 1914*, Oxford, Osprey, 1999.

Ludendorff, E, *My War Memories, Volume I*, London, Hutchinson, 1929.

McCarthy, Chris, *The Third Ypres–Passchendaele, the Day-by-Day Account*, London, Arms and Armour, 1995.

Macdonald, Lyn, *They Called it Passchendaele*, London, Michael Joseph, 1978.

Mangin, Général Charles, *Comment Finit la Guerre*, Paris, Plon, 1920.

Marix Evans, Martin, *Battles of World War I*, Ramsbury, Airlife, 2004.

Marix Evans, Martin, *Passchendaele and the Battles of Ypres*, Oxford, Osprey, 1997.

Mockler-Ferryman, A F, *The Oxfordshire and Buckinghamshire Light Infantry Chronicle, 1917–1918*, London, Eyre and Spottiswoode, no date.

Moser, Otto von, *Die Württemberger im Weltkriege*, translated by Michael French.

Nicholson, G W L, *Canadian Expeditionary Force 1914–1919*, Ottawa, Queen's Printer, 1962.

Parker, E W, *Into Battle*, London, Longmans Green, 1964.

Prior, Robin, and Trevor Wilson, *Passchendaele, the Untold Story*, New Haven and London, Yale University Press, 1996.

Sources and Bibliography

Pope, Stephen, and Elizabeth-Anne Wheal, *Dictionary of the First World War*, London, Macmillan, 1995.

Quigley, Hugh, *Passchendaele and the Somme*, 1928, reprinted Naval and Military Press, 2004.

Sheffield, Gary, *Forgotten Victory, the First World War Myths and Realities*, London, Headline, 2001.

Sheffield, Gary, *The Somme*, London, Cassell, 2003.

Sheffield, Gary, and John Bourne (eds), *Douglas Haig: War Diaries and Letters 1914–1918*, London, Weidenfeld & Nicolson, 2005.

Smith, Aubrey (A Rifleman), *Four Years on the Western Front*, London, Odhams, 1922, reprinted Naval & Military Press.

Spagnoly, Tony, *The Anatomy of a Raid*, London, Multidream, 1991.

Terraine, John, *The Road to Passchendaele*, London, Leo Cooper, 1977.

Terraine, John, *The Smoke and the Fire: Myths and Anti-Myths of War 1861–1945*, London, Sidgwick & Jackson, 1980 and Leo Cooper, 1992.

Travers, Tim, *The Killing Ground*, London, Allen & Unwin, 1987, reprinted Barnsley, Pen & Sword, 2003.

Vaughan, Edwin C, *Some Desperate Glory*, London, Frederick Warne, 1981.

Walker, Jonathan, *The Blood Tub*, Staplehurst, Spellmount, 1998.

Watson, W H L, *A Company of Tanks*, London and Edinburgh, William Blackwood, 1920.

Wedd, A F (ed), *German Students' War Letters*, Philadelphia, Pine Street Books, 2002.

Williams-Ellis, Clough, and A Williams-Ellis, *The Tank Corps*, London, Country Life & Newnes, 1919.

Wolff, Leon, *In Flanders Fields*, London, Longmans Green, 1959.

Zabecki, David T, *Steel Wind: Colonel Georg Bruchmüller and the Birth of Modern Artillery*, Westport, Praeger, 1994.

Index

Campaign Chronicle

Index